AD

ARCHITECTURAL DESIGN

GUEST-EDITED BY
GEORGE L LEGENDRE

MATHEMATICS OF SPACE

04|2011

ARCHITECTURAL DESIGN
VOL 81, NO 4
JULY/AUGUST 2011
ISSN 0003-8504

PROFILE NO 212
ISBN 978-0470-689806

WILEY
wiley.com

AD

ARCHITECTURAL DESIGN

GUEST-EDITED BY
GEORGE L LEGENDRE

MATHEMATICS OF SPACE

5 EDITORIAL
   Helen Castle

6 ABOUT THE GUEST-EDITOR
   George L Legendre

8 INTRODUCTION
   The Mathematics of Sensible Things
   George L Legendre

18 Mathematics and the Sensible
   World: Representing,
   Constructing, Simulating
   Amy Dahan–Dalmedico

36

28 Architecture and
   Mathematics: Between
   Hubris and Restraint
   Antoine Picon

   Architecture's and mathematics'
   enduring relationship is one of
   vicissitudes — embrace and estrangement
   — as charted by Antoine Picon.

36 Continuity and Rupture
   Dennis R Shelden and Andrew J Witt

44 IJP Explained: Parametric
Mathematics in Practice
George L Legendre

54 A Sense of Purpose:
Mathematics and Performance
in Environmental Design
*Martha Tsigkari, Adam Davis and
Francis Aish, Specialist Modelling
Group, Foster + Partners*

70

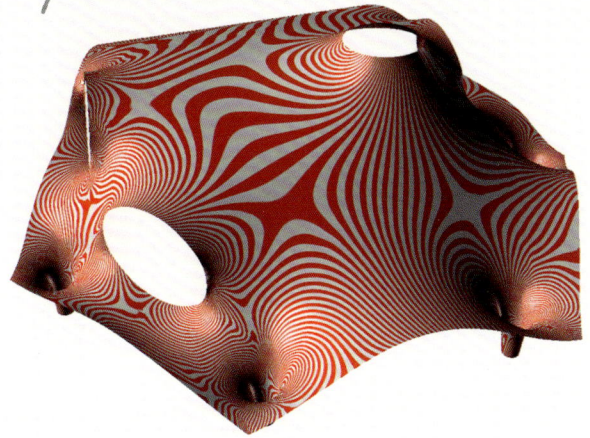

58 Long Form and Algorithm
Daniel Bosia

66 Intuitive Material Distributions
*Panagiotis Michalatos and
Sawako Kaijima, Adams Kara
Taylor (AKT)*

66

70 Lost in Parameter Spacc?
*Fabian Scheurer and
Hanno Stehling*

80 Geometry Working Beyond Effect
Mark Burry

*Is descriptive geometry on the wane?
Or as suggested by Mark Burry, does
it enable us to make some significant
distinctions between disciplines?*

90 Desargues and Leibniz:
In the Black Box –
A Mathematical Model of
the Leibnizian Monad
Bernard Cache

100 Pasta by Design
George L Legendre

102 The Metabolism of the City:
The Mathematics of Networks
and Urban Surfaces
Michael Weinstock

108 Rising Masses, Singapore
Max Kahlen

112 The Hinging Tower
*Ana María Flor Ortiz and
Rodia Valladares Sánchez,
Rising Masses Studio, Harvard
Graduate School of Design*

118 Implicit Fields – MOCAPE
Shenzhen PRC
*George L Legendre and Max
Kahlen*

122 Sense and Sensibilia
Philippe Morel

130 COUNTERPOINT
Less Answers More Questions
Will McLean

ΛD

ARCHITECTURAL DESIGN
JULY/AUGUST 2011
PROFILE NO 212

Editorial Offices
John Wiley & Sons
25 John Street
London
WC1N 2BS

T: +44 (0)20 8326 3800

Editor
Helen Castle

Managing Editor (Freelance)
Caroline Ellerby

Production Editor
Elizabeth Gongde

Design and Prepress
Artmedia, London

Art Direction and Design
CHK Design:
Christian Küsters
Hannah Dumphy

Printed in Italy by Conti Tipocolor

Sponsorship/advertising
Faith Pidduck/Wayne Frost
T: +44 (0)1243 770254
E: fpidduck@wiley.co.uk

Reprinted April 2013

Subscribe to ΛD

ΛD is published bimonthly and is available to purchase on both a subscription basis and as individual volumes at the following prices.

Prices
Individual copies: £22.99 / US$45
Mailing fees may apply

Annual Subscription Rates
Student: £75 / US$117 print only
Individual: £120 / US$189 print only
Institutional: £200 / US$375
print or online
Institutional: £230 / US$431 combined
print and online

Subscription Offices UK
John Wiley & Sons Ltd
Journals Administration Department
1 Oldlands Way, Bognor Regis
West Sussex, PO22 9SA
T: +44 (0)1243 843272
F: +44 (0)1243 843232
E: cs-journals@wiley.co.uk

Print ISSN: 0003-8504;
Online ISSN: 1554-2769

Prices are for six issues and include postage and handling charges. Individual rate subscriptions must be paid by personal cheque or credit card. Individual rate subscriptions may not be resold or used as library copies.

All prices are subject to change without notice.

Rights and Permissions
Requests to the Publisher should be addressed to:
Permissions Department
John Wiley & Sons Ltd
The Atrium
Southern Gate
Chichester
West Sussex PO19 8SQ
England

F: +44 (0)1243 770620
E: permreq@wiley.co.uk

Front cover: IJP, Punctual Klein Bottle, 2003.
© George L Legendre
Inside front cover: Concept CHK Design

Many of us glaze over at the very mention of the word 'mathematics'. It brings to mind too many years of forced learning in stuffy classrooms. Moreover as 'creatives', many designers feel themselves to be entitled to be free from the strictures of such a highly demanding and logical discipline. In his introduction (see pp 8–17), guest-editor George L Legendre compares mathematics to 'plumbing' – the essential but unappealing system underlying architectural thought. Certainly, it is the more humdrum application of mathematics in operational processes that architects have had an ongoing problem with, even today when algorithms enable scripting and the design agility that it brings. When acknowledging this deep ambivalence to the discipline, it is also necessary to recognise the enduring romance that architecture has had with one particular branch of mathematics – geometry. This is a wholly natural affinity, as geometry is the most visual manifestation of mathematics. It is a liaison that has held sway across continents and time, most apparent in ancient temples, Renaissance churches, Islamic structures and contemporary digital surfaces; it reached perhaps its point of greatest infatuation with 'sacred geometry' in 15th-century Italy, when certain numbers and patterns were attributed as having symbolic divine qualities.

So why this sudden interest in 'plumbing' in △? There has been what Antoine Picon so aptly phrases an 'estrangement' between architecture and mathematics for several centuries (see pp 28–35). The onset of computation has, however, offered us the chance not only to reconnect architecture with geometry and pursue the possibilities of non-Euclidean geometries, but also to realise the opportunities that other branches of mathematics, such as calculus and algorithms, afford. This places an important emphasis on looking beneath the surface, providing architects with a fuller understanding of the processes and software that they use and solving problems from the baseline. George L Legendre exemplifies this approach, not only disseminating an understanding of the discipline through his teaching at Harvard Graduate School of Design, but also rigorously working with parametric analytic equations across the design process in his London-based practice IJP Corporation (see pp 44–53). This requires an aptitude and stringency that is not possible for most practices to embrace, but it also recognises a real need to question the given and problem solve at a higher level. △

IJP with John Pickering, F01(b), 2009
top: Projective sculpture (detail). F01(b) features two overlapping cylinders inversed relative to the same centre. The resulting figure is encased in a translucent box which crops the infinite surfaces produced by a transformation known as inversion.

IJP with RSP Architects Planners and Engineers, Henderson Waves, Singapore, 2008
above: Study model of structure.

IJP with RSP Architects Planners and Engineers, Henderson Waves, Singapore, 2008
opposite: The tallest pedestrian bridge in Southeast Asia is located in the Southern Ridges area of Singapore. The 304.8-metre (1,000-foot) long footbridge was designed with a single periodic equation. The doubly curved parts of the deck form a tapestry of 5,000 modular boards, each varying by a single degree every few metres and all tapered to measure.

George L Legendre's fusion of design, mathematics and computation took off in print starting with *IJP: The Book of Surfaces* (AA Publications, 2003). Part publisher's spread and part mathematical surface, this playful manifesto was closely followed by the Henderson Waves project (2004–8), in which his newly minted, eponymous office IJP deployed similar principles to design and tender the tallest pedestrian bridge in Southeast Asia. The contractor borrowed the book's original notation to identify the project's parts – bridging the gap between theory and practice. Since graduating from Harvard, Legendre's work has been defined by the full-time decade he spent in academia. An Assistant Professor of Architecture at the Harvard Graduate School of Design (GSD) from his mid-20s, he has been a visiting professor at ETH Zurich and Princeton University, and master of Diploma Unit 5 at the London-based Architectural Association School of Architecture, where he undertook for eight years (alongside Lluís Viu Rebès) the intense educational experiments for which the place was famed. He returned to Harvard in 2008 as a visiting design critic before being appointed Adjunct Associate Professor.

Freely inspired by analytic mathematics, computer programming, the literary pranks of Oulipo and other less highbrow forms of automatic writing, the work of IJP is closely identified with the emergent computational avant-garde. While cherishing this brotherly affiliation, IJP's attachment to traditional values of instrumentation and artistic probity has been equally important. To date the office has won a competition to cover a central London street with glass (with Adams Kara Taylor), and completed Henderson Waves (with RSP) in Singapore. In 2011, the practice was a finalist of the MoMA-PS1 design competition. The influential weekly *Building Design* recently elected the firm as one of the top five practices in the UK led by principals under the age of 40. The work of the firm has been featured on the cover of *AA Files*, the *RIBA Journal*, *Mondo Arc Perspective +* and *Icon Magazine* among others. A regularly published lecturer and essayist, in addition to *IJP: The Book of Surfaces*, Legendre is also the author of *Bodyline: the End of our Meta-Mechanical Body* (AA Publications, 2006) and a critical essay, 'JP's Way', in Mohsen Mostafavi's *Mathematical Form: John Pickering and the Architecture of the Inversion Principle* (AA Publications, 2006). His next research piece, *Pasta by Design* (see pp 100–1 of this issue) will be published by Thames & Hudson in September 2011. ⌀

Figure 1. Fdecomite, Laughing Cow Inverted
Humorous deployment of projective geometry in the graphic space of a famous food brand, instantly recognisable among French schoolchildren past or present. This piece is based on a projective transformation known as inversion (developed in the 1820s); that is, scaling relative to a fixed point, but with a variable coefficient.

THE MATHEMATICS OF SENSIBLE THINGS

Architecture and Mathematics have constantly balanced between two extremes: an experiential dimension often imbued with contemplative connotations, and the quest for operative techniques that do not necessarily present a spatial meaning. Hence the ambiguity we find ourselves in today, faced simultaneously with architecture's estrangement from mathematics and the spectacular diffusion of computational tools.
— Antoine Picon, 'Between Intuition and the Quest for Operative Techniques', public lecture, Symposium on 'Mathematics in Space', Harvard Graduate School of Design, 5 March 2010

Over the past 15 years, architecture has been profoundly altered by the advent of computation and information technology. Design software and numerical fabrication machinery have recast the traditional role of geometry in architecture and opened it up to the wondrous possibilities afforded by topology, parametric surface design and other areas of mathematics. From the technical aspects of scripting code to biomorphic paradigms of form and its association with genetics, biology, phylogeny and other branches of natural science, the impact of computation on the discipline has been widely documented.[1] What is less clear, and has largely escaped scrutiny so far, is the role mathematics itself has played in this revolution.

While our design culture has firmly embraced the innovations of computing, it has decidedly less time for the formulated thought lying at the very root of the breakthrough. There are several reasons behind this paradox. Mathematics is a deeply abstract discipline, and as such it is easily misunderstood. On a personal level, mathematics is likely to summon memories of hard graft, frustration and perhaps even of failure. Critically for designers (at first glance at least), the instrumentality of computation seems easier to grasp than that of mathematics, which good design software will render 'transparent' anyway. This transparency comes at a price. The underlying essence of formulated thought is often wrongly perceived to be no better than plumbing, and as such unworthy of being separated from the higher-

Figure 2. Fdecomite, Third Stellation of Cuboctahedron
A cuboctahedron, also known as a dymaxion according to Buckminster Fuller, is a uniform polyhedron with a specific number of faces.

$$M := \texttt{READ\_IMAGE}(\,\texttt{"G2L.tga"}\,)$$

$$S1 := \texttt{submatrix}\left(M, 0, 299, 0, 299\right)$$

$$D := \texttt{cols(S1)} \qquad m := 0 \,..\, D - 1 \qquad n := 0 \,..\, D - 1$$

$$I_{m,n} := \frac{m + i \cdot n}{D - 1} - \frac{1 + i}{2}$$

$$f(z) := 1.4 \cdot z \cdot \exp\,3i \cdot \pi \cdot \left(|z|\right)^2$$

$$Q2 := \overrightarrow{f((I))} \cdot \frac{D - 1}{2} + \frac{D - 1}{2} \cdot (1 + i)$$

$$rd(x) := \texttt{floor}\left(x + .5\right)$$

$$F2_{m,n} := S1_{\,rd\left(\text{Re}\left(Q2_{m,n}\right)\right),\, rd\left(\text{Im}\left(Q2_{m,n}\right)\right)}$$

S1

F2

Figure 3. George L Legendre, Self Portrait As Photoshop Filter, 2006
The mapping rotates the complex coordinates of a pixel by an amount proportional to the square of its distance from the origin to produce a swirl. Mathematics is typically pervasive under the software hood – in this case, matrix algebra applied to a pixel grid.

Far from being a bonus or a side-effect, architectural geometry is a discipline in its own right, forming a long and complex continuum subdivided into distinct historical segments with vastly different instrumental priorities.

level functionality of design computing that has ultimately smothered it. As a result, in our software-saturated design environments the formulated syntax of mathematics is all too easily amalgamated with the functionality of digital tools, which mathematics enable – but also predate by thousands of years.

At this critical juncture in time, it is therefore important for us architects, designers, computational designers, historians and engineers to tease the mathematics out of our respective disciplines, not to show how it is done – a hard and futile challenge for the reader – but to reflect on the shared roots of our process, and the multiple ways these roots shape our practices and intellectual agendas while helping us define new directions. Strangely neglected since the onset of the digital design era, the impact of mathematics on contemporary creativity may now be explored in its own terms.

Dualities
Mathematics, as Amy Dahan-Dalmedico reminds us in the historical account that opens this issue (see pp 18–27), is hardly a 'stable and well-defined' object. In effect, the term applies to a greatly diverse collection of practices and 'cognitive constructions' spanning various practical, historical and philosophical contexts. Wading through this collection of theoretical and applied reflections on mathematics in space, we are indeed struck by the many themes our subject can simultaneously embody, by the many dualities it is apt to represent. Duality is a 'native' concept in its own right, designating a state of equivalence between objects in projective geometry, such that a given transformation involving two terms will remain valid if we swap them around (replacing a point with a line and a line with a point in the plane, for instance, as established by Jean-Victor Poncelet's 1822 *Principle of Duality*).[2]

Hence, for the historian Antoine Picon (see pp 28–35), the relationship of architecture to geometry since the 18th century reflects alternate polarities of 'hubris' and 'restraint' in relation to a formal, conceptual, and even mystical design project. For Amy Dahan-Dalmedico, geometry can be understood either as a realistic practice rooted in human perception and the world itself, or as a Platonist realist collection of concepts totally independent of the human mind. For Dennis Shelden and Andrew Witt, recent developments in digital computation posit the emergence of a higher geometry at once continuous and discrete – until the very distinction is

itself abolished (see pp 36–43). In Bernard Cache's account of the work of French mathematician Girard Desargues (pp 90–9), projective geometry represents a practical expedient to determine metric relationships, as well as an embodiment of Gottfried Leibniz's mystical monad. And so on. Throughout the 16 essays and projects collected here, we are presented with a productive tension between mathematics understood as an autonomous set of questions and speculations (a 'well-ordered ceremonial'), and mathematics as an open, problem-solving-oriented force of creation and praxis.

Which Mathematics?
Mathematics is a broad topic that we must necessarily restrict, for the purpose of brevity and coherence, to the subject of geometry. As Martha Tsigkari, Adam Davis, and Francis Aish of Foster + Partners' Specialist Modelling Group demonstrate in their thoughtful essay on the 'invisible' mathematics of environmental performance (pp 54–7), the formal and perceptual aspects of architecture best abetted by geometry are not the only game in town; but they are the primary one. Compare, for the sake of argument, two structures as far apart in scope and scale as Foster + Partners' Swiss Re Building (the Gherkin) and Philippe Morel's Universal House (see p 122). Regardless of emphasis (algorithmic or otherwise) and despite the occasional claims to the contrary, the overwhelming geometric implications of any structured design process will not go away – so we may as well discuss them seriously.

Far from being a bonus or a side-effect, architectural geometry is a discipline in its own right, forming a long and complex continuum subdivided into distinct historical segments with vastly different instrumental priorities. What distinguishes these segments, qualitatively speaking, is less *what* they do, than *how* they do it; and in this sense, the key difference between contemporary architectural geometry and, say, that of Andrea Palladio (1508–80), is not only that we no longer believe in the ideal figure of the circle, but that when we do use it we choose to construct it with Cartesian or polar (parametric) coordinates, rather than with a ruler and a compass.

The difference is not only technical. As the consolidation of symbolic algebra and its emancipation from the figures of geometry began around the middle of the 16th century, the Renaissance architect (born in 1508) whose villas embody the ultimate expression of classical geometry lies on the wrong side of modernity by a couple of decades. The algebraists of the 16th and 17th centuries set out the future innovations of analytic and differential geometry, this new geometry of symbols and operators rather than lines and figures, which subtends our contemporary understanding of mathematics in space and, of course, enables the recent innovations of computation. With the notable exceptions of Desargues's projective transformations profiled by Bernard Cache, and to some extent (though not exclusively), Mark Burry's analysis of ruled and developable surfaces in the work of Antoni Gaudí and Félix Candela (see pp 80–9), analytic geometry is, in all its subsequent forms, the brand of mathematics discussed here. Hence the architectural, engineering and computational proposals illustrating our theme (as well as most geometry produced and consumed today in the world at large) can be said to be calculated rather than figured, and written rather than drawn.

Sadly no trained architect since Desargues in the 17th century has managed to contribute disciplinary knowledge to mathematics, but the movement across the (increasingly wide) boundary between geometry and architecture has nonetheless been continuous. In the 18th century, a further seismic shift towards calculus, detailed by Antoine Picon in his account of the turbulent relationship between geometry and architecture, alienated our profession's narrowly intuitive dimensional sensibility, leading to a protracted estrangement from mathematics, only weathered today, thanks in part to the advent of computation, which has imbued the relationship with a new lease of life.

Mathematics or Computation?

The relationship between computation and architectural geometry looms large in the collective argument exhumed in this issue. To explore the terms of a fair and mutual rapport, this collection of essays departs from the habitual emphasis on computational morphogenetic design that has dominated theoretical discourse in the last one and a half decades. The simplistic notions that computation constitutes an 'automation' of mathematics (a probable side effect of the introduction and popularity of early CAD systems), or conversely that mathematics is only a slower, static expression of computational activity, must be dispensed with. As Fabian Scheurer and Hanno Stehling demonstrate in

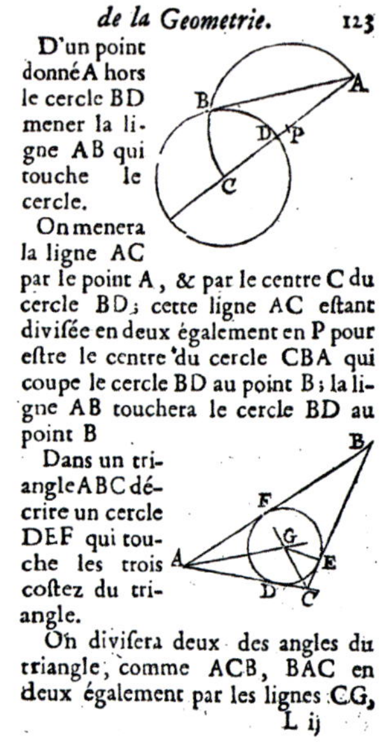

de la Geometrie. 123

D'un point donné A hors le cercle BD mener la ligne AB qui touche le cercle.

On menera la ligne AC par le point A, & par le centre C du cercle BD; cette ligne AC eſtant diviſée en deux également en P pour eſtre le centre du cercle CBA qui coupe le cercle BD au point B; la ligne AB touchera le cercle BD au point B.

Dans un triangle ABC décrire un cercle DEF qui touche les trois coſtez du triangle.

On diviſera deux des angles du triangle, comme ACB, BAC en deux également par les lignes CG,

L ij

Figure 4. Euclidean geometry at work
The applied mathematics of space in the 17th century consists in bisecting the triangle and other Euclidean concerns. From *L'Ecole des arpenteurs où l'on enseigne toutes les pratiques de géométrie qui sont nécessaires à un arpenteur* (The Survey School where all Manners of Geometry Needed by Surveyors Are Taught), Thomas Moette (Paris), 1692.

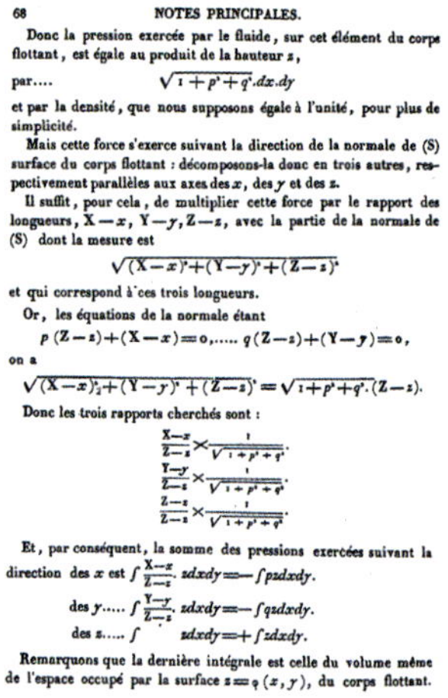

68 NOTES PRINCIPALES.

Donc la pression exercée par le fluide, sur cet élément du corps flottant, est égale au produit de la hauteur z,

par.... $\sqrt{1+p^2+q^2}.dx.dy$

et par la densité, que nous supposons égale à l'unité, pour plus de simplicité.

Mais cette force s'exerce suivant la direction de la normale de (S) surface du corps flottant : décomposons-la donc en trois autres, respectivement parallèles aux axes des x, des y et des z.

Il suffit, pour cela, de multiplier cette force par le rapport des longueurs, $X-x$, $Y-y$, $Z-z$, avec la partie de la normale de (S) dont la mesure est

$$\sqrt{(X-x)^2+(Y-y)^2+(Z-z)^2}$$

et qui correspond à ces trois longueurs.

Or, les équations de la normale étant

$$p(Z-z)+(X-x)=0, \ldots\ldots q(Z-z)+(Y-y)=0,$$

on a

$$\sqrt{(X-x)^2+(Y-y)^2+(Z-z)^2}=\sqrt{1+p^2+q^2}.(Z-z).$$

Donc les trois rapports cherchés sont :

$$\frac{X-x}{Z-z}\times\frac{1}{\sqrt{1+p^2+q^2}}.$$
$$\frac{Y-y}{Z-z}\times\frac{1}{\sqrt{1+p^2+q^2}}.$$
$$\frac{Z-z}{Z-z}\times\frac{1}{\sqrt{1+p^2+q^2}}.$$

Et, par conséquent, la somme des pressions exercées suivant la direction des x est $\int\frac{X-x}{Z-z}.zdxdy=-\int pzdxdy.$

des y..... $\int\frac{Y-y}{Z-z}.zdxdy=-\int qzdxdy.$

des z..... $\int zdxdy=+\int zdxdy.$

Remarquons que la dernière intégrale est celle du volume même de l'espace occupé par la surface $z=\varphi(x,y)$, du corps flottant.

Figure 5. Analytic geometry at work
The applied mathematics of space in the 19th century is no longer concerned with drawn figures: all steps are now written (and calculated). From Charles Dupin, *Applications de géométrie et de mécanique à la marine, aux ponts et chaussées etc. pour faire suite aux développements de géométrie* (Application of the Latest Developments in Geometry and Mechanics to Marine Engineering and all Manners of Infrastructure), Bachelier (Paris), 1822.

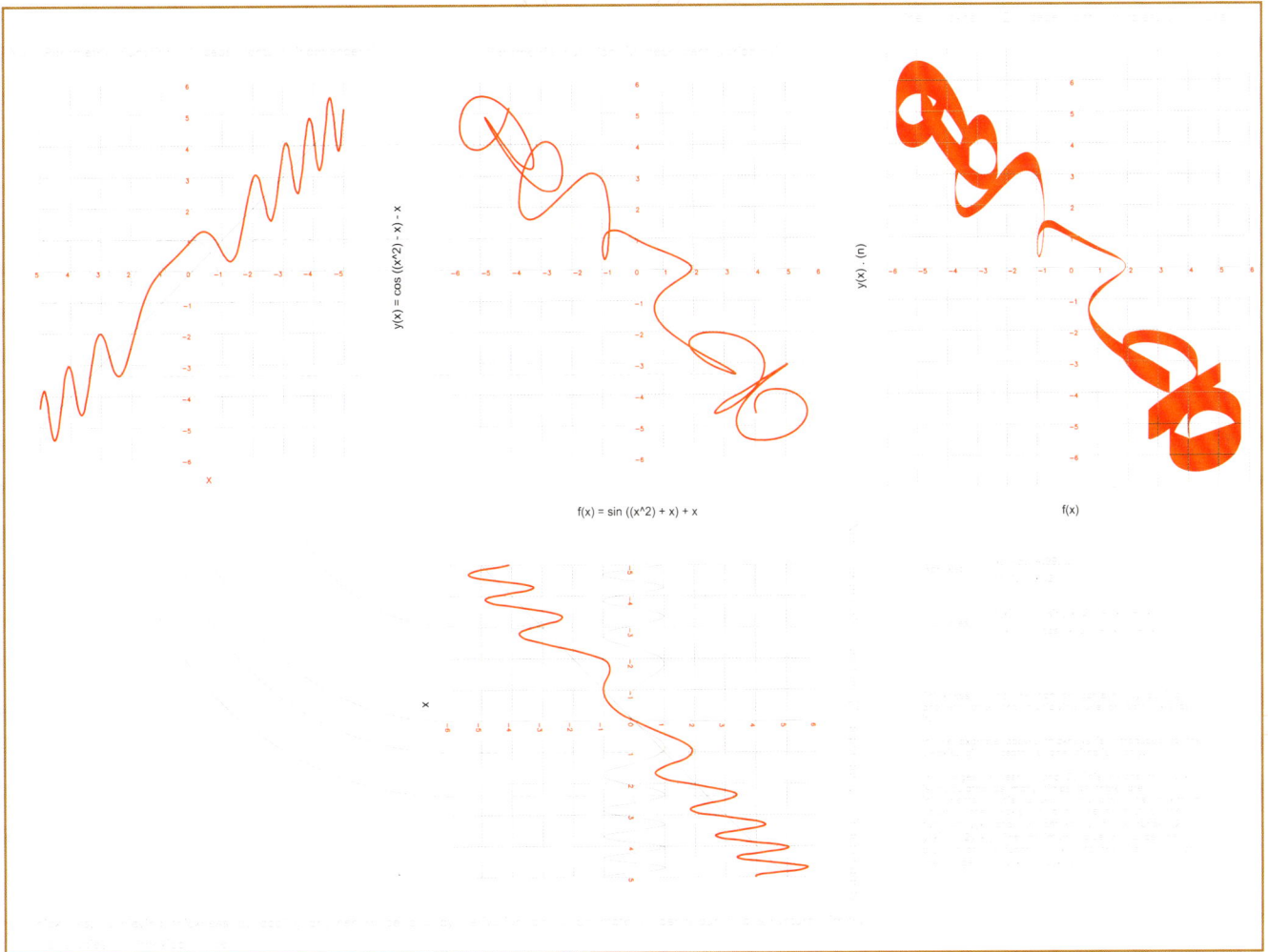

$y(x) = \cos((x^2) - x) - x$

$f(x) = \sin((x^2) + x) + x$

$y(x) \cdot (n)$

$f(x)$

Figure 6. Omar Al Omari, Superficial Thickness I, Diploma Unit 5 (Learning Japanese), Architectural Association, London, 2004
Analytic geometry at work. Parametric periodic curves subjected to a 'thickening' function that reproduces the inflections of a calligrapher's brushstroke.

Figure 7. Omar Al Omari, Superficial Thickness II,
Diploma Unit 5 (Learning Japanese), Architectural Association, London, 2004
Periodic pleating. Discontinuous parametric surfaces are subjected to a 'pleating'
function that produces a highly controlled instance of superficial depth.

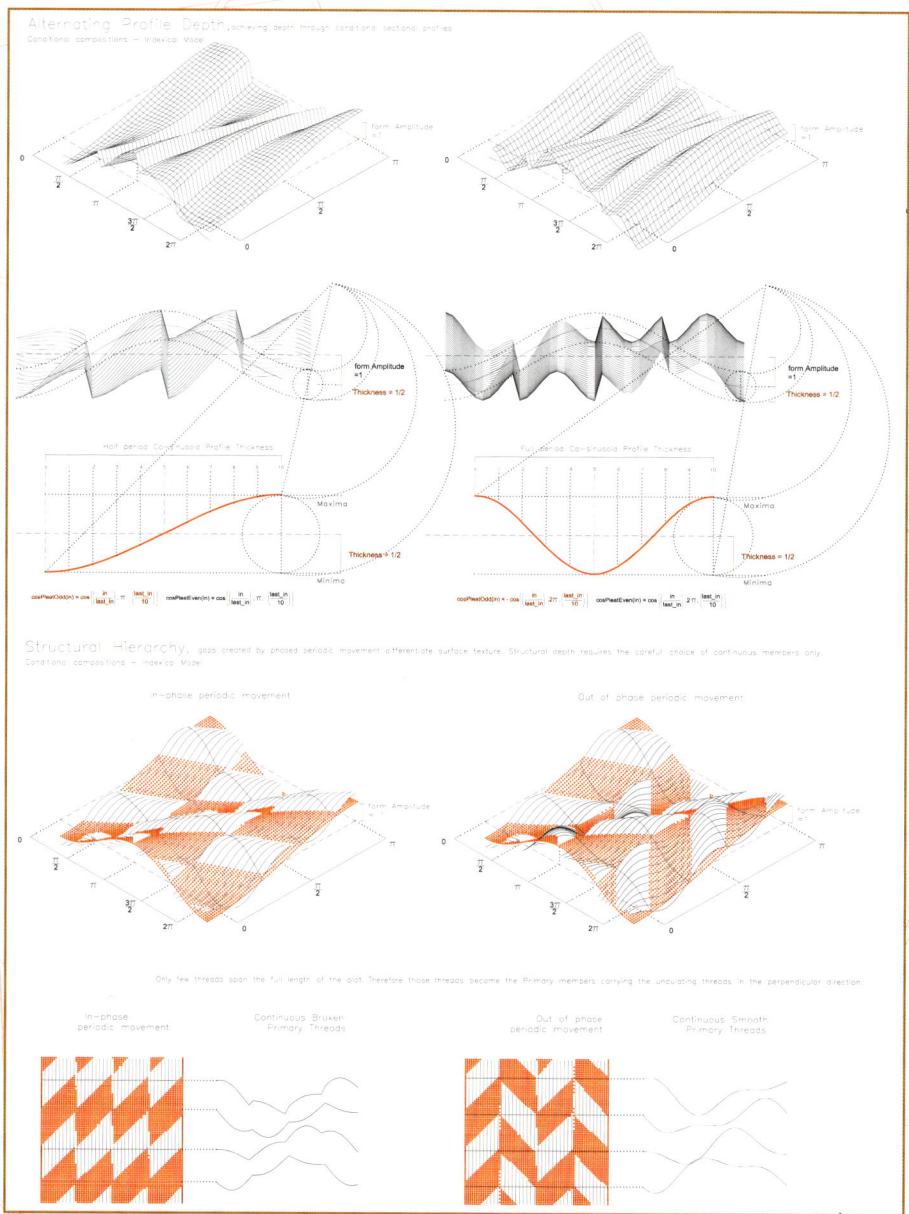

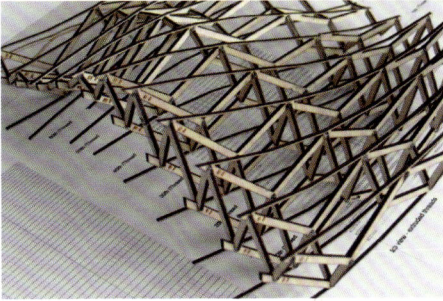

Figure 8. Omar Al Omari, Superficial Thickness II, Diploma Unit 5 (Learning Japanese), Architectural Association, London, 2004
Periodic Pleating. Detail of material model.

their masterful analysis of the applied relationship between mathematics and theoretical computer science (pp 70–9), the relative transparency of mathematics when subsumed under the interface of standard software is merely an illusion. The essential issues of representation, abstraction and reduction of data are still very much there, and must be disentangled through a careful interplay of mathematical and computational resources, driven to a large extent by the unforgiving bottlenecks of machinic performance and physical materiality. Scheurer and Stehling's essay outlines in great detail the interdependence of the two realms when faced with problems of increasing complexity, while reaffirming their respective specificities.

In a similar vein, Dennis Shelden's and Andrew Witt's article demonstrates how recent developments in computation have re-actualised established yet hitherto exceptional non-Euclidean configurations, usually treated in general and simplistic form, and turned them into something applicable to architecture, 'and indeed [to] everyday experience'. Recalling Felix Klein's and David Hilbert's famous theoretical consolidations of geometry in the 19th century (also mentioned by Amy Dahan-Dalmedico), Shelden and Witt suggest that the recent breakthroughs of computing may demand a similar approach; that innovation may bring about a further generalisation of historical precedent, that the feedback loop between the development of technology and the history of mathematics is still up and running, and hence that the relationship between them is alive and well, despite the more cautious prognoses spelled out by historian of science Dahan-Dalmedico at the close of her article.

Praxis

This issue would not be relevant without an applied survey of what mathematics can actually do for practice. More than efficiency or technique, mathematics in design is ultimately about individual authority. When it comes to solving problems and creating new things, working with mathematical concepts and equations, rather than with the standard modelling software disseminated by the industry, implies a direct recourse to generative symbols and marks. Writing forms and processes in this manner requires an authorial mindset. Modelling software being generally built by 'chunking', or consolidating lower-level steps into higher-level ones – like

Figure 9. Ema Bonifacic, Suk-Kyu Hong and Jung Kim, Degenerate Weave, Diploma Unit 5 (Engineering the Immaterial), Architectural Association, London, 2003
The iterative summation of a complex periodic function causes a weave of indicial threads to veer into a hyperactive, disorderly pattern.

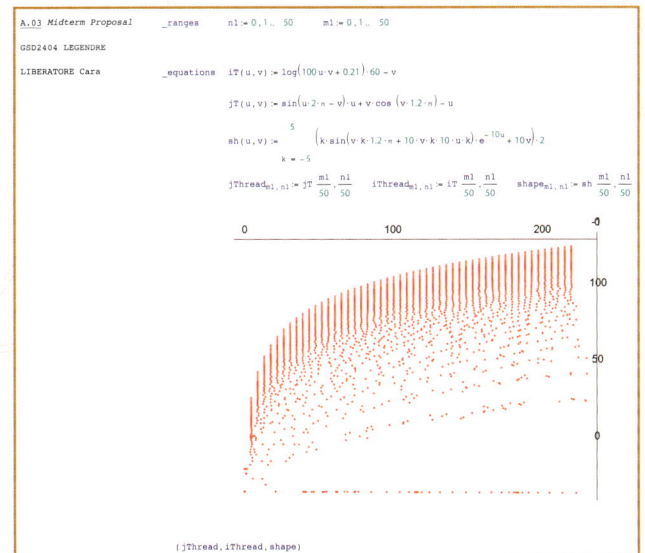

In all these projects the material considerations and an intimate knowledge of physical behaviour go hand in hand with a rigorous mathematical formalisation, abetted by the latest computational facilities.

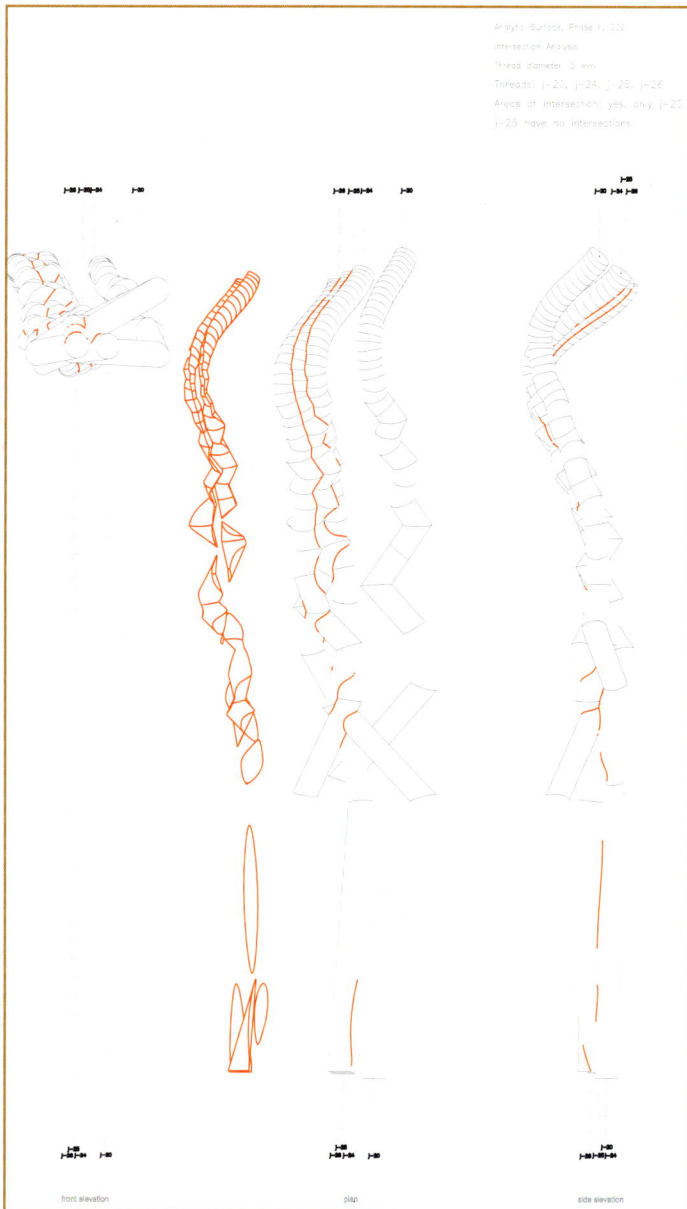

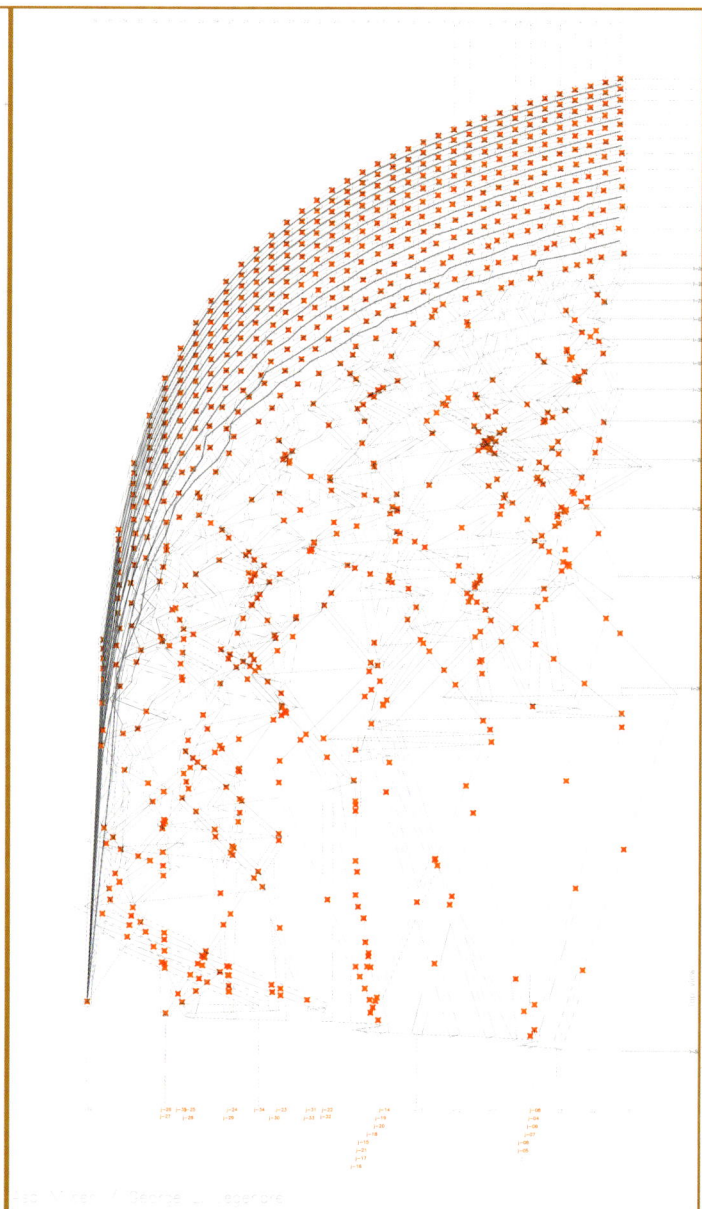

Figure 10. Ema Bonifacic, Suk-Kyu Hong and Jung Kim, Degenerate Weave, Diploma Unit 5 (Engineering the Immaterial), Architectural Association, London, 2003
Detail of thickened parametric threads.

Figure 11. Ema Bonifacic, Suk-Kyu Hong and Jung Kim, Degenerate Weave, Diploma Unit 5 (Engineering the Immaterial), Architectural Association, London, 2003
The woven arrangement of indicial threads veers into a hyperactive, disorderly pattern. Threads that used to be parallel are now secant (the intersections are flagged in red).

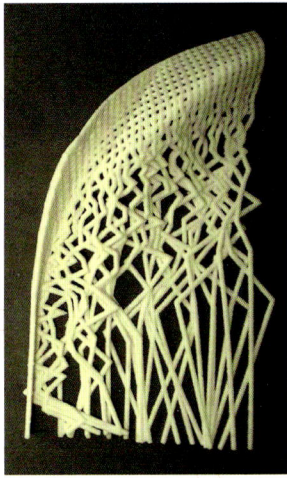

Figure 12. Ema Bonifacic, Suk-Kyu Hong and Jung Kim, Degenerate Weave, Diploma Unit 5 (Engineering the Immaterial), Architectural Association, London, 2003
Thanks to the multiple intersections, half of the form is becoming potentially self-structural. The other half is removed, and the remainder laminated into a self-supporting structure that shares the morphological characteristics of half and whole.

a pyramidal structure – to work with commercial software is to work at the top of the pyramid, where the interaction is intuitive but the decisions have already been made. To write equations, on the other hand, is to work, if not at the bottom of the pyramid, at least pretty down low, where most of the room lies but little if anything is predefined. Hence to design with mathematics in 2011 is not to design free of software, a futile if not wholly impossible claim in an age where software is the only idiom available. To work with mathematics is to work without interface, and the difference matters: like any channel of communication, the interface conveys as much as it fashions the message itself, ultimately undermining the authority of the designer.

The pattern-oriented design strategies devised by Daniel Bosia's Advanced Geometry Unit (AGU) at Arup (pp 58–65) provide a strong survey of the incredible creativity and pragmatic application, in different contexts and at different scales, of non-linearity, branching, recursion, complex proportional relationships and mathematical parametricism in practice. In all these projects the material considerations and an intimate knowledge of physical behaviour go hand in hand with a rigorous mathematical formalisation, abetted by the latest computational facilities. Similar concerns about spatial and organisational patterns, networks and scaling animate Michael Weinstock's masterful study of territorial growth and self-organisation (pp 102–7), reconciling the latest heuristic paradigms of flow and network topologies with a time-honoured progressivist model of city growth, where the mathematics of space operate at a large scale.[3]

Another line of argument unfolds in Scheurer and Stehling's practice, designtoproduction, where such issues are taken at the other end of the spectrum to the micro-level of component fabrication, resulting in ground-breaking structures in collaboration with architect Shigeru Ban. Tsigkari, Davis and Aish at Foster + Partners use projective geometry, chaotic/probabilistic algorithms and statistical analysis to calibrate the environmental performance of some of the largest buildings erected by the practice in the last decade. And Adams Kara Taylor (AKT) research associates Panagiotis Michalatos and Sawako Kaijima have devised an application of topology optimisation theory to facilitate an intuitive yet rigorous approach to structural scheme design in the early parts of the design process (pp 66–9).

Similar concerns abound in our own work at the London-based IJP (see the articles pp 44–53, 100–1 and 118–21). IJP explores the deployment of parametric analytic equations at all stages of the design and construction process, from scheme design to tender; and at all scales, from urban infrastructure to numerically fabricated installations. Over the past six years it has developed a unique body of knowledge about periodic equations, variously consistent with the constraints of numerical fabrication machinery (some better suited to sheet cutting, others to lamination). This direct mathematical approach to practice has already inspired a new generation of outstanding young architects, including Max Kahlen (see his Rising Masses project on pp 108–11) and Ana María Flor Ortiz and Rodia Valladares Sánchez (The Hinging Tower, pp 112–17), who studied under myself at the Architectural Association in London and Harvard University's Graduate School of Design (GSD), and whose recent final theses are in part reproduced in this issue. Among other things, these school projects for a new type of global high-rise building demonstrate the application of periodic equations and Fourier summations to the production of building diagrams while pointing to many new future directions.

In March 2010, Bernard Cache, Amy Dahan-Dalmedico, Antoine Picon, Dennis Shelden and myself participated in a conference on a related subject that I convened at Harvard, during which many ideas presented in this issue were initially discussed. The variety, scope and strength of this collection of projects and essays testify to the continued vitality of mathematics in space, an age-old discipline finding itself at a defining moment of acute re-actualisation and renewed relevance. ∆

Notes
1. Among others, see Antoine Picon, *Digital Culture in Architecture*, Birkhäuser Architecture (Basel), 2010; Michael Hensel, Achim Menges and Michael Weinstock, *AD Techniques and Technologies in Morphological Design*, Vol 76, No 2, 2006; Michael Hensel and Achim Menges, *AD Versatility and Vicissitude*, Vol 78, No 2, 2008; Michael Hensel, Achim Menges and Michael Weinstock, *Emergent Technologies and Design: Towards a Biological Paradigm for Architecture*, John Wiley & Sons (London), 2010; Michael Hensel, Achim Menges and Michael Weinstock, *AD Emergence: Morphogenetic Design Strategies*, May/June 2004.
2. Jean Victor Poncelet, *Traité des propriétés projectives des figures*, Bachelier (Paris), 1822.
3. Françoise Choay, *L'Urbanisme: Utopies et réalités* (Urban Planning: Utopia and Reality), Editions du Seuil (Paris), 1979.

Amy Dahan-Dalmedico

MATHEMATICS AND THE SENSIBLE WORLD
REPRESENTING, CONSTRUCTING, SIMULATING

Figure 1. Fdecomite, Perfect Colouring of Zv2 on the Riemann Sphere
The Riemann sphere (or extended complex plane in algebra and analysis) is the sphere obtained from the complex plane by adding a point at infinity.

The Paris-based scientific historian **Amy Dahan-Dalmedico** asks why a knowledge of numbers, algebra and abstract forms should be key to our understanding of the sensible world. As she reveals, mathematics, like the world itself, has shifted and fluctuated over time since its earliest origins in ancient Egypt. Evolving and morphing as a discipline, it has covered a diverse range of practices and theories.

Throughout its long history, the bond between mathematics and the sensible world has always fluctuated between three key philosophical attitudes: representation, construction and simulation. Beyond the immediate notions summoned by these simple terms, deeper meanings emerge, constantly shifting and reconfiguring one another at key moments of the history of mathematics.

Mathematics are not a stable and well-defined object, but rather a plurality of objects, practices, theories, cognitive and collective constructions, which have a history and great diversity. Scientific theories speak of neurons, atoms, celestial bodies, but also of numbers, groups or functions, most of them couched in the language of mathematics. Hence mathematics is applied to the natural world, to its forms, to space and to reality at large. Why does the knowledge of abstract objects, such as numbers or algebraic structures, help us better understand, control and master the sensible world and its forms? Several philosophical responses are conceivable, which have more or less always coexisted, and are the focus of this introductory essay to the subject.

Geometry originated in Egypt and Mesopotamia with the survey of land, until the Greeks assumed that an interest could be taken in exact forms that are only vaguely represented by objects: thus no longer a tree trunk, for instance, but a cylinder; no longer the edge of a plank, but a truly straight line; or an absolutely flat plane without dents or bumps, and so on. Geometry manipulated these ideal forms and around 300 BC built an impressive edifice out of them, Euclid's *Elements*, demonstrating the necessarily true properties of exact forms. Philosophy seized on this and declared that reality was an imperfect image of this exact world: the tree trunk became a defective cylinder, and the plank an adulterated plane. With Galileo, geometry entered the world and became reality itself. The totality of nature became a geometric edifice, an edifice we could learn to see. According to this realist point of view, mathematical objects really exist and the 'great book of the universe […] is written in the language of mathematics'.[1] In this sense, applied mathematics is verified by experience and constitutes an inherent and indispensable part of the empirical sciences.

Figure 2. Fdecomite, With a Little Help from my Polyhedron
Building the origami version of five intersecting tetrahedra is a real puzzle. The Wenninger model is of great help for assembling all parts in the right order. The term 'polyhedron' refers to a solid with flat faces.

By contrast, a large number of mathematicians, notably the prestigious members of Bourbaki, the Paris-based collective which developed highly abstract and theoretical mathematics from 1930 to 1970, defended a so-called Platonist realism, rooted in the belief that a mathematical reality exists independently of the human mind. The fact that mathematicians often reach the same results with similar objects through separate paths greatly incites them to believe in the independent existence of these objects. Hence, statements about mathematical objects such as Euler's theorem (the number of vertices and edges minus the number of faces of the polyhedron is equal to 2), seem to present themselves to mathematicians who merely 'discover' their properties.

A further philosophical divide opposes Platonist realism to a tradition of Constructivist philosophy of mathematics. Constructivism posits that all truth is constructed, without reference to whatever it conforms to. For Austrian philosopher Ludwig Wittgenstein, for example, the mathematical understanding of a statement does not exist outside of its proof, and in this sense the mathematician is merely an inventor (as opposed to a discoverer) who establishes connections and forms descriptions, but does not describe real facts.[2]

Mathematics is certainly characterised by an impressive coherence, seemingly superhuman, that distinguishes it from other human practices. Practitioners of mathematics frequently express a strong subjective sense of discovery or of the exploration of a terra incognita that is already extant and consistent. However, while the universality of mathematical objects does speak in favour of some kind of realism, the discoveries of logic in the 20th century have made this position difficult to defend. In 1931, Kurt Gödel showed that any coherent axiomatic system, a system without contradictions, features propositions that cannot be proven true or false; while other mathematical results from set theory reinforce the sentiment of the 'unreality' of the world of mathematics.

For the proponents of a Platonist realist view, mathematical objects are figments of the human imagination, and mathematical theories principally useful fictions. The philosopher Hartry Field went as far as proposing that mathematical theories are literally false since their objects do not really exist. Yet what characterises a fiction is not so much its logical status (whether it is true or false), but its cognitive function. As representations whose purpose is less to provide an accurate description of reality than to help us imagine possibly unreal situations, fictions are assisting our imagination, and that

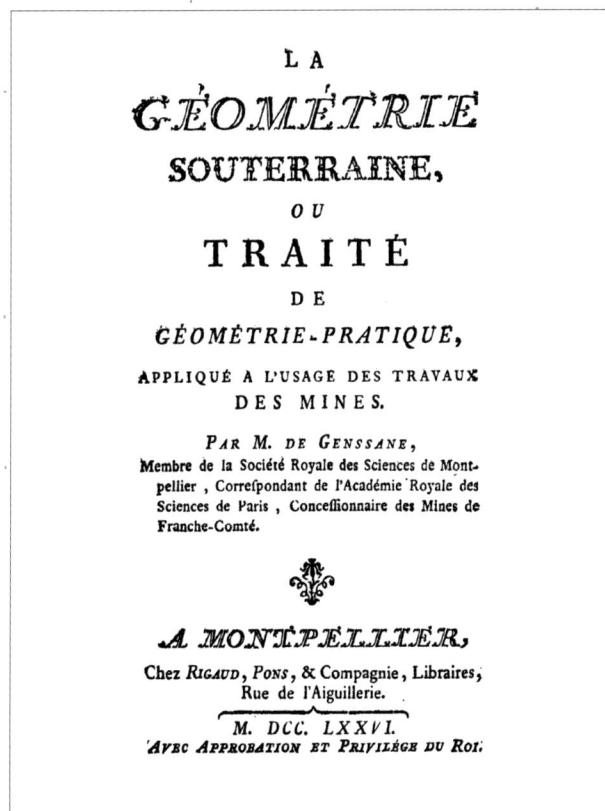

Figure 3. M de Genssane, *La Géométrie Souterraine ou Traité de géométrie pratique appliqué à l'usage des travaux des mines* (Subterranean Geometry or Applied Geometry Treatise Intended for All Manners of Mining Works), 1776
Works such as this treatise of applied geometry by a well-known French mining engineer in the 18th century disseminated the emerging paradigm of analytic geometry.

is where their scientific pertinence lies, science being more than a mere collection of facts. To produce theories we must envision hypotheses and explore their consequences; we must build models of phenomena, and formulate idealisations. Imagining is not only representing an unreal situation, but simulating it; all simulations must be represented in a hypothetical 'as if' mode, which fiction and imagination support. Thus, in constant interaction with one another, representing, constructing and simulating form three inseparable moments of mathematical activity: to represent an object, other objects must be constructed from it; to construct an abstract object (a function, a transformation), we must represent it; and to simulate an object, we must elaborate fictitious representations which mobilise more constructions at will.

A.02 *Where the Truly Formless Lives*

GSD2404 L. LEGENDRE

LIBERATORE Cara

$n1 := 0, 1 .. \ 24$ $m1 := 0, 1 .. \ 24$

$iT(u,v) := \dfrac{u}{\pi} \cdot 30$ $jT(u,v) := \dfrac{v}{\pi} \cdot 30$ $sh(u,v) := 10 \cdot \cos\sqrt{2\left(\dfrac{u}{\pi}-\dfrac{1}{2}\right)^2 \cdot 2\left(\dfrac{v}{\pi}-\dfrac{1}{2}\right)^2 \cdot 200 \cdot \pi}$

$iThread_{m1,n1} := iT\left(\dfrac{m1}{24}\cdot\pi, \dfrac{n1}{24}\cdot\pi\right)$ $jThread_{m1,n1} := jT\left(\dfrac{m1}{24}\cdot\pi, \dfrac{n1}{24}\cdot\pi\right)$ $shape_{m1,n1} := sh\left(\dfrac{m1}{24}\cdot\pi, \dfrac{n1}{24}\cdot\pi\right)$

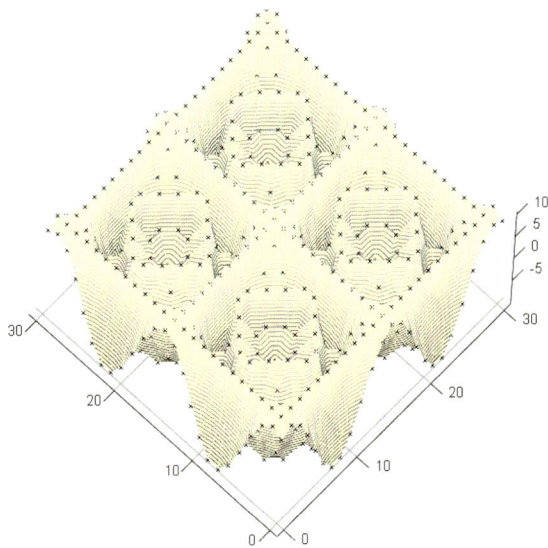

(jThread, iThread, shape)

_PROFILE OF 2 ITHREADS (BLUE) AND 1 JTHREAD (RED)

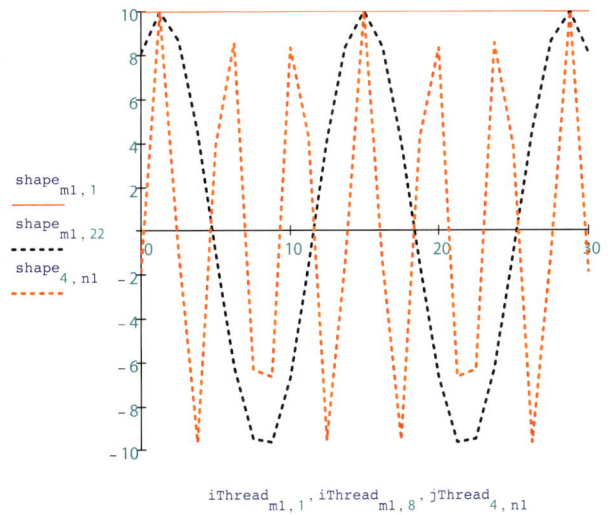

$shape_{m1,1}$
$shape_{m1,22}$
$shape_{4,n1}$

$iThread_{m1,1}, iThread_{m1,8}, jThread_{4,n1}$

Figure 4. Cara Liberatore, Where the Truly Formless Lives, Superficial Spaces, Harvard Graduate School of Design, Cambridge, Massachusetts, 2010
Analytic geometry at work: a coarse quadruple parametric ripple with sectional parametric curves. This warm up piece was submitted in response to a question on form and formlessness.

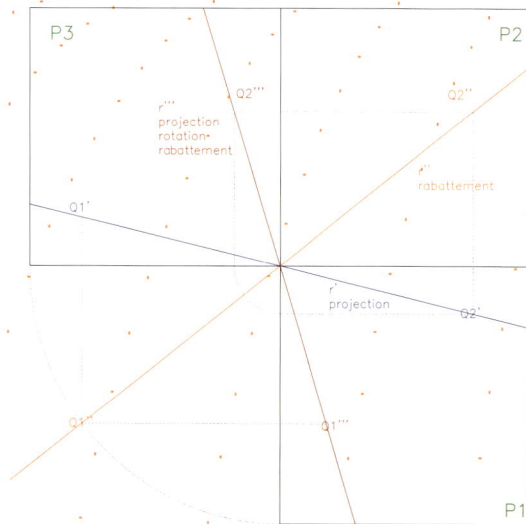

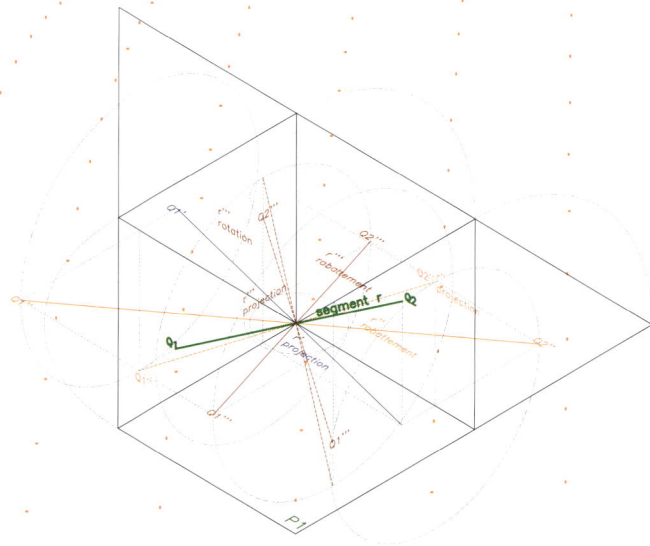

Figure 5. Stefano Rabolli-Pansera, Stereotomic Self-Portrait, Diploma Unit 5
(Engineering the Immaterial), Architectural Association, London, 2003
Descriptive geometry at work, submitted in response to an undergraduate
design brief on self-representation. The Mongean representation of the drawing
plane demonstrates a technique unchanged since the late 18th century.

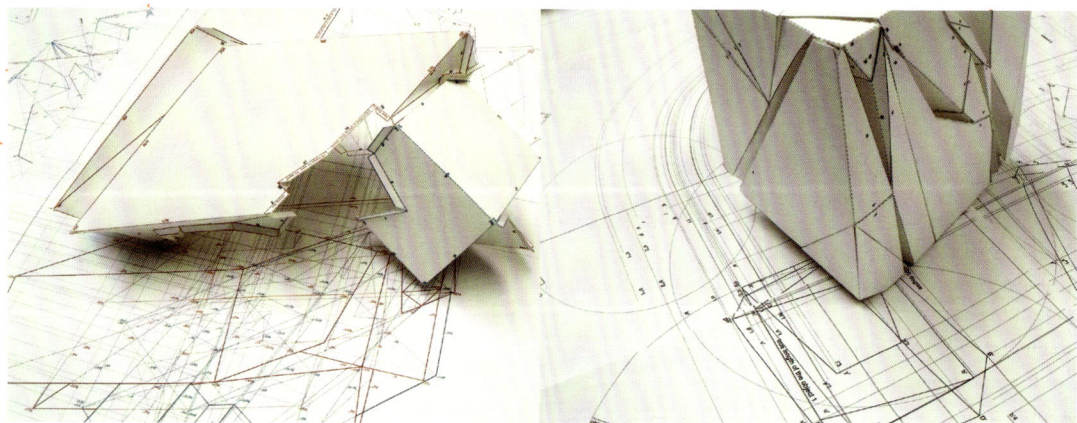

Figure 6. Matthew Chan, Stereotomic Self-Portrait,
Diploma Unit 5, Architectural Association, London, 2003
Several successive derivations of stereotomic projection
(projective geometry applied to stone cutting) result
in a highly articulated prismatic object recording, in
metaphorical and narrative terms, an argument between
the author and his girlfriend.

Figure 7. Harold Tan, Stereotomic Self-Portrait, Diploma
Unit 5, Architectural Association, London, 2003
In this particular narrative, the deployment of stereotomic
projection to subtract portions of matter from a solid
cube offers a metaphor of the application of colour
inversion within the cubic red-green-blue (RGB) space
of the additive light colour model (a slice of which we
casually experience when using the 'colour-picker' of
digital imaging software).

In conclusion, is mathematical realism independent of sensible reality? Is mathematics to be found in the world, or in our minds and imagination? The argument is without a doubt impossible to settle and, unless one is a philosopher, a bit of a waste of time: the question of mathematical realism is a metaphysical problem, forever unanswerable or irrefutable. The development of the neurosciences has hardly made a difference in this regard. For the defenders of an ideal (or Platonist) realism, the brain may possess structures that give it access to the independent universe of mathematics. For those who envision a realism inscribed in sensible reality, mathematics is simply in the world, and since our brains are tailored by the process of evolution to understand the world, we are naturally drawn to doing mathematics.

The historian not directly immersed in creative mathematical activity (nor prone to making philosophical statements) will contend that the historical and cultural contexts are key to the emergence of certain concepts. Mathematics being a human construction inscribed in a temporal dimension, it is difficult to conceive of a mathematical reality out of time and out of touch with its surroundings. And since the very essence of cultural facts is to emerge among small human groups and amalgamate in larger families while preserving their specificity, mathematics aspires to working with universal structures, which is one of its lasting characteristics. It is also unbelievably diverse. Because of the hegemony of the form inherited from Greek mathematics, it took some time to recognise the great diversity of forms of mathematical expression. Yet, strikingly, such diverse forms are comparable, and it is possible to rigorously reinterpret the mathematical knowledge of one civilisation within the context of another.

Furthermore an understanding of mathematical reality inscribed in history, space, time and culture imbues the work needed to reconstruct and analyse mathematical practices with veritable meaning. Thinking, for example, of complex numbers as eternal members of a Platonic heaven of mathematical ideas, leads us to conceptualise the development of this key concept as a series of increasingly accurate approximations of its present-day formulation, always presumed to be its perfect embodiment. Such a deterministic history may be useful to the mathematician and the student, but it does not take into account the highly contingent aspects of the formation of mathematical knowledge, with its generally chaotic course and winding paths of discovery. The historians of mathematics with a finite amount of time to dedicate to each phase of history cannot embrace all of the meanderings of mathematical practice as it historically developed. They must compromise between a dimension of historicity proper to mathematical knowledge and mathematics' potential objectivity and universality.

A (Very) Brief History of the Mathematics of Space

With the notable exception of Archimedes' treatise 'On Spirals' (225 BC), the mathematics of Greek antiquity was only concerned with immobile objects contemplated in a sort of universe of ideas. The Ancients did use some analogous curves to explore intractable problems (for example, the duplication of the cube), but discounted such findings as unworthy of what they would have hoped to obtain using a ruler and a compass.

The 17th century witnessed the concurrent birth of infinitesimal calculus and the science of movement, bringing radically different conceptions of mathematics to a head. Concerned with methodological rigour and the need for generality, René Descartes did not see curves as spatial realities for their own sake, but as the set of solutions to a given equation. For Isaac Newton, on the other hand, all measurements were a function of time. A curve derived through the Newtonian Method of Fluxions was a reality that moved and animated. The tension opposing the two titans of the 17th century was not only a matter of temperament, or a historical fluke. It expressed the very nature of mathematics, torn between two opposed yet inseparable trends: on the one hand we have rigour, an economy of means and an aesthetic standard. On the other, a will to conquer and the desire to force one's way down new paths. From the latter's point of view, mathematics should not only be a well-ordered ceremonial, but a tool for controlling and creating things.

Geometry's original aim was the measurement of angles, lengths and surfaces, but from the Renaissance onwards, artistic curiosity began to represent the real to better understand it. For the geometers of the 19th century, a period witnessing the explosion of a realist understanding of the discipline, descriptive geometry was essentially a graphical procedure for tackling numerous real practical problems. In 1822, however, Jean-Victor Poncelet explored the properties of figures remaining invariant by projection with the systematic help of infinite or imaginary elements, endowing projective geometry with a far greater degree of abstraction and generality. Many more developments were to come. Working independently during the first decades of the 19th century, Nikolai Lobachevski and János Bolyai reached the conclusion (already intuited by CF Gauss after

1813) that a geometry of space did 'exist' and conform on many points to Euclidean geometry, with the exception of the so-called Fifth Postulate (through a point outside of a line pass an infinity of parallels to that line). By the middle of that century, numerous constructions of Euclidean models of non-Euclidean geometries provided these discoveries with intuitive support and accelerated their ultimate acceptance. In 1872, studying the properties of figures left invariant by a given class of transformations, Felix Klein reorganised the body of all known geometries. By identifying curves in space with binary quadratic forms, Klein advocated the merger of geometry and algebra, now an established tendency of contemporary mathematics.

After the prodigious development of geometry in the 19th century, the time had come to rebuild the foundations of mathematics, which the advent of non-Euclidean geometries had shaken. A powerful research movement converged towards the axiomatisation of geometry, led by David Hilbert and his *Foundations of Geometry* (1899).[3] Beginning with undefined objects whose nature hardly mattered – points, lines, planes or chairs, tables or spoons – Hilbert specified relations between them through axioms, or given rules, no longer seeing the elements of geometry as intuitively realistic objects, but as variables of a formal language (or their symbols). The *Foundations* owes its radical novelty to its capacity to integrate the general with the technical and mathematical philosophy with practice. Hilbert was the first to fully consider space as a mathematical concept, rather than as the site of our experience, declaring geometry a formal science rather than a set of propositions about 'reality', and breaking, for the first time, the bond between this foundational discipline and the sensible world.

In stark contrast to the Hilbertian project, the Frenchman Henri Poincaré dedicated himself to what he called 'problems that are formulated' as opposed to 'problems that we formulate'. Scorning problems artificially fabricated by mathematicians, Poincaré privileged above all the large questions arising in the natural sciences, such as the study of celestial mechanics, which led him to develop qualitative methods for the study of dynamic systems. By combining local and general points of view, such methods explored the relative relationships and general behaviour of trajectories, their stability and complexity, allowing one to look for mathematical solutions even when they were not quantifiable. From these new methods, other mathematicians have been able to develop current theories of complexity and chaos.

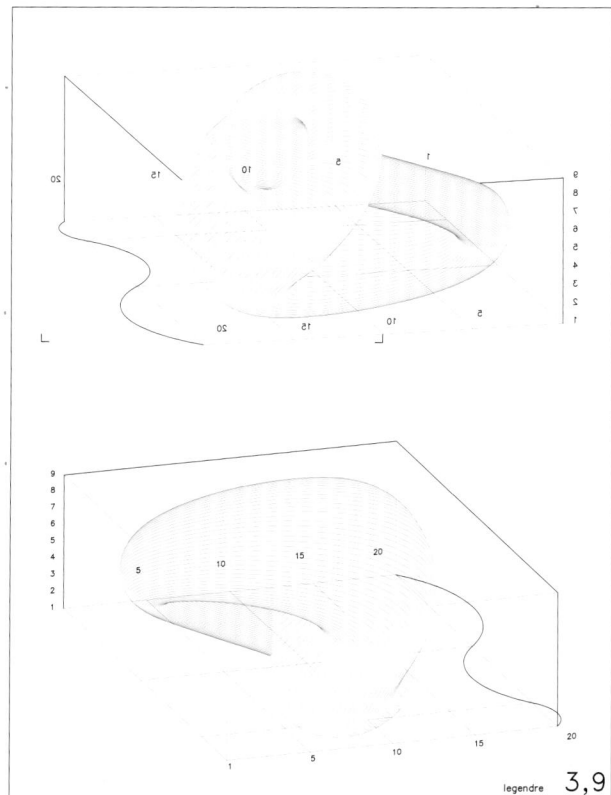

Figure 8. George L Legendre, Mono-Linear Klein Bottle, 2003
Ribbing along the direction of the warp emphasises the cross-section of the bottle's tubular body and its variable girth, from thin neck to thick midriff. Ribbing along the other way enhances the perception that the bottle turns in on itself. The weft outlines the notional continuity between interior and exterior for which the Klein bottle is famed.

Recent Developments

Today the image of mathematics ruled by structures and the axiomatic method is a matter of the past. In a technological environment characterised by the omnipresence of computers, a different set of domains – those precisely excluded by the axiomatic and structuralist programme – have acquired an increasing importance: discrete mathematics, algorithms, recursive logic and functions, coding theory, probability theory and statistics, dynamical systems and so on. When the disciplinary hierarchy is upset in such a way, the role of past mathematicians must be re-evaluated, and mathematics' own methodology re-examined. With the recent advance of the science of chaos, for example, mathematics eclipsed by the Hilbertian heritage, such as Poincaré's qualitative methods, have _ranges $n1 := 0, 1 \dots 20$ $m1 := 0, 1 \dots 128$

_equations $iT(u,v) := \cos(u) \cdot 6$ $jT(u,v) := \sin(u) \cdot 6 + \frac{3}{2} + -\sin\left(v + \frac{\pi}{2}\right) + 2.5 \cdot \cos\left(v + \frac{\pi}{2}\right) - 1.3 \cdot \cos\left(v + \frac{\pi}{2}\right)$ $sh(u,v) := \frac{v}{\pi} \cdot 20$

$iThread_{m1,n1} := iT\left(\frac{m1}{128} \cdot 2\pi, \frac{n1}{20} \cdot 2\pi\right)$ $jThread_{m1,n1} := jT\left(\frac{m1}{128} \cdot 2\pi, \frac{n1}{20} \cdot 2\pi\right)$ $shape_{m1,n1} := sh\left(\frac{m1}{128} \cdot 2\pi, \frac{n1}{20} \cdot 2\pi\right)$

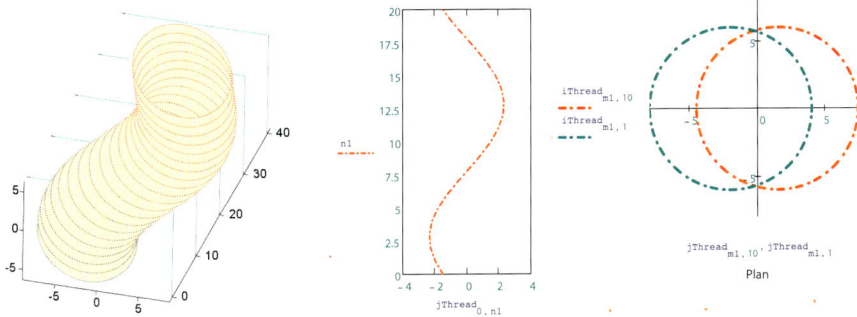

$iThread_{m1,10}$
$iThread_{m1,1}$

n1

$jThread_{m1,10}$ $jThread_{m1,1}$
Plan

(jThread, iThread, shape)

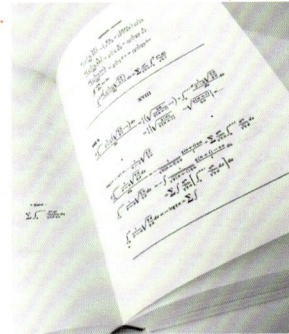

Figure 9. George L Legendre, High-Rise Sketch, 2011
Analytic geometry at work: a parametric circle swept
along a periodic curve.

Figure 11. Evariste Galois, *Ecrits et
mémoires Mathématiques* (Collected
Writings on Mathematics), fragment from
unpublished manuscript, 1832
Galois made significant contributions to the
emergence of algebraic structures in the
19th century.

_ranges $n1 := 0, 1 \dots 360$ $m1 := 0, 1 \dots 4$

_equations $iT(u,v) := \left(\cos\left(2 \cdot u + \frac{\pi}{4}\right) + 6\,\text{asin}\left(\cos\frac{v}{2} + \frac{\pi}{2}\right)\right) \cdot 45$ $jT(u,v) := \left(\sin\left(2 \cdot u + \frac{\pi}{4}\right) + 2\,\text{asin}(\cos(5v + \pi))\right) \cdot 45$ $sh(u,v) := \text{asin}(\cos(6v)) \cdot \frac{840}{3}$

$iThread_{m1,n1} := iT\left(\frac{m1}{4}\pi, \frac{n1}{360}\pi\right)$ $jThread_{m1,n1} := jT\left(\frac{m1}{4}\pi, \frac{n1}{360}\pi\right)$ $shape_{m1,n1} := sh\left(\frac{m1}{4}\pi, \frac{n1}{360}\pi\right)$

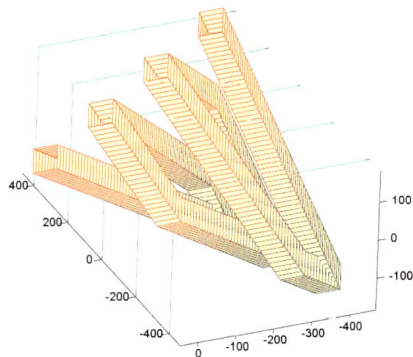

(jThread, iThread, shape)

Figure 10. Mark Lewis, George L Legendre, Richard Liu and Kazuaki
Yoneda, Parametric Seed, Option Studio Rising Masses II, Harvard
Graduate School of Design, Cambridge, Massachusetts, 2010
The deployment of the arcsine function discretises and 'straightens out' a
translated solid with a smooth, periodic profile. The seed was eventually
developed into a high-rise proposal by Richard Liu and Kazuaki Yoneda.

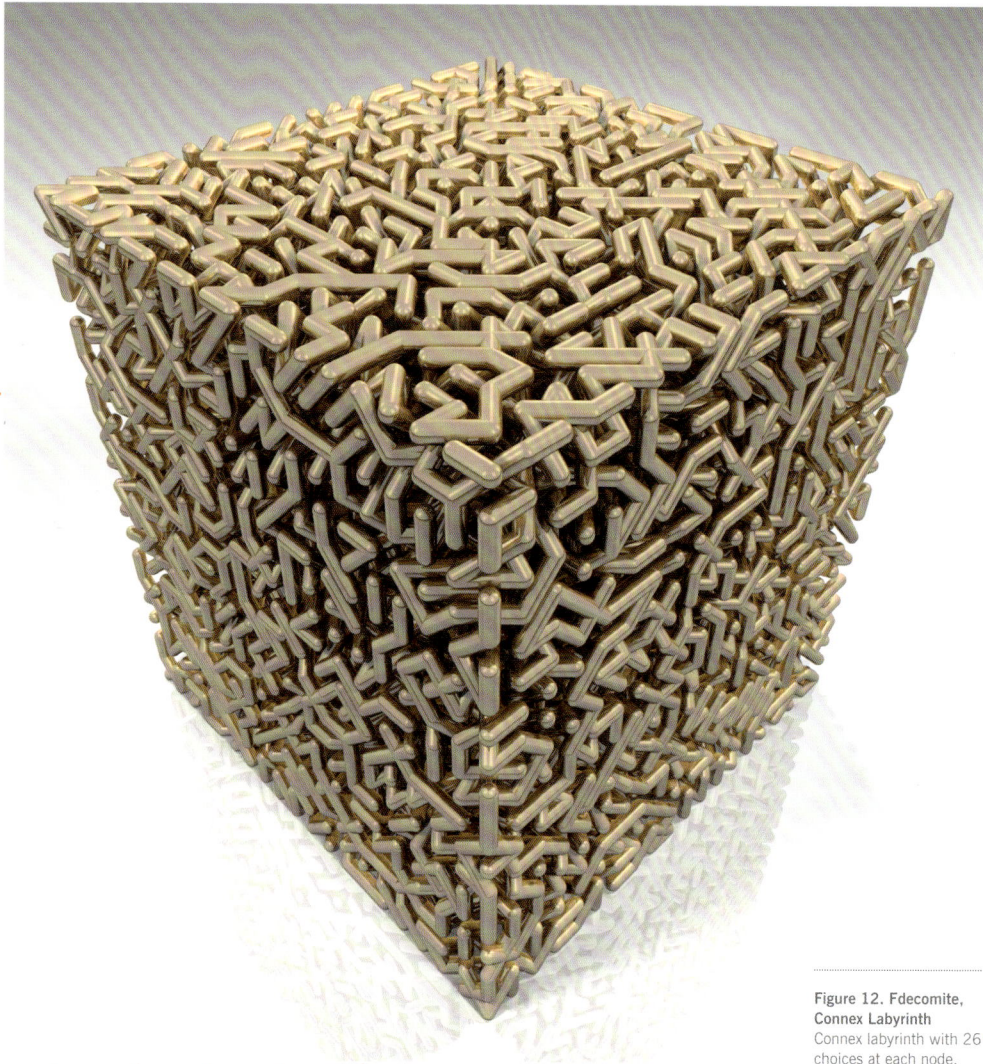

Figure 12. Fdecomite,
Connex Labyrinth
Connex labyrinth with 26
choices at each node.

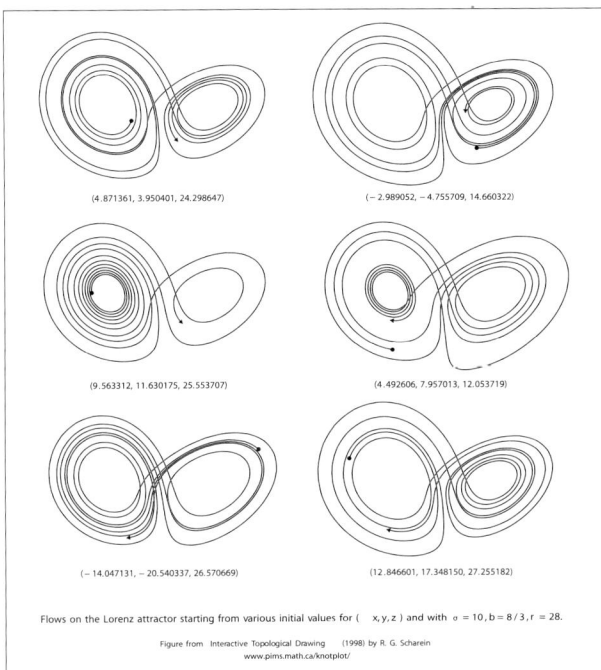

(4.871361, 3.950401, 24.298647)

(−2.989052, −4.755709, 14.660322)

(9.563312, 11.630175, 25.553707)

(4.492606, 7.957013, 12.053719)

(−14.047131, −20.540337, 26.570669)

(12.846601, 17.348150, 27.255182)

Flows on the Lorenz attractor starting from various initial values for (x, y, z) and with σ = 10, b = 8 / 3 , r = 28.

Figure from Interactive Topological Drawing   (1998) by R. G. Scharein
www.pims.math.ca/knotplot/

Figure 13. Rob Scharein, Chart of the unpredictable states of the Lorenz attractor, 2007
The Lorenz attractor is a non-linear dynamic system simulating the two-dimensional flow of fluid for given temperature, gravity, buoyancy, diffusivity, and viscosity factors.

regained an important position. Similarly, the experimental method is no longer regarded as an antinomy to mathematics. While in the 1950s or 1960s structure was the emblematic paradigm of science, the notion of model is more typical of today's knowledge, even if it is premature to affirm that it will ultimately prevail.

In the 1980s, under the joint influence of technological progress and the increased awareness of the social dimension of mathematical practice, questions emerged in the community that, a few years earlier, would have been deemed totally incongruous. A new type of demonstration heavily reliant on the computer, such as the four-colour theorem by K Appel and W Haken (1986), called into question the very nature of proof in mathematics: how could a human mind grasp a demonstration which filled nearly 400 pages and distinguished close to 1,500 configurations by means of long automatic procedures? Starting from computer-generated proofs, the discussion soon moved to other types of demonstrations, either unusually expansive or mobilising an extremely complex architecture of conjectures stemming from various domains – the work of Edward Witten on knot theory and string theory (after 1997) comes to mind.

The computer's contribution to mathematical research was not, however, a new development; the evolutionary pattern of exploring results using the machine was already established and irreversible. A large number of conjectures emerging from extensive computational activity had been used for years before they could be rigorously proved, as was the case, for instance, with the topological properties of the Lorenz attractor. The founders of the journal *Experimental Mathematics*[4] summed up this trend unequivocally: 'The role of computers in suggesting conjectures and enriching our understanding of abstract concepts by means of examples and visualisation is a healthy and welcome development.'[5]

From the 1980s onwards the increasingly pressing theme of the social dimension of mathematics gradually brought the discipline back to earth. As the great mathematician William Thurston wrote: 'Mathematical knowledge and understanding [are] embedded in the minds and in the *social fabric* of the community of people thinking about a particular topic …. In any field, there is a strong social standard of validity and truth ….'[6] Similarly, René Thom claimed that 'rigour can be no more than a local and sociological criterion'.[7] When called upon to check Andrew Wiles's proof of Fermat's theorem in 2001, several mathematicians recognised that the social and institutional dimension of the confidence vested in them were at least as decisive a factor as the rigour of the verification they could perform. Hence, advocated since the 1960s by both philosophers and historians of science, the sociological dimension of mathematics eventually caught up with those thinkers so far least amenable to it. ∞

Notes
1. Galileo Galilei, *Il Saggiatore*, Edition Nationale Barberin (Florence), Vol 6, 1896, p 322.
2. Ludwig Wittgenstein, *Lectures on the Foundations of Mathematics*, Cambridge 1939. ed Cora Diamond, University of Chicago Press (Chicago, IL), 1975.
3. David Hilbert, *Foundations of Geometry*, 1899. Trans EJ Townsend, PhD, University Of Illinois Reprint Edition, The Open Court Publishing Company (La Salle, IL), 1950.
4. The journal *Experimental Mathematics* was founded in 1991 by D Epstein and S Levy.
5. D Epstein and S Levy, 'Experimentation and Proof in Mathematics', *Notices of the American Mathematical Society*, Vol 42, No 6, 1995, pp 670–4.
6. WP Thurston, 'On Proof and Progress in Mathematics', *Bulletin of the American Mathematical Society*, Vol 30, No 2, 1994, pp 161–77.
7. R Thom, 'Mathématique et Théorisation scientifique', in M Loi (ed), *Penser les mathématiques*, Le Seuil (Paris), 1982, pp 252–73.

Figure 1. Philibert De L'Orme, *The Good Architect,* from *Le Premier Tome de l'Architecture de Philibert De L'Orme* (Paris), 1567
Restraint is clearly among the characteristics of the good architect.

Antoine Picon

ARCHITECTURE AND MATHEMATICS

BETWEEN HUBRIS AND RESTRAINT

The introduction of calculus-based mathematics in the 18th century proved fatal for the relationship of mathematics and architecture. As **Antoine Picon**, Professor of History of Architecture and Technology at Harvard Graduate School of Design, highlights, when geometry was superseded by calculus it resulted in an ensuing estrangement from architecture, an alienation that has persisted even with the widespread introduction of computation. It is a liaison that Picon characterises as having shifted between hubris and restraint.

Until the 18th century, following the Renaissance's preoccupations with perspective and geometry, the relations between mathematics and architecture were both intense and ambiguous. Mathematics was sometimes envisaged as the true foundation of the architectural discipline, sometimes as a collection of useful instruments of design. Mathematics empowered the architect, but also reminded him of the limits of what he could reasonably aim at. Inseparably epistemological and practical, both about power and restraint, the references to mathematics, more specifically to arithmetic and geometry, were a pervasive aspect of architecture.

Towards the end of the 18th century, the diffusion of calculus gradually estranged architecture from mathematics. When they looked for foundations, 19th-century architects like Eugène-Emmanuel Viollet-le-Duc were more interested by the sciences of life than by the new calculus-based mathematics of their time. While arithmetic and geometry remained highly useful practical tools, they gradually lost their aura of cutting-edge design techniques.

This estrangement has lasted until today, even if the computer has enabled architects to put calculus to immediate use. Actually, today's situation is quite paradoxical insofar that under the influence of digital tools architecture has never used so many mathematical objects, from Bézier curves to algorithms, while remaining indifferent to the question of its relation to mathematics. A better understanding of the scope and meaning that mathematics used to have for architects might very well represent a necessary step in order to overcome this indifference. The purpose of this article is to contribute to such an understanding.

Mathematics as Foundation

From the Renaissance onwards, the use of mathematical proportions was widespread among architects who claimed to follow the teachings of Roman architect and engineer Vitruvius. This use was clearly related to the ambition to ground architecture on firm principles that seemed to possess a natural character. For the physical world was supposed to obey proportions, from the laws governing the resistance of materials and constructions to the harmonic relations perceived by the ear.

The interest in proportions was related to the intuitive content that arithmetic and geometry possessed. As we will see, the strong relation between mathematics and the intuitive understanding of space was later jeopardised by the development of calculus. But it bore also the mark of two discrepant points of view.

Proportion could be first interpreted as the very essence of the world. Envisaged in this light, proportion possessed a divine origin. The 17th-century French theologian and philosopher Jacques Bénigne Bossuet gave a striking expression of this conception when he declared in one of his treatises that God had created the world by establishing the principles of order and proportion.[1] In this perspective, proportion was about power, about the demiurgic power of creation, and the architect appeared as the surrogate of God when he mobilised, in his turn, this power to plan his buildings.

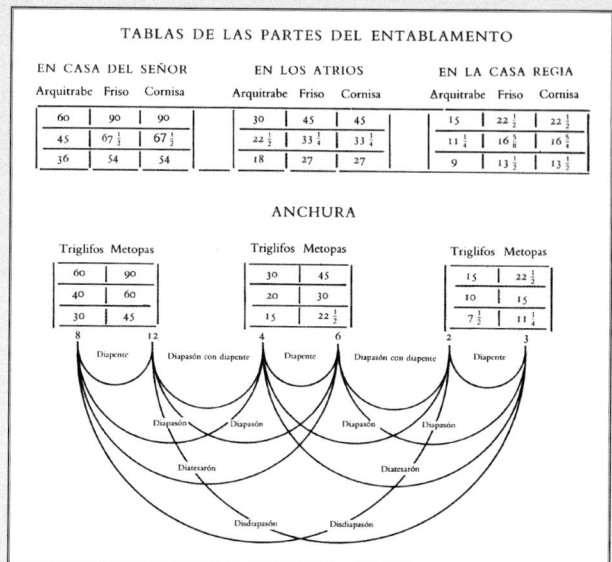

Figure 2. Juan Bautista Villalpandus, Chart of the proportions of the entablature of the Temple of Jerusalem, from *El Tratado de la Arquitectura Perfecta en La Última Visión del Profeta Ezequiel* (Rome), 1596–1604
The architectural discipline was supposed to emulate the creative power of the Divinity by following those very rules of proportion that were constitutive of the Creation and that had been dictated by God to the builders of the Temple of Jerusalem.

Following Spanish Jesuit Juan Bautista Villalpandus's detailed reconstruction of the Temple of Jerusalem based on an interpretation of Prophet Ezekiel's vision and published between 1596 and 1604, the large array of speculations regarding the proportions dictated by God to the builders of the temple stemmed from the belief that architectural design was ultimately an expression of demiurgic power. Historian Joseph Rykwert has shown how influential these speculations were on the development of the architectural discipline in the 16th and 17th centuries.[2] Through the use of proportions the architect experienced the exhilaration of empowerment.

But proportion could also be envisaged under a different point of view, a point of view adopted by Renaissance theorist Leon Battista Alberti for whom the purpose of architecture was to create a world commensurate with the finitude of man, a world in which he would be sheltered from the crude and destructive light of the divine. In this second perspective, proportion was no longer about the hubris brought by unlimited power, but about its reverse: moderation, restraint. Philosopher Pierre Caye summarises this second attitude by stating that the aim of architects like Alberti was to rebuild something akin to Noah's Ark rather than to emulate the Temple of Jerusalem.[3] It is worth noting that such a conception was to reappear much later with Le Corbusier and his Modulor, which was inseparable from the attempt to conceive architecture as the core of a totally designed environment that would reconcile man within his inherent finitude.[4]

Exhilaration of power on the one hand, and the restraint necessary to protect man from the unforgiving power of the divine on the other: the reference to mathematics in the Vitruvian tradition balanced between these two extremes. Such polarity was perhaps necessary to give proportion its full scope. Now, one may be tempted to generalise and to transform this tension into a condition for mathematics to play the role of a basis for architecture. Another way to put it would be to say that in order to provide a truly enticing foundational model for architecture, mathematics must appear both as synonymous with power and with the refusal to abandon oneself to seduction of power. For this is what architecture is ultimately about: a practice, a form action that has to do both with asserting power and refusing to fully abandon oneself to it. On the one hand the indisputable presence of the built object is synonymous with the permanence of power; on the other the same built object opposes its opacity, and a certain form of instability, at least if we are to follow Peter Eisenman's analyses, to the sprawling domination of power.

To conclude on this point, one may observe that this polarity, or rather this balance, has been compromised today. For the mathematical procedures architects have to deal with, from calculus to algorithms, are decidedly on the side of power. Nature has replaced God, emergence the traditional process of creation, but its power expressed in mathematical terms conveys the same exhilaration, the same risk of unchecked hubris as in prior times. What we might want to recover is the possibility for mathematics to be also about restraint, about stepping aside in front of the power at work in the universe.

It is interesting to note how the quest for restraint echoes some of our present concerns with sustainability. The only thing that should probably not be forgotten is that just like the use of mathematics, sustainability is necessarily dual; it is as much about power as about restraint. Our contemporary approach to sustainability tends to be as simplistic as our reference to mathematics, albeit in the opposite direction.

Tools for Regulation and/or Invention

Let us turn now to mathematics as tools. From an architectural standpoint, the same mathematical principle can be simultaneously foundational and practical. Vitruvian proportion corresponded both to a way to ground architecture theoretically and to a method to produce buildings. In this domain also, a duality is at work.

This second duality has to do with the fact that tools may be seen as regulatory instruments enabling coordination and

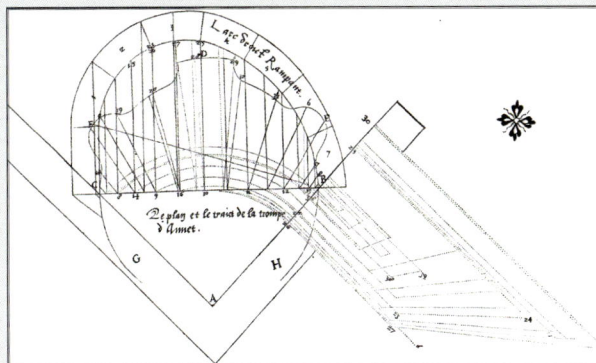

Figure 4. Philibert De L'Orme, geometrical construction of the squinch of Anet, from *Le Premier Tome de l'Architecture de Philibert De L'Orme* (Paris), 1567
For De L'Orme, mathematics, and geometry in particular, was the foundation of architectural invention.

control, giving precedence to standardisation upon invention. Until the 18th century, most uses of mathematics and proportion had in practice to do with coordination and control rather than with the search for new solutions. But tools can be mobilised to explore the yet unknown; they can serve invention. From the Renaissance on, the geometry used for stone-cutting, also known as stereotomy, illustrates perfectly this ambivalence.

On the one hand, from Philibert De L'Orme to Gaspard Monge, this geometry of a projective nature was seen by its promoters as a means to exert greater control on architectural production. But this ambition was accompanied with the somewhat contradictory desire to promote individual invention. De L'Orme epitomises this contradiction. Besides major architectural realisation like the castle of Anet or the Tuileries royal palace, his main legacy was the first comprehensive theoretical account of the geometric methods enabling designers to master the art of stereotomy. Until De L'Orme, this art was a secret transmitted from master mason to apprentice, a secret based on recipes and knowhow. De L'Orme was actually the first to understand some of the underlying projective principles at work in such a practice. For the architect, the aim was twofold. First, he wanted to achieve a better control of the building production. It is not fortuitous that De L'Orme was the first architect to be entrusted with major administrative responsibility by the crown. But the objective was also to invent. The best demonstration of this art of invention was in his eyes the variation of the Montpellier squinch that he designed for Anet. The identification of the true regulatory principles at work in a given practice could lead to truly innovative combinations.[5]

Control and invention, these two objectives were also on the agenda of mathematician Gaspard Monge, the inventor of descriptive geometry. Descriptive geometry actually derived from the geometry used for stereotomy that had been explored by De L'Orme at the dawn of the French Renaissance. For Monge, descriptive geometry was both about standardisation and invention.[6]

In a similar vein to the hypothesis concerning mathematics as a theoretical foundation for architecture, the following can be proposed: in order to provide truly enticing tools for designers, mathematics must be about both control and invention. Today, what might be often lacking is not so much

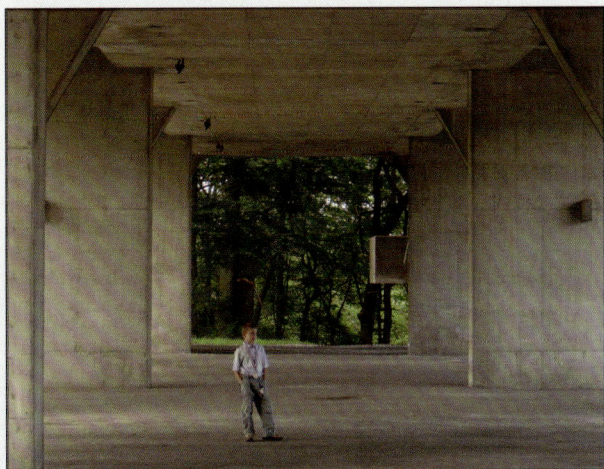

Figure 3. Le Corbusier, Unité d'Habitation de Firminy, France, 1946–52
Le Corbusier's objective is to place man within a totally designed environment.

. . . calculus would also be instrumental in the development of economic theory by providing the means to study the circulation of goods and capitals.

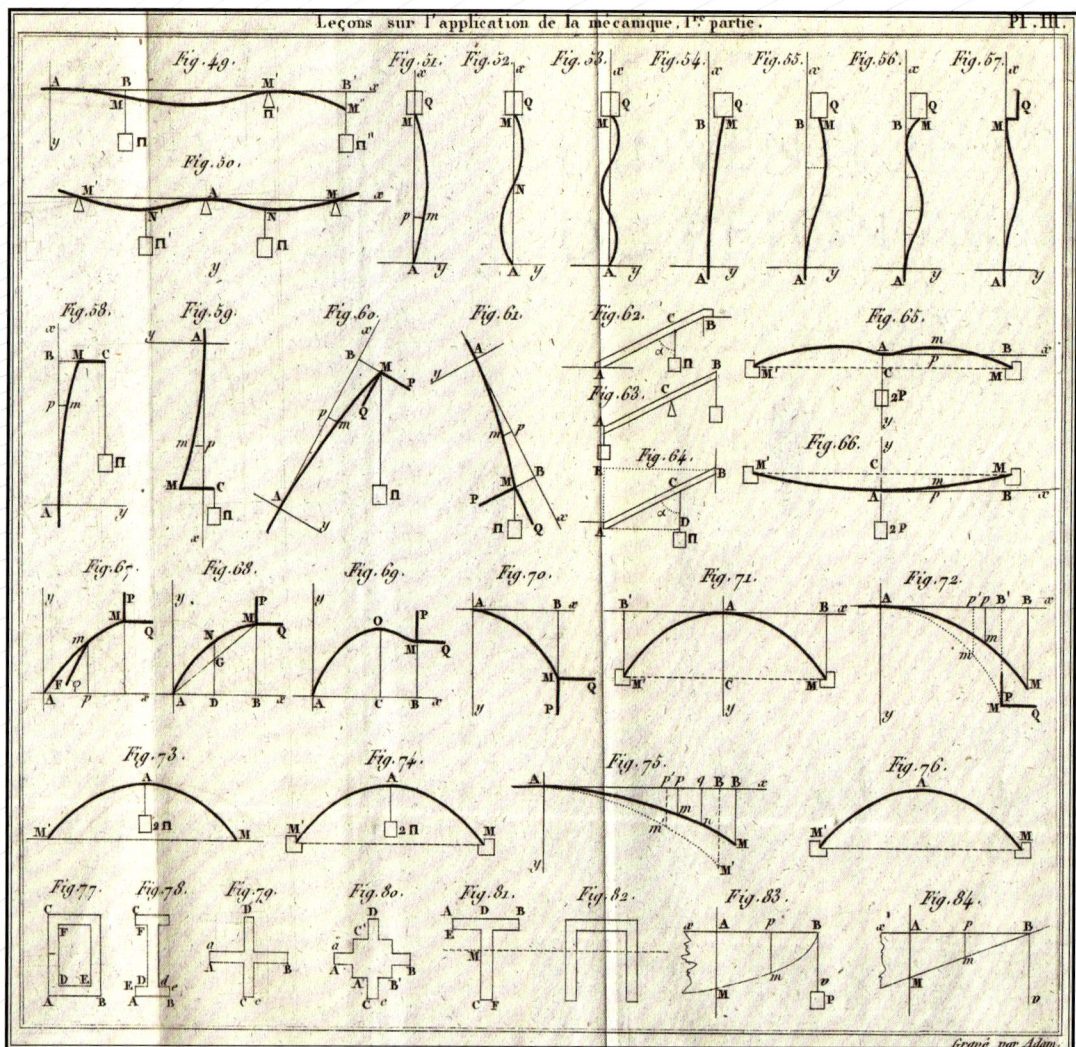

Figure 5. Claude Navier, Study of the bending of elastic curves, from *Résumé des Leçons (…) sur l'Application de la Mécanique à l'Etablissement des Constructions et des Machines* (Paris), 1826
Navier's work marks the triumph of calculus in the science of constructions.

the capacity of mathematics to be on the side of invention, but rather its contribution to the framing and standardisation of design problems. In contemporary cutting-edge digital practices, mathematical entities and models are most of the time mobilised in a perspective that has to do with emergence, with the capacity to amaze, to thwart received schemes.

One of the best examples of this orientation lies in the way topology has been generally understood these days. What has most of the time retained the imagination of designers are topological singularities, what mathematician René Thom has dubbed as 'catastrophes'. This explains the fascination exerted on architects by topological entities like the Möbius strip or the Klein bottle. This interpretation of topology is at odds with what mathematicians consider as its principal objective, namely the study of invariance. Whereas architects are usually interested in extreme cases that allow surprising effects to emerge, the mathematicians' perspective is almost opposite. It has to do with conservation rather than sheer emergence. It might be necessary to reconcile, or at least articulate these two discrepant takes on the role of mathematics to fully restore their status.

The Calculus Breaking Point

The end of the 18th century clearly marks a breaking point in the relationship between architecture and mathematics. Until that time, arithmetic and geometry had been a constant reference for the architect, as foundational knowledge as well as practical tools, as empowerment and as incentive for restraint, as a means of control and standardisation as well as a guideline for surprising invention.

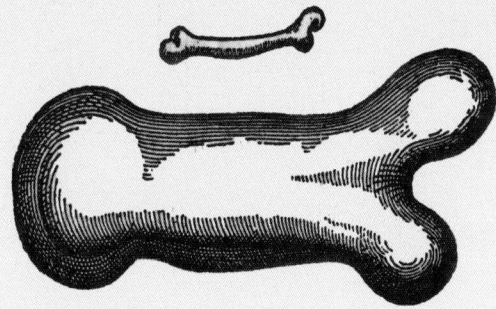

Figure 7. Galileo Galilei, Animal bones, from *Discorsi e dimostrazioni matematiche intorno a due nuove scienze*, 1638
The example is used by Galileo to illustrate how strength is not proportional to size, contrary to what proportion-based theories assumed.

In all these roles, mathematics had a strong link with spatial intuition. Arithmetic and geometry were in accordance with the understanding of space. This connivance was brought to an end with the development of calculus and its application to domains like strength of materials. First, calculus revealed the existence of a world that was definitely not following the rules of proportionality that architects had dwelt upon for centuries. Galileo, for sure, had already pointed out the discrepancy between the sphere of arithmetic and geometry and domains like strength of materials in his *Discorsi e dimostrazioni matematiche intorno a due nuove scienze* (Discourses and Mathematical Proofs Regarding Two New Sciences) published in 1638. But such discrepancy became conspicuous to architects and engineers only at the end of the 18th century.

The fact that some of the operations involved in calculus had no intuitive meaning was even more problematic. It meant that the new mathematics were like machines that possessed a certain degree of autonomy from intuitive experience. A century later, nascent phenomenology would return to this gap and explore its possible philosophical signification.

Among the reasons that explain such a gap, the most fundamental lies in the fact that calculus has generally to do with the consideration of time instead of dealing with purely spatial dimensions. What was the most puzzling, like the so-called infinitely small, were actually elementary dynamic processes rather than static beings. Calculus's most striking results were by the same token related to dynamic phenomena like hydraulics and the study of flows. Later on, calculus would also be instrumental in the development of economic theory by providing the means to study the circulation of goods and capitals.

Another reason explaining the growing gap between architecture and mathematics was the new relation between theory and practice involved in the transition from arithmetic and geometry to calculus. In the past, mathematical formulae were seen as approximate expressions of a higher reality deprived, as rough estimates, of absolute prescriptive power. One could always play with proportions for they pointed towards an average ratio. The art of the designer was all about tampering with them in order to achieve a better result. As indicators of a higher reality, formulae were an

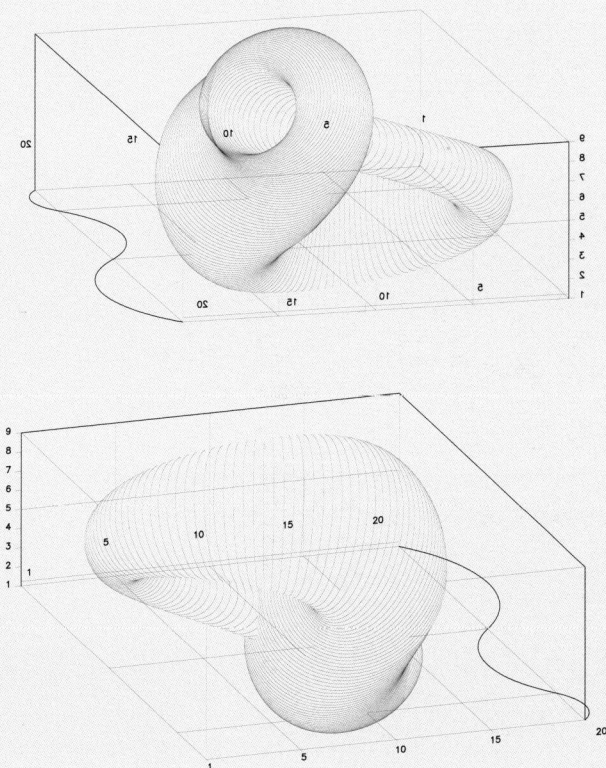

Figure 6. IJP, Klein Bottle
An intriguing topological singularity.

Figure 8. Jenny Sabin + Jones LabStudio, Branching Morphogenesis, 2008
Complex organisation is today found at every level of living organism, from macro- to microstructures. Computer simulation is instrumental in the exploration of such complex organisational patterns.

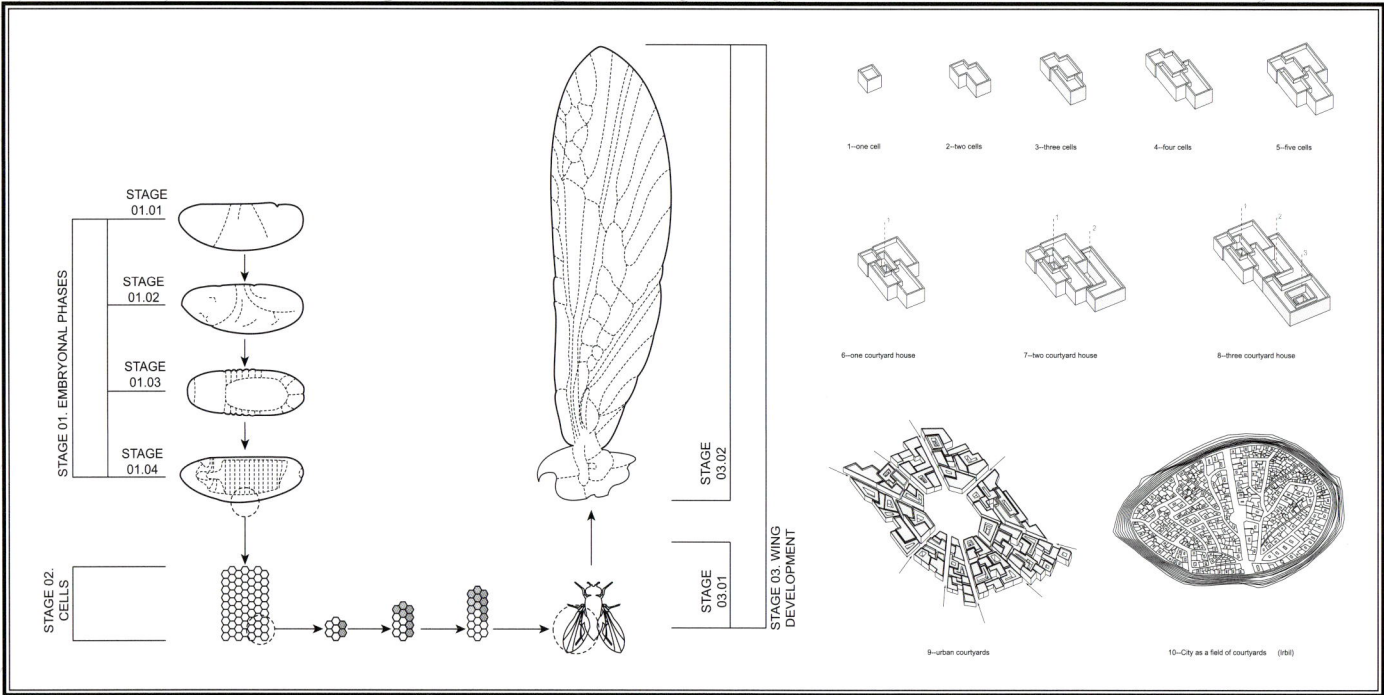

Figure 9. Michael Weinstock, Drosophilia Wing Development, 2010
The emergence of small complex anatomical organisations makes possible the emergence of ever larger and even more complex organisations. Complexity builds over time by a sequence of modifications to existing forms.

Figure 10. Michael Weinstock, Architectural and urban forms in Mesopotamia
The organic property of emergence is supposed to apply to both the natural and the human realms.

expression of power, as average values that could be tampered with; they went along with the notion of restraint.

In the new world of calculus applied to domains like strength of materials or hydraulics, mathematics no longer provided averages but firm boundaries that could not be tampered with. From that moment onwards, mathematics was about setting limits to phenomena like elasticity, then modelling them with laws of behaviour. Design was no longer involved. Theory set limits to design regardless of its fundamental intuitions.[7]

As a consequence, 19th-century architects became far less interested in the new mathematics of their time than in history, anthropology and the biological sciences. Theorists like Viollet-le-Duc or Gottfried Semper are typical of this reorientation. Despite claims to the contrary made by architects like Le Corbusier, this indifference to mathematics was to remain globally true of modern architecture.

The Ambiguities of the Present

Today the computer has reconciled architecture with calculus. For the first time, architects can really play as much with time as with space. They can generate geometric flows in ways that transform architectural forms into sections or freezes of these flows. But this has not led so far to a new mathematical imaginary. To put it in the historical perspective adopted here, mathematics appear neither as foundational nor as tools.

Various reasons may account for this situation. First, the mathematical principles are very often hidden behind their effects on the screen. In many cases the computer veils the presence of mathematics. This is a real issue that should be overcome in the perspective of truly mastering what is at stake in computer-aided design.

Second, one has the disturbing nature of the underlying mathematical principles mobilised by design. In computer-aided design, one no longer deals with objects but with theoretically unlimited series of objects. One deals also with relations. This is what parametric design is about: considering relations that can be far more abstract than what the design of objects usually entails. Scripting and algorithmics reinforce this trend. With algorithmics, one sees the return of the old question of the lack of intuitive content of some operations.[8]

However, the main reason may have to do with the pervasiveness of a new kind of organicism, vitalism or, rather, materialism, a materialism postulating an animated matter, a matter marked by phenomena like emergence, a matter also in which change is as much qualitative as quantitative.[9] Mathematics serves this new materialism, but is not seen as the most profound layer of it. This might result from the fact that the polarities evoked earlier have not been reconstituted.

In architecture, today's mathematics is about power and invention. Restraint and control through the establishment of standards have been lost so far. The reconstitution of this polarity might enable something like the restoration of an essential vibration, something akin to music. Architects need mathematics to embrace the contradictory longing for power and for restraint, for standardisation and for invention.

To achieve that goal, one could perhaps follow a couple of paths. One has to do with parametricism, but parametricism understood as restraint and not only as power, and also parametricism as having to do with the quest for standards and not only of invention.

Another path worth exploring is simulation. Simulation goes with the new importance given to scenarios and events. In this perspective, architecture becomes something that happens, a production comparable to a form of action, an evolution that lies at the core of today's performalist orientation.[10] Mathematics and architecture might meet again in the name of action, under the aegis of an ethics prescribing when to use power and when to adopt restraint. ⌂

Notes

1. Jacques Bénigne Bossuet, *Introduction à la Philosophie, ou de la Connaissance de Dieu, et de Soi-Mesme*, R-M d'Espilly (Paris), 1722, pp 37–8.
2. Joseph Rykwert, *On Adam's House in Paradise: The Idea of the Primitive Hut in Architectural History*, Museum of Modern Art (New York), 1972.
3. Pierre Caye, *Empire et Décor: Le Vitruvianisme et la Question de la Technique à l'Age Humaniste et Classique*, J Vrin (Paris), 1999.
4. See Christopher Hight, *Architectural Principles in the Age of Cybernetics*, Routledge (New York), 2008, pp 55–69.
5. Philippe Potié, *Philibert De L'Orme: Figures de la Pensée Constructive*, Parenthèses (Marseilles), 1996.
6. Joël Sakarovitch, *Epures d'Architecture: De la Coupe des Pierres à la Géométrie Descriptive XVIe-XIXe Siècles*, Birkhäuser (Basel), 1998.
7. See Antoine Picon, *L'Invention de l'Ingénieur Moderne: L'Ecole des Ponts et Chaussées 1747–1851*, Presses de l'ENPC (Paris), 1992, pp 498–505.
8. Antoine Picon, *Digital Culture in Architecture: An Introduction for the Design Professions*, Birkhäuser (Basel), 2010.
9. Michael Weinstock, *The Architecture of Emergence: The Evolution of Form in Nature and Civilisation*, John Wiley & Sons (Chichester), 2010.
10. Yasha Grobman and Eran Neuman (eds), *Performalism: Form and Performance in Digital Architecture*, Tel Aviv Museum of Art (Tel Aviv), 2008.

Dennis R Shelden
Andrew J Witt

CONTINUITY AND RUPTURE

Figure 1. A medial surface
discretised by parallelepipeds
The medial surface represents a class of
surfaces that synthesise global topology
with local discretisation.

There is currently a disjoint between the enthusiasm that is expressed for geometry in architecture and the disparate manner in which it is applied spatially. **Dennis R Shelden and Andrew J Witt** of Gehry Technologies here seek to address this by reconnecting theory and practice with developments in modern mathematics.

It can be argued that architecture's contemporary embrace of the geometries of modern mathematics has occurred derivative of, but largely removed from, the corresponding evolution in the foundational basis of space and shape that these advances propose. As algorithmic design has emerged through application of a collection of discrete geometric techniques, the contemporary language of form has become a disparate archipelago of geometries with unique topological signatures, collectively instantiated into space but otherwise disconnected from any unifying framework.

The project featured here is twofold. First, it seeks to reconnect the theory and discourse of contemporary architectural form to its origins in the development of modern mathematics, and in doing so bring to light the radical implications these theoretical developments offer to the epistemology of form. From the basis of this emergent theoretical foundation, a framework for the examination of form is proposed that reveals the distinct topologies of contemporary architectural form as aspects of a synthetic and unifying problematic. As a central example, the framework is applied to the oppositions of continuous and discrete topologies, and demonstrates that these apparently contrary signatures can be seen as duals, co-emerging from a common origin.

Space and Shape

From antiquity until the present, architecture has been founded on the principles, constructs and, to no small extent, the ontologies of the Euclidean and Cartesian systems. Often used interchangeably, these systems both individually and in concert make specific assertions on the nature of geometry and its relationship to space. Euclid's *Elements*[1] establish geometry through assertions on constructions of shapes – the lines and arcs, their measurements, angles and intersections – without directly referencing a spatial medium. They establish 'shape as construction'.

The Cartesian system declares shape as an algebraic function on points in real numbered coordinate space (R^n). The fact that the Euclidian constructions hold when described

as coordinates is one of the remarkable achievements of the Cartesian system. However, no less remarkably, the Euclidean axioms do not presume or require the presence of any space, real numbered or other, to be complete.

The nature of space, in which the constructions occur and the axioms hold, has been debated throughout the history of spatial ontology,[2] and specifically whether space is absolute, discrete from geometries it contains, or relational, sufficiently defined by relationships between spatial phenomena. Despite the complexity of Descartes's position,[3] and Euclid's silence on the topic, the Euclidean/Cartesian system has become identified with geometry as functions on points in three-dimension, real numbered space, and of 'shape as occupancy' of three-dimensional space. This containing space is presumed Euclidean: linear, continuous, absolute and singular; there is only one such space in which all shape occurs.

Shape grammar theory, as established by George Stiny,[4] provides an important counterpoint to this largely pervasive view of design shape as occupancy of point set topology. This work re-prioritises shape over space, and re-establishes an axiomatic system of shape as an algebraic topology of shapes and their parts. As with the Euclidean elements, shape grammars form a complete system of shape description whose closure is independent of any containment space. While much of the application of this system has been concerned with developing substitution grammars of Euclidean transformations implicitly deployed in the context of a Euclidean spatial medium, the shape grammar system has demonstrated applicability to problems involving non-Euclidean elements and their transformations as well.

In the last half-decade, the available descriptions of architectural form have radically expanded beyond the Euclidean to include new geometries: the non-Euclidean, the fractal, the procedural and the parametric. The existence of such geometries has been supposed over the past three centuries, but prior to digital computation they could be treated only in their most general forms and through their most simplistic examples,

$x = s(u)$

$u' = t^{-1}(x)$

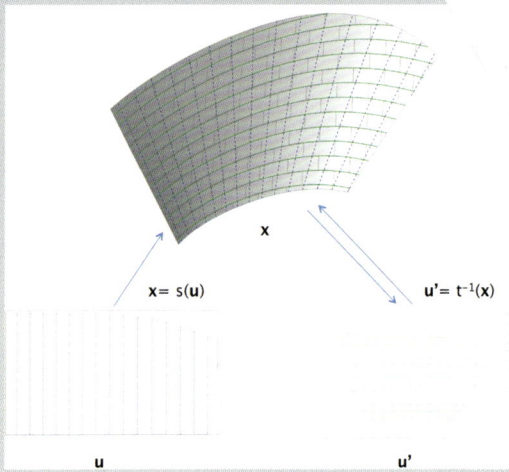

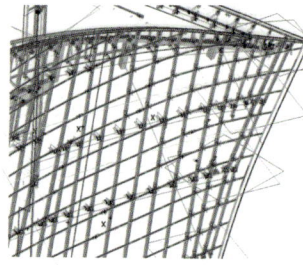

Figure 2. Gehry Partners, Walt Disney Concert Hall, Los Angeles, 2002
The enclosure detailing connects features from two distinct mappings between 2-D and 3-D space: the ruling lines of the global developable surface, and a patterning of lines in the unfolded surface space, injected back into 3-D space as geodesic curves.

Figure 3. The tangent developable surface
The tangent developable surface is a locally continuous surface that has a global singularity at the edge of regression.

largely inaccessible to anyone beyond topologists. These geometries are no longer seen as monstrous or pathological, devised to challenge the limits of the Euclidean, but rather as generalisations of the classic geometries, formalisms of utility and applicability to architecture, and indeed of everyday experience. Collectively they can be seen as positing a view of 'shape as space'; moreover as connections via mappings among a disparate network of Euclidean, non-Euclidean and more general topologies.

The most visible examples are the tensor manifolds of non-uniform rational b-spline (NURBS) surfaces. These geometries occur as R2 *x* R3 mappings between two or more distinct topological spaces: an intrinsic two-dimensional parametric space, and the containing three-dimensional space outside the surface. The extrinsic space contains the shape as points of occupancy, while the intrinsic space – the space of the surface – is the basis by which its shape is described, measured and traversed, and the perspective from which its continuity emerges. Its signature as a continuous surface emerges from both its real numbered Cartesian intrinsic and extrinsic structures, and by the specific coordinate relationships defined across its mapping. By extension to alternative dimensions, the two- and three-dimensional Euclidean and non-Euclidean shapes including points, lines, curves, surfaces and volumes are described. This mapping is itself a space – the product space of the intrinsic and extrinsic – and an instance in the space of the family of all similarly structured mappings. This framework extends directly to the parametric, wherein shapes are instances of geometric functions driven from spaces of discrete parametric values. The spaces are not atomic, but in turn disaggregate into subspaces of individual parameters, subshapes and their products. As shapes aggregate through their combinatorics, so do their individual connected spaces connect into larger networks. Shape exists in – and as – this network of spatial connection.

In the purely digital realm, both intrinsic and embedding spaces are by necessity Euclidian – real numbered coordinate

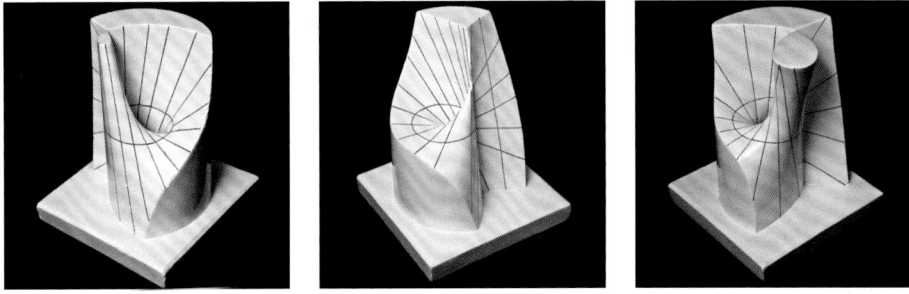

Figure 4. Mathematical models from Institut Henri Poincaré, Paris, France, late 19th century
Models illustrating three possible cubic ruled surfaces. These surfaces each demonstrate remarkable singularities in the form of self-intersections. The geometry and formal structure of the self-intersections may not be immediately obvious from the standard analytic representation of these surfaces.

systems within the machine. However, this manifold structuring applies in a formally rigorous manner when extended to a much wider spectrum of embedding topologies. Manifolds can be embedded into any topological space where locally continuous measurement by real numbered coordinates holds. This broad class of admissible embedding topologies includes the affine, vector and tensor spaces among many others. We can in fact rigorously consider manifolds that bridge from the digital into the 'worldly' topologies and transformations of physical space. The measurements and mappings, historically the realm of craft, are now conducted through increasingly sophisticated machines providing direct and continuous transformation between numerical coordinates and physical location.

What emerges is a view of space and shape that is a radical expansion of the Cartesian system. Space and shape are no longer distinct, but synonymous. Shapes emerge from, within and as a system of spatial networks of heterogeneous dimension and signature, no longer inert but active and dynamic, continuously created, connected and destroyed by design. Within this system, Euclidean geometries and spaces take a natural place as the restricted class of linear transformations in the more general class of differentiable mappings. The Euclidean re-emerges locally within the network as a regularising structure wherever Cartesian product spaces of independent real variables and their linear transformations occur.

In the context of such an expanding constellation of interconnected space, the notion of a singular and privileged containing space loses hold as a necessary or even relevant construct. Special relativity dictates that the container view of space cannot hold, but we do not need to recourse to the very large, very small or very fast to witness the efficacy of the relational space–time view. At the scale of human experience, we may arbitrarily select a containing Euclidean space worldview – of specific dimensionality, measured by a specific coordinate system, etc, and normalise shape by its embedding into this arbitrarily privileged frame. But this reductionism erases the

syntactic structure of shape that can only be seen through its nature as the connective tissue in and among the relational spaces in which shape participates, both generating and inhabiting.

This evolution of the spatial fabric presupposed by contemporary geometry, of shape as space, and of space as relational, localised and connected, is arguably the central ontological advance of contemporary form-making and associated architectural description. Most significant for design is the migration of form's locus, which emerges not simply as the occupancy of any specific Cartesian space, nor its numerical description, but resides in and as the connection between spatial frames – the intrinsic and the extrinsic, the Euclidean and non-Euclidean, the continuous and the discrete, the digital and the physical.

Continuous Maps and Their Epistemic Limits

The new geometries are uneasily classified as either continuous or discrete, a dichotomy whose simple and axiomatic distinction in the classical view – between the real and the integer – no longer so simply holds. The non-Euclidean shapes are intrinsically continuous, but can demonstrate folds and singularities in the embedding space. The procedural shapes of subdivision surfaces may be extrinsically continuous but arise out of discrete intrinsic operations. Parametric shapes may be both continuous in state space and their extrinsic instantiation, but may exhibit singularities in either, and no longer maintain any topological similarity between intrinsic and extrinsic views.

The impulse to equate continuous maps to complete definitions of architectural elements is compelling because it has proven so germane to problems of constructability, rationalisation and parametric control (Figure 2). If one understands the surface as a purely functional space, problems of design rationalisation become more precise and tractable. Unfortunately the lure of such problems has kept recent applications of mathematical approaches within architecture focused on technical problems of surface resolution and

Figure 5. Amiens Cathedral, Amiens, France, 13th century
left and opposite top: As systems of one logic are sequentially propagated along surfaces of a divergent logic, ruptures inevitably occur. Such ruptures are common in Gothic design, for example here in the vaults of Amiens Cathedral.

modularisation, rather than on broader questions of spatial structure and design coherence. Fascinating as issues of surface differential geometry are, the more fundamental formal issues play out at the scale of the global surface – that is, how surfaces enclose and partition spaces, how one circulates among them, and resolution of spatial connectedness and separation. How can we bridge the gap between the mathematics of continuous discretisation and the syntax of architectural spaces?

To answer, we must consider why the functional definition of surface geometry has become so distinct from the topological one. It follows from the axiomatisation of mathematics in the 19th century. During this time the mathematician Felix Klein was preoccupied with the question of unifying a multiplicity of theoretical geometries. Klein's ambition was to classify the varieties of surfaces through the sets of maps or functions that left these surfaces invariant.[5] Continuous maps themselves form a space which can be transformed, and these second-order sets of transformations can themselves also be transformed, and so on, creating an infinitely nested sequence of continuous function sets that indirectly describe the properties of the first set of surfaces. Klein's proposal for a unified classification of surfaces through their nested invariant functional meta-behaviour is known as the Erlangen programme.

While the Erlangen programme opened profound new understandings in the mathematics of geometric group theory, it also effectively divorced geometry from spatial intuition: since facts about commutative algebra became facts about the surface itself, spatial visualisation became superfluous to the mathematical study of surfaces. By distancing geometry from visualisation, Klein's Erlangen programme lay the seeds of the divorce between geometry and design.

This split is fundamental because continuous mathematical functions, algebraically expressed, often obscure rather than reveal spatial or topological facts. The local, closed, analytic representation of the surface does not communicate its key spatial properties – the moments of self-intersection, self-tangency, the way it partitions space. Consider, for example, the functional expression of the tangent developable

surface $s(u,v)=c(u) + v(c'(u))$ (Figure 3).[6] The function is by definition continuous, but it is difficult, a priori, to observe that such a surface has a singularity, precisely at the curve of its generation. Thus for designers, a purely functional approach obscures as much as it illuminates.

What designers need are descriptors of shape and space that encompass, but move beyond, notions of functional continuity to include singularities, ruptures and exceptional conditions. What we need are richer descriptions of topology that embed also implicit logics of construction and concurrent local discretisation that emerge organically from the global topology itself. Of course the tools we have are new, but this synthetic ambition for deductive relationships of local parts to global whole is a fundamental tension within the project of design itself (Figure 4).

Continuous Maps and the Topological Exceptions of the Gothic
The dialectic between global continuity and local discontinuity forms a clear thread within design history, emerging from material laws of aggregation and deformation. Certain designers strive for perfect and unobstructed continuity, and others for punctuated discontinuity. The tension is illustrated in the topological exceptions of Gothic vaults – moments where continuity is frustrated by ruptures in the logic of module propagation itself. Gothic builders attempted to build complex vault surfaces with modules – bricks – with no explicit mathematical relationship to the vault geometry. The divergence of each successive row of aggregation from the ideal design surface accumulated to the point of system rupture – the necessary introduction of a distinct material and module. As the logic of discrete material confronts the desire of global continuous expression, the need for more integrated descriptors of shape emerges (Figure 5).

Semantic Descriptors of Global Ruptures
Mathematics seduces with its promise of rigorous synthesis to otherwise contradictory systems of rules. To control the logic of ruptures, architects need a semantic set of descriptors that are not merely parametric but topological, which represent,

Geodesic Parallel
Operational Definition

On Developable Surface
(May be equivalent to isoparms)

On Hyperbolic Surface
(Negative Gaussian Curvature)

On Spherical Surface
(Positive Gaussian Curvature)

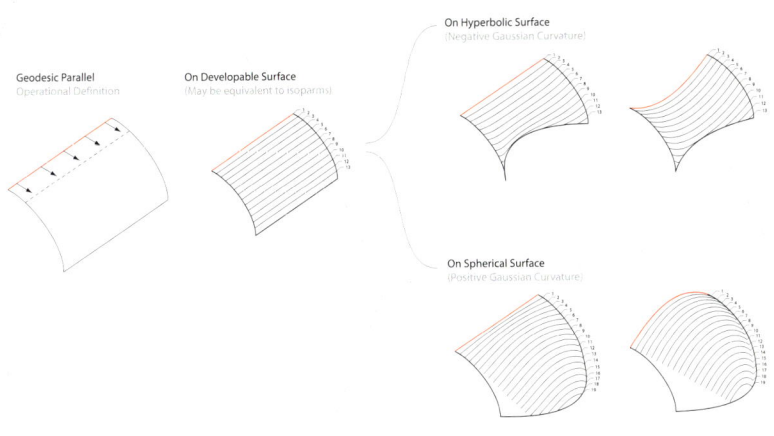

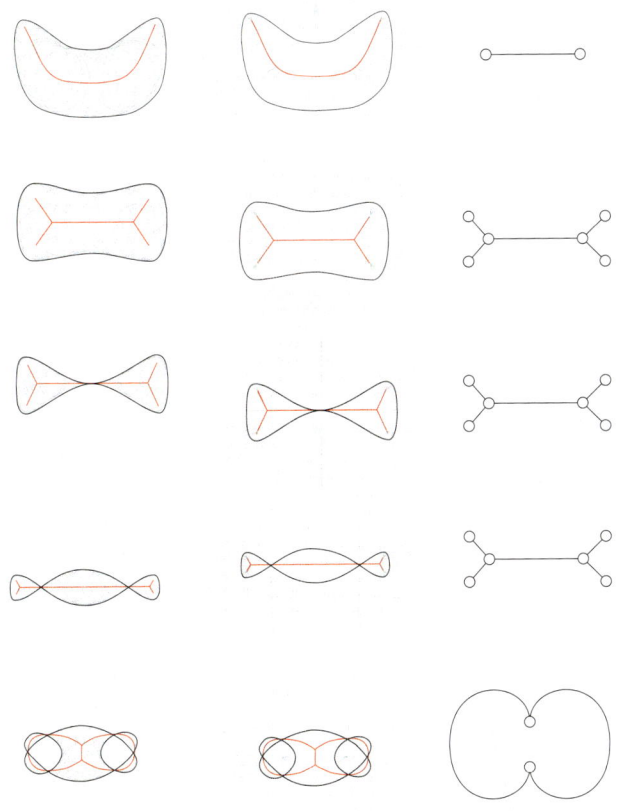

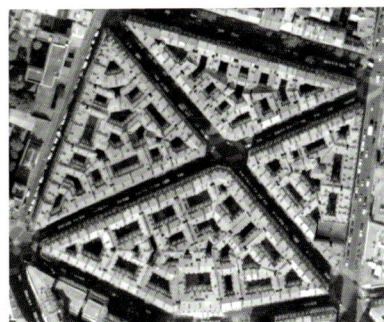

Figure 7. Skeletal subdivision of Paris housing, late 19th century
Curve skeletons arise naturally in discretisations and packings, and as such recur in unexpected contexts. For example, the packing of regularly shaped apartments into irregular block shapes in Paris's urban plan induces a curve skeleton that is legible in the plan even if the original designers did not intend it.

Figure 6. Curve skeletons of closed curves
The curve skeletons (below) of various closed curves (above). The skeleton metaphor is apt; the skeleton represents a sort of minimum distribution or circulation network for the interior of the shape. It also represents the locus of singularities as a boundary is continuously and uniformly offset. This shape descriptor, which is broadly applicable in design analytics, was first described by Harold Blum in his 1967 paper 'A Transformation for Extracting New Descriptors of Shape'.

Architecture is the design of a felicitous relationship of parts to whole, a synthetic project of multi-objective invention. The promise of mathematics is that those diverse relationships and constraints can be made conceptually or notationally explicit, and their manipulation can be precise.

essentialise and make operative the basic tensions of contrary and contested conditions in design. In this context we mention two constructs – the curve skeleton and the medial surface – that suggest generative topological tools and semantic descriptors of shape.

Computer vision scientists began the search for such semantic descriptors to distil shapes to their computer-readable fundamentals. In the 1960s, interest in syntactic structure for the human senses produced operators that would take any shapes and automatically generate information about their fundamental spatial or topological configuration. A pioneer among these researchers was Harry Blum, of the US Air Force Research Laboratories. During the 1960s, Blum devised a construct which, given a particular shape, would generate a second encoded shape that would distil the key formal features of corners, changes in curvature and general configuration. This second, encoded shape often indirectly revealed features of the first shape that were difficult to detect directly. Blum called his shape descriptor the 'curve skeleton' (Figure 6).[7]

The significance of Blum's curve skeleton for design is that one can deductively calculate the topological singularities of a broad range of shapes, surfaces and spaces from a non-analytic description of global shape. Instead of operating on the functional notation of the shape, it operates on the shape itself, regardless of its notational representation. The curve skeleton appears in many contexts – as a diagram of circulation, as an aid to smooth subdivision, as an emergent property of circle and shape packings.

The urban form of Paris is an example of the surprising uses of the curve skeleton. In post-Haussmann Paris, designers pack regularly shaped apartments into irregularly shaped city blocks. This quasi-uniform packing – not unlike the packing of stones in a Gothic vault – must be reconciled with the irregular block shapes of the global urban plan. The solution is remarkable: the curve skeleton, this essential diagram of shape, appears not as a planned structure but as an emergent trace, an inevitable consequence of uniform packing within a non-uniform boundary (Figure 7).

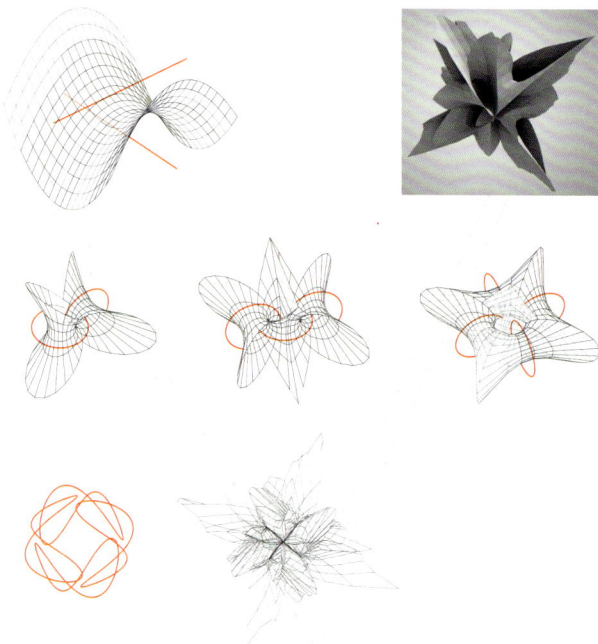

Figure 8. Medial surfaces generated from sets of curves
The surface is generated so that there is always a wall between two distinct curves. Remarkably, the logic of discretisation for these surfaces follows directly from the diagram of their circulation, namely the curves here indicated in red. They could in fact be seen as generalisations of hyperbolic paraboloids. Thus one may generate designed spaces of a given circulation logic that, at the same time, are also simply discretisable into flat panels. In addition, the discretisation has a direct connection to the implicit logic of self-intersection of the surface.

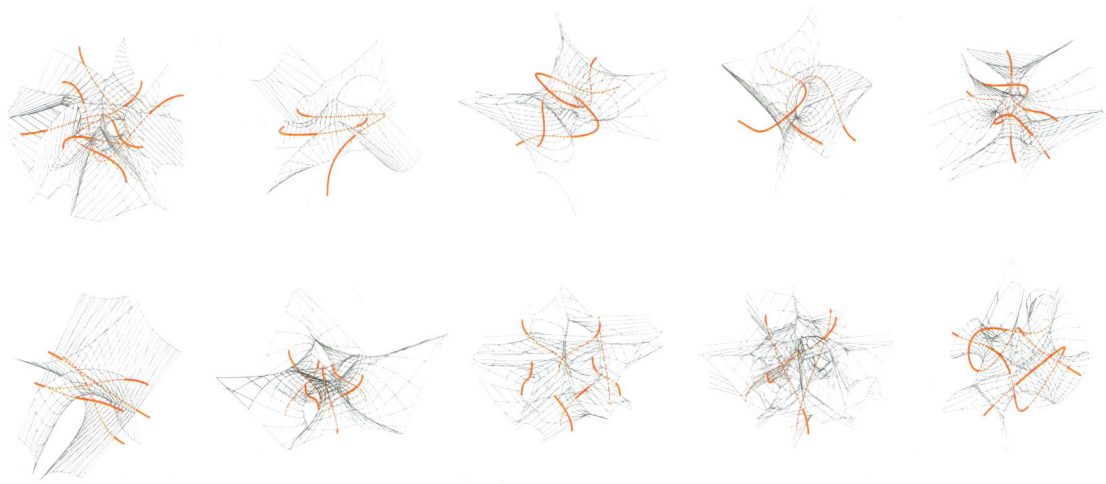

Curve skeletons can be generalised from planimetric to surfacial constructs. Applying the logic of the curve skeleton to a collection of curves in space produces a surface wall between each pair of curves in the set; a configuration called a 'medial surface' (Figure 8). The medial surface is the precise surface that would induce a given set of circulation paths around and through it.

The curve skeleton, and to some extent the medial surface, are nearly self-dual: they can represent either circulation paths, or the surfaces and walls that enclose circulation paths. From wall boundaries the skeleton describes a circulation path through them. Conversely, from a circulation path the skeleton will describe walls that induce that circulation. The curve skeleton thus represents something fundamental about space and circulation, a reciprocity between the singularities that structure both.

What is more, for medial surfaces there is post-rational surface discretisation; their definition guarantees that they are rationalisable in a quad-dominated way. In fact, there is an elegant connection between the global and local forms of these medial surfaces since the joint lines between different surfacial domains extend continuously from one to the next. Medial surfaces thus represent a sort of synthesis of continuity and rupture, in one simple descriptor.

With these curve skeleton diagrams and medial surfaces, the topological properties of space – connectivity, passage, edge and rupture – follow directly from the connective paths of the designed promenade. These surfaces represent a deductive relationship between parts and whole. Our contemporary opportunity is to broaden the connection of mathematics to architecture beyond intensive application of continuous surface functions to a disciplinary project that is more synthetic and spatially specific. In short, we can broaden our vision beyond analysis and generative procedures to design.

Conclusion

Architecture is the design of a felicitous relationship of parts to whole, a synthetic project of multi-objective invention. The promise of mathematics is that those diverse relationships and constraints can be made conceptually or notationally explicit, and their manipulation can be precise. A logic of continuous maps is an aspiration towards that comprehensive quality – a precise description of the local, topologically global and structurally recursive. But these maps, limited as they are by the semantics of their symbolic notation, hold the seed of their own rupture, particularly when iteratively applied. Continuous maps can fold, intersect with themselves, exhibit singularities; what is continuous from one point of view or notational representation may not be so from another. The identification of these ruptures, both at the local scale and at the global, topological scale, becomes key to understanding space itself and the descriptive, analytic and designed project of architecture – the description of the thing itself, beyond its multiple notational representations. In particular, architecture can begin to move beyond empty ideological distinctions that rest on notational distinctions, beyond simple dichotomies between pre-rationalisation and post-rationalisation, towards a more profound and codetermined logic of space. What is required is a more synthetic approach of global–local reciprocity, and an embedded logic of mathematical design. ∆

Notes
1. TL Heath, *Euclid: The Thirteen Books of The Elements*, Dover Publications (New York), 1956.
2. GV Leroy, *Die philos. Probleme in dem Briefwechsel Leibniz und Clarke*, Giessen, 1893.
3. N Huggett, 'Cartesian Spacetime: Descartes' Physics and the Relational Theory of Space and Motion', *British Journal for the Philosophy of Science* 55(1), 2004, pp 189–93.
4. G Stiny, *Shape: Talking about Seeing and Doing*, MIT Press (Cambridge, MA), 2008.
5. F Klein, *Elementary Mathematics from an Advanced Standpoint: Geometry*, Dover Publications (New York), 2004.
6. E Kreysig, *Differential Geometry*, Dover Publications (New York), 1981.
7. Harry Blum, 'A Transformation for Extracting New Descriptors of Shape', in W Wathen-Dunn, *Models for the Perception of Speech and Visual Form*, MIT Press (Cambridge, MA), 1967, pp 362–80.

IJP EXPLAINED
PARAMETRIC MATHEMATICS IN PRACTICE

Mathematics provides the underlying principles for IJP Corporation, the London-based practice, led by △ Guest-Editor **George L Legendre**. Eschewing packaged software, IJP develops its own equations, while its spatial model is underwritten by mathematical surfaces. Legendre describes the pervasive influence of the discipline across the office's output.

Figure 1. IJP with John Pickering, F01(b), London, 2009
In this project, IJP explored the parametric deployment of a simple
homothetical (scaling) transformation known as inversion, to
which the Wolverhampton-based artist John Pickering has devoted
several decades of work. IJP determined the analytic equations
of the transformation and used them to invert, under Pickering's
guidance, a pair of ordinary cylinders into an intricate aggregation
of (partial) cycloid surfaces.

GSD2404 LEGENDRE

LIBERATORE Cara

_ranges $n1 := 0, 1 .. \ 20$ $m1 := 0, 1 .. \ 20$

_equations $iT(u, v) := 6 \cdot \dfrac{u}{\pi}$ $jT(u, v) := 6 \cdot \dfrac{v}{\pi}$ $sh(u, v) := \left(\cos(u)^{2000} + \cos(v)^{2000} \right) \cdot -4 + 4 + 1$

$\Pi_{m1, n1} := iT \dfrac{m1}{20} 2\pi, \dfrac{n1}{20} 2\pi$ $\Theta_{m1, n1} := jT \dfrac{m1}{20} \cdot 2\pi, \dfrac{n1}{20} 2\pi$ $K_{m1, n1} := sh \dfrac{m1}{20} \cdot 2\pi, \dfrac{n1}{20} \cdot 2\pi$

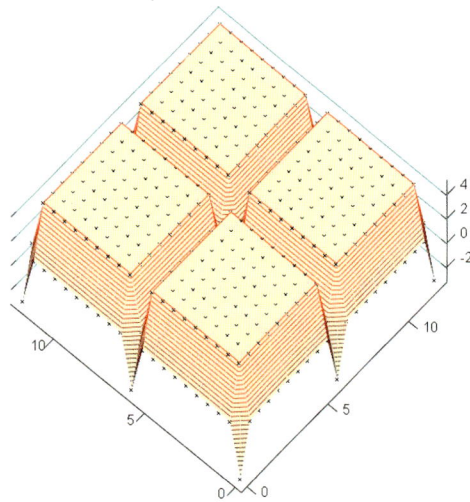

(Θ, Π, K) (Θ, Π, K)

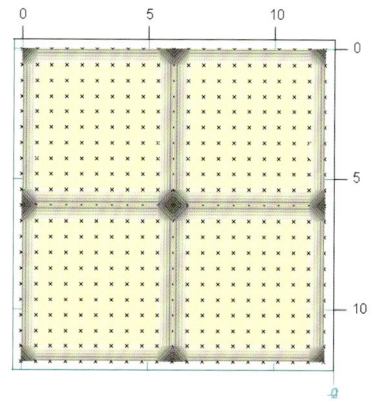

Figure 2. IJP, Asymptotic Box, Parametric equations, 2004–10
The Asymptotic Box© is an implicit 3-D surface derived by analytic
means. A blob trying to pass itself off as a box, this curious surface
is produced by raising a periodic product to a (very) high exponent
in order to deform an ordinary pliant surface into a 'near box'. There
are algebraic limits to this kind of game, as infinite tangents are
inadmissible. Hence the term 'Asymptotic', whereby the box tends
towards orthogonality – without reaching it.

Since its inception in 2004, the London-based practice IJP Corporation has been using a mathematical knowledge model as a blueprint for the design of novel structures. Proposals that are drastically different in size and scope follow the same instrumental premises. This is evident in F01(b) (2009), a collaboration with the artist John Pickering; in the Art Fund Pavilion (2009); Yeosu 2012 Thematic Pavilion (2009); the Shenzhen Museum of Contemporary Art and Planning (2007), with architect Max Kahlen; and the Henderson Waves Bridge (2004–9) with RSP Architects, Planners and Engineers. Bypassing the conveniences of modelling software in favour of elemental mathematics, these projects share a common basis of analytic geometry. Rather than simply consuming software, IJP produces the very material software is made of – raw equations – usually taken for granted under the hood, and hence maintains a far greater amount of control over what it designs and manufactures. In this sense, the office turns its back on a dazzling technological design agenda, preferring to work at an infra-technological level, where a symbolic language common to all computational design processes exists.

IJP's model of spatial cognition is based on the notion of mathematical surface. In analytic terms, all mathematical parametric surfaces form and deform in direct response to numerical relations they hold in their midst. To the observer who knows what to look for, the conformation of a parametric surface exhibits the traces of these internal motions as markedly as the plump figure of midlife will subsume the sharper inflections of a youthful physique. Parametric surfaces surge upwards because of a genetic antecedent of linearity, a pattern of linear growth exhibited to some degree by one of the dependent relations they quite literally incorporate. They undulate by peaks and depressions because of a periodic internal makeup, pointing to the presence of cyclical behaviours in one of their three respective antecedents. Finally, they spiral up and down under the confluence of linearity, periodicity and transposition. Each term follows a distinct pattern and determines the overall form of the surface in tandem with the other two, through a composite process yielding the most complex results.

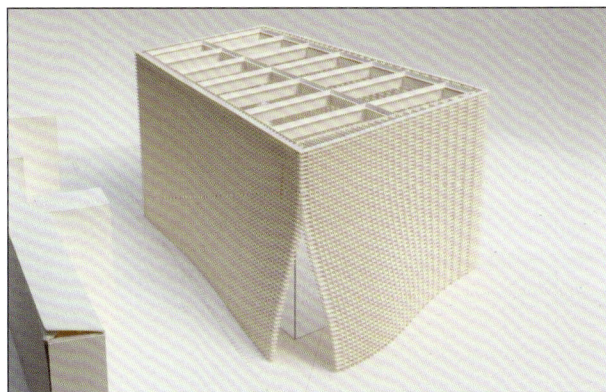

Figure 4. IJP, The Art Fund Pavilion, Woking, Surrey, 2009
Schematic plan. On busy nights, the short ends of the timber honeycomb (and the acrylic panels behind) swing open to let visitors overflow through the space.

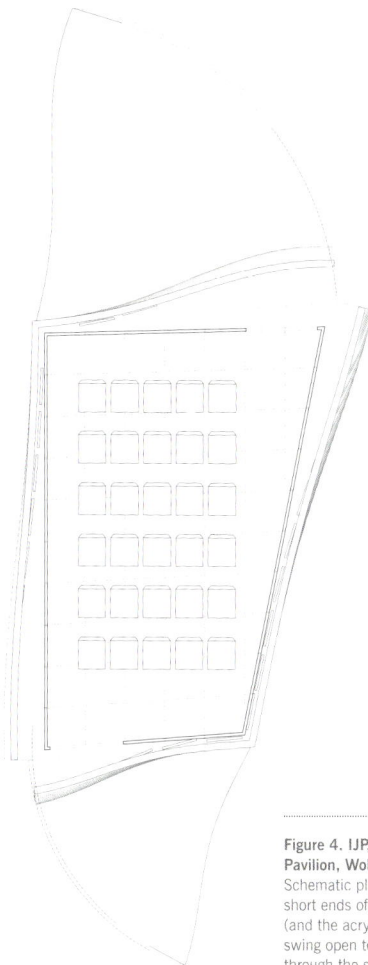

Figure 3. IJP, The Art Fund Pavilion, Woking, Surrey, 2009
This lightweight structure is clad with a prefabricated timber lattice of highly variable, side-specific density. A single room enclosed by four rigid panels of extruded acrylic, the Art Fund Pavilion may be endlessly reconfigured into a temporary support space for the neighbouring Light Box contemporary art museum for which it was commissioned. The pavilion is designed to be assembled and taken apart in 72 hours by a team of just two. View of laser-cut model.

Variable Densities

A commitment to mathematics is not consistent with a bias towards a given style or Gestalt. For IJP, variable curvature is not a matter of architectural vocabulary, but a heuristic device, an operative tool to conceptualise space. The office develops plain boxes, for instance, while remaining equally committed to meeting the challenge of continuity, which gets surprisingly tricky where mundane conditions of orthogonality (or proper tectonic corners) are concerned. Hence the tendency is to avoid discontinuous, piecemeal assemblies where each side of a notionally continuous envelope is dealt with separately, considering instead alternative holistic options such as plotting circles or ellipses with only four points, raising periodic expressions to a high exponent (IJP's trademark Asymptotic Box©), or substituting Fourier summations for ordinary periodic functions, all of which involve bona fide blobs (successfully) trying to pass themselves off as a box.

For reasons related to the programmatic requirements spelled out by the organising body of the open international competition for a new temporary art space sited by the Light Box Art Museum in Surrey, UK, the Art Fund Pavilion (2009) is the exception to the rule. Here the overriding issue is the differential filtering of natural daylight, so the emphasis is kept on each individual side, and the practical possibility of redistributing its indexical threads without altering the form

> Geometry and algebra, the study of figures and that of symbols, separated more than 400 years ago; as noted in the introduction to this issue, this separation lies at the root of mathematical modernity, and reminds us that unlike art history, or even technology, progress in mathematics is extremely fast paced.

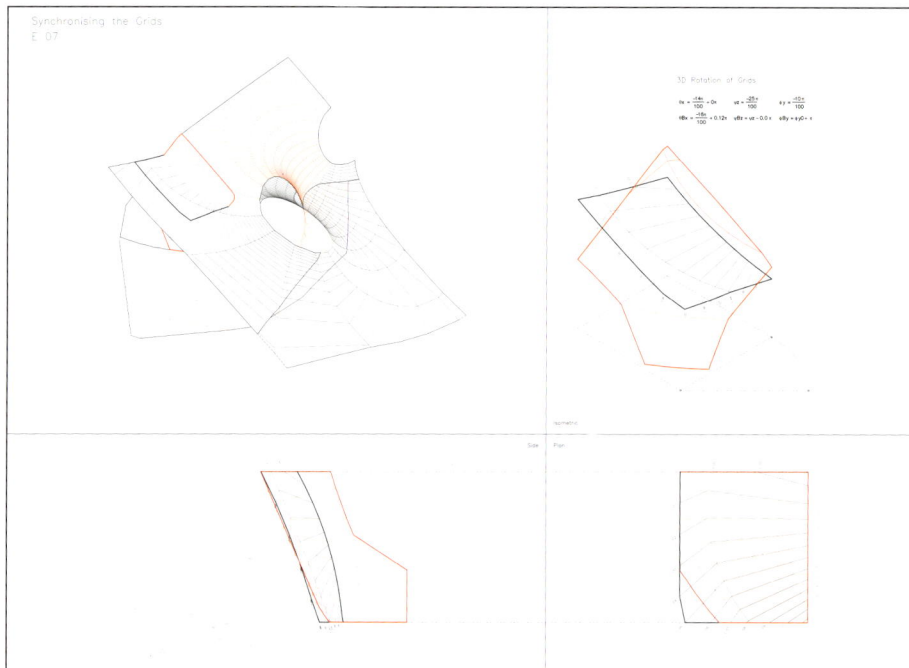

Figure 5. IJP with John Pickering, F01(b), London, 2009
Study diagram of intersection between the solid and reticular portions of the model. The multiple intersections of surface threads establish a material continuity between discrete figures in space and enhance the cohesiveness – and stability – of the final piece.

Figure 6. IJP with John Pickering, F01(b), London, 2009
Close-up view. The figure is encased in a translucent box that crops the infinite surfaces produced by the transformation. The rapid-prototyped silicate and engraved acrylic give the finished model a light and reflective quality.

Figure 7. IJP, The Art Fund Pavilion, Woking, Surrey, 2009
Model of northwest corner, with zip-up entrance.

itself. The proposal consists of a single room with four walls and a roof. This temporary structure is meant to support its host institution by variously housing cultural seminars, temporary exhibitions or fundraising events. It is orientated like a traditional artist's studio for a maximum intake of northern daylight, and its envelope is made of pliant parametric surfaces extruded into a honeycomb, behind which a lightweight thermal barrier of acrylic panels marks the boundary of the exhibition space proper.

Each of the pavilion's walls is designed by altering the sequence of a numerical range through the deployment of equations. The rhythm of the south-facing studs follows a periodic distribution that aggregates proximate threads to within an inch of one another, closing the honeycomb and blocking direct sunlight. On the north side, the distribution is precisely inversed. 'Stitching' overlapping edges secures the water-tightness of contiguous walls, whereas pulling the edges apart produces zipper-shaped entrances and exits at the opposite corners of the room. The materiality of the honeycomb is based on a lattice of flat, CNC-cut profiles of shallow radii meeting at a right angle, and the profiles are notched to maximise adherence without chemical bonding. The completed honeycomb is dense, stiff and so redundant structurally that other forms of support, including steel posts or panel frames, are unnecessary. In this project it is the curtains that carry the 3.6-metre (12-foot) high wall, frame and roofing material, and not the other way around. High ranges are always used to solve parametric surface equations offering the opportunity of experimenting with the sturdiness of redundant lattices at drastically different scales, from a single room like the Art Fund Pavilion, to a 2.4-metre (8-foot) wide, 152.4-metre (500-foot) tall high-rise building.

Curvature as Fragmented Flatness

From small installations to extra-large infrastructure, this mathematical knowledge model migrates seamlessly across scales and contexts. Working, for instance, with the brand of geometry pioneered by the British sculptor John Pickering has uncovered unexpected forms of tectonic efficiency. Based on a projective transformation known as inversion (or scaling relative to a fixed point, but with a variable coefficient), Pickering's art

is an exercise in absolute reduction. IJP has worked on three short projects in collaboration with the artist, resulting initially in the production of licensed similes of his original artwork with state-of-the art software and numerically controlled fabrication, with a view to soliciting a grant from the Arts Council in order to rebuild them as large-scale installations in a gallery. The first two pieces re-created at his behest closely follow his working blueprint, canning Pickering's manual approach into a scripting routine and exporting the result to a rapid-prototyping device. As such, the resulting pieces are little more than copies (or forgeries, depending on one's point of view) of the original.

The third instalment of the collaboration, on the other hand, an installation titled F01(b) commissioned by Pickering for his own collection, disregards the manual two-dimensional strategy favoured by the artist, using instead the parametric equations of a relatively simple homothetical transformation in space. Developing F01(b) through equations rather than drawings was not only a matter of re-evaluating the Modernist sensibility of the previous installations, but of taking a profoundly different approach that involved a shift from figures to symbols, in line with an argument more at home in the 17th century than in the 21st. Geometry and algebra, the study of figures and that of symbols, separated more than 400 years ago; as noted in the introduction to this issue, this separation lies at the root of mathematical modernity, and reminds us that unlike art history, or even technology, progress in mathematics is extremely fast paced. Hence, rather than recasting the static geometry favoured by the artist in a new technical idiom, deploying the analytic equations of inversion in F01(b) opens up the possibility of a contemporary re-evaluation of his modus operandi itself.

F01(b) has two parts, both made of overlapping cones inversed relative to the same centre. For purely formal reasons, the top part is solid and the bottom reticular. The resulting figure is encased in a translucent box that crops the infinite surfaces produced by inversion, and the choice of materials (rapid prototyping and engraved acrylic) give the finished model a light and reflective quality. Critically F01(b) secretes an exciting discovery. Inversion is a transformation: it does not create anything new, it just alters what is already there. In this context circles invert (mostly) into circles, and spheres (mostly) into spheres. Planes invert into spheres too. However, unlike the standard polar variety (which must be rationalised through triangulation if it is to be built), these spheres are made of flat quadrilaterals. When the right conditions are met, standard primitives such as planes, cones or cylinders invert into non-standard surfaces, such as spheres, cycloids or cross-caps, without the need to rationalise, triangulate or develop the result.

Inverse Configurations

An operative shift from geometry to algebra – and the surprising tectonic properties uncovered in F01(b) – are wont to accelerate the cycle of design experimentation, making it possible to deploy the principle of inversion to full-blown building scale. As the point of convergence of the Yeosu 2012 World Expo, the form of IJP's Thematic Pavilion is simple, yet memorable, involving a simple spherical form

Figure 8. IJP, Yeosu 2012 Thematic Pavilion, Yeosu, South Korea, 2009
Masterplan. IJP's Thematic Pavilion features an elementary spherical form sitting on the edge of the sea, and topped with a large circular opening. It is located on the geographic centre of the boundary defined by the six public access points of the Yeosu 2012 World Fair.

notated I and J (after which IJP is named). This conceptual model ensures a stable transition to materiality: if the threads are two-dimensional, they are used to define centre lines for laser-cut material profiles. If the indexical threads are not two-dimensional, they are used to print double-curved members in depth (the threads are effectively laminated from the ground up with rapid prototyping, stereo-lithography or casting). Eventually all morphogenetic results can be traced back to fundamental issues of algebraic modulation; there are various machinery-consistent equations, in other words some better suited to sheet-cutting, others to lamination.

IJP's first built project (in collaboration with RSP), the Henderson Waves Bridge is a project commissioned by the Urban Redevelopment Authority (URA), Singapore, following an open international competition. It involves an infrastructural intervention with a complex structure and a simple brief: to link two ridge summits with a continuous plane on the southern coast of the island of Singapore. The equation that was used here offers a direct application of IJP's research in periodicity[1] where, like the rhetorical algebra of medieval Arabia, it is narrated without symbols. The 'parametric pillow' is the product of three space-relations: the first may be diagrammed as an oblique plane; the second is more complex and produces a flowing periodic oscillation; and the third (and most intricate) represents a product of periodic out-of-phase

topped with a large circular opening; in turns sea creature, beached monster or fishing basket, the form brings to mind disparate but related associations. The pavilion sits near the geographic centre of the area defined by the six public access points of the fair. The programme is housed on circular floor plates distributed around a large atrium, and the interiors are naturally lit through windows and internal openings. The large circular oculus pours ambient daylight levels throughout the building (perceived at the end of the public exhibition route, this gigantic opening looms over the visitor like a rising orb). On the ocean side, the Floating Island extends the pavilion to create an artificial shoreline, further extended underwater by a man-made Marine Life reef.

The mathematical subtleties of inversion help resolve the complementary demands of the brief by providing a common spatial blueprint that unites the two main features of the proposal – the spherical exhibitions volume and the fanning surface dedicated to marine life. The two figures are derived by inverting two primitives relative to the same centre, but with a different coefficient. The inverse figures intertwine in a seemingly continuous way about a single focal point, coinciding with a public observatory. The fanning outline of the Marine Reef illustrates how a closed primitive positioned next to the centre of the transformation will invert into an open superficial expanse for the same geometric reason that a circle passing though the centre of inversion will map onto an (infinite) straight line. The principle of continuity between solid and reticulated form established in F01(b) carries over seamlessly to this project, where the very same superficial geometry is given alternate material expressions above and below the variable flood line.

Material Efficiencies

Ultimately, the key question raised by the deployment of analytic mathematics in design is whether it produces material efficiencies. The surface of discrete analytic mathematics does not actually exist: what the parametric formulas produce is only a discrete array of indexical threads grouped in two sets,

Figure 9. IJP, Yeosu 2012 Thematic Pavilion, Yeosu, South Korea, 2009
Model seen from the northwest. Side view of Floating Island and Marine Life reef.

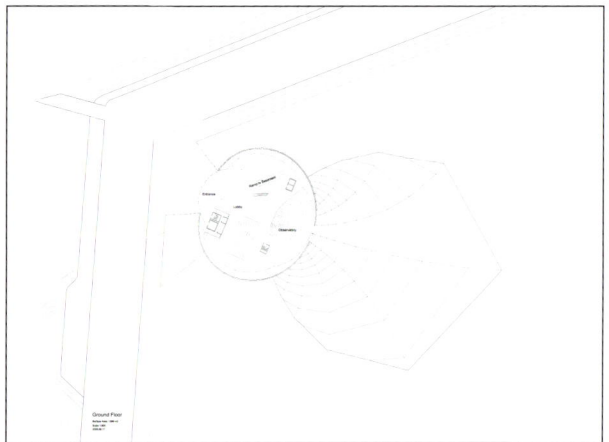

Figure 10. IJP, Yeosu 2012 Thematic Pavilion, Yeosu, South Korea, 2009
Ground-floor plan of the pavilion showing the entrance lobby, the Floating Island and the Marine Life reef that surrounds it.

_matrices

$$TTx := \begin{vmatrix} i \leftarrow last\_in + 1 \\ j \leftarrow last\_jn + 1 \\ a \leftarrow matrix(i,j,FinalX) \\ a \end{vmatrix} \qquad TTy := \begin{vmatrix} i \leftarrow last\_in + 1 \\ j \leftarrow last\_jn + 1 \\ a \leftarrow matrix(i,j,FinalY) \\ a \end{vmatrix} \qquad TTz := \begin{vmatrix} i \leftarrow last\_in + 1 \\ j \leftarrow last\_jn + 1 \\ a \leftarrow matrix(i,j,FinalZ) \\ a \end{vmatrix}$$

_INVERSION CONE B   _modulo of point/inverse

$$MOD\_B_{in,jn} := \frac{invR}{\sqrt{\left(COM\_Y\_B_{in,jn} - INVy\right)^2 + \left(COM\_X\_B_{in,jn} - INVx\right)^2 + \left(COM\_Z\_B_{in,jn} - INVz\right)^2}}^2$$

_equations

$$FinalX\_B(x,y) := \left(COM\_Y\_B_{x,y}\right) \cdot MOD\_B_{x,y} - INVy \cdot \left(MOD\_B_{x,y} - 1\right)$$

$$FinalY\_B(x,y) := \left(COM\_X\_B_{x,y}\right) \cdot MOD\_B_{x,y} - INVx \cdot \left(MOD\_B_{x,y} - 1\right)$$

$$FinalZ\_B(x,y) := COM\_Z\_B_{x,y} \cdot MOD\_B_{x,y} - INVz \cdot \left(MOD\_B_{x,y} - 1\right)$$

_matrices

$$TTBx := \begin{vmatrix} i \leftarrow last\_in + 1 \\ j \leftarrow last\_jn + 1 \\ a \leftarrow matrix(i,j,FinalX\_B) \\ a \end{vmatrix} \qquad TTBy := \begin{vmatrix} i \leftarrow last\_in + 1 \\ j \leftarrow last\_jn + 1 \\ a \leftarrow matrix(i,j,FinalY\_B) \\ a \end{vmatrix} \qquad TTBz := \begin{vmatrix} i \leftarrow last\_in + 1 \\ j \leftarrow last\_jn + 1 \\ a \leftarrow matrix(i,j,FinalZ\_B) \\ a \end{vmatrix}$$

■ inversion

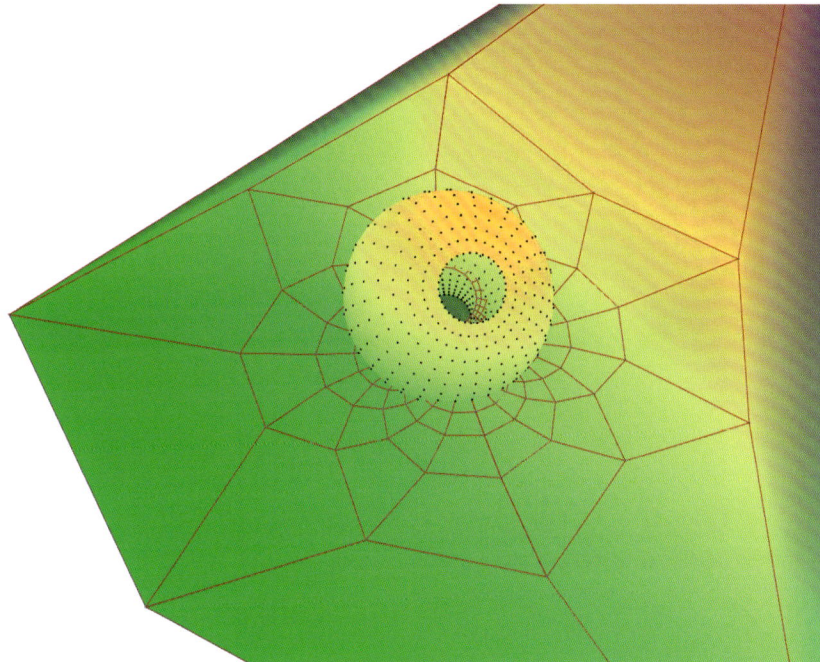

(TTy,TTx,TTz) , (TTBy,TTBx,TTBz)

Figure 11. IJP, Yeosu 2012 Thematic Pavilion, Yeosu, South Korea, 2009
Partial mathematical formulation. Such worksheets (greatly simplified here
for purposes of publication) lie at the heart of the office's methodology.
The upper half of the sheet features the parametric surface calculations
that are the true engine of the process; the lower, a read-only illustration of
the result. For designers skilled in this methodology, visualising the act of
'writing form' is not strictly necessary, but it is useful in helping to alleviate
the abstraction of the process.

Figure 12. IJP and RSP Architects Planners and Engineers, Henderson Waves, Singapore, 2008
Location plan of the bridge and timber end-works by IJP (competition stage). The project begins with a timber pathway linking the springing point of the bridge to the busy vehicular loop on Mount Faber –shown in the lower-right corner of the plan. The project continues with the bridge itself and concludes with a ramp that connects the bridge to another existing circular path, winding its way around the summit of Telok Blangah Hill (in the upper-left corner of the plan). The entrance pathway, bridge deck and connecting ramp are given the same steel and timber treatment and can hardly be distinguished.

Figure 13. IJP and RSP Architects Planners and Engineers, Henderson Waves, Singapore, 2008
View of the central span and completed deck in May 2008.

Figure 14. IJP and RSP Architects Planners and Engineers, Henderson Waves, Singapore, 2008
Timber deck of the main span under construction. This central arch spans 57 metres (187 feet), and rises to more than 6 metres (19.6 feet) at its apex. Too large to be prefabricated off-site and craned into position, it was assembled on a makeshift platform directly above Henderson Road, then raised into position by a battery of hydraulic jacks. The centre-lines of the steel members shown (central arch, edge member, mid-height member and curved ribs) are determined by a single set of parametric equations.

oscillations spreading in perpendicular dimensions. In space, the pillow resembles an egg-crate-like arrangement of peaks and depressions. As the ranges vary, it divides like a cell into two, three, or N swelling bulges, as if held in place by knots.

The structural considerations driving this morphogenetic process determined a comparatively rational scheme that leverages the structural integrity of the surface's indexical threads, a scheme formulated as a succession of arches and catenaries, behaving like a dual, differentiated beam. In terms of structural expression, the bridge systematises and amplifies the problem of converting selected indexical threads into centre lines of material members with structural roles. Named after the ubiquitous index I (reappearing here as a steel beam), the iThreads provide the physical edge and lateral stability of the surface form. Along the other dimension, the J threads fulfil the gravitational demands of the structure, and the piles sit at both ends of each span where the surface self-intersects and the section of the structure is reduced to a single beam.

The timber deck presents a subtler challenge. Largely in evidence in its completed form, the recurrence of kinks along its surface indicates that it is discontinuous. To accommodate wheelchair access, the deck is bent, sheared, oblique and punctuated with thresholds that break its continuity at regular intervals. Every flight and threshold is computed by a specific variant of the equation, and the numbers collected from 160 different formulas in a spreadsheet. At competition stage, this super-surface was envisioned as a thin timber veneer stretched over the steel members, peeling off the structure to provide seating and playing areas. Eventually the form of the

veneer was given by the same overall equation, with minor adjustments for the seating areas, which required their own custom calculations. The 1,500-square-metre (16,145-square-foot) expanse of tropical hardwood is the fulcrum of Henderson Waves. Its double-curved areas form a tapestry of 5,000 modular boards, each varying by a single degree every few metres and all tapered to measure.

The Relational Body

IJP's methodology is no different from a traditional approach based on precedent, otherwise known as 'type', but with the proviso that its types are abstract rather than figurative, and invisible rather than conspicuous. Its commitment to typological reduction goes hand in hand with a rejection of traditional modes of composition, as the traditional understanding of form begins and ends with what is, from the standpoint of its mathematical model, an unnecessary premise: the separation of the whole into parts. Parametric surfaces are naturally inured to this mode of thought because their constitutive parts are not fragments, in the sense that a cornice would constitute a fragment of an elevation, but relationships.

Relationships act as parts only in a loose, strictly functional sense, inasmuch as they can be manipulated independently to alter a whole. Their role is neither 'pure' nor distinct, and the combined impact they visit on the body muddles their respective areas of influence. A form shaped by modulation has no discrete limbs; one cannot chop it off into pieces nor indulge in the permutation and scaling of parts to which parametric 'invention' is often reduced. Consider, for instance, the parametric seed of the pillow that in time hatched into Henderson Waves. What exactly is it made of?

This common surface is obtained by composing one linear transformation with two periodic ones. The three relations determine the motions that shape it in breadth, width and depth, and clarify – if their interplay can be unravelled – why it looks the way it does. The symmetries of the pillow can be traced back to periodic cycles with identical beginnings and ends; its upright stance will be traced back to a linear range increase. And the pillow's subsequent cell-like division into two, three or more swellings reflects the number of phases fed to a periodic function.

None of these surfaces looks like the pillow itself. None resembles the form, yet all jointly determine it. Had they not been there, the form could not have been produced because it cannot be modelled simply by deforming other, ready-made surfaces, however sophisticated the software may be. Had they not been identified as antecedents, it could not have been retrospectively read. With their dependent functions, variable parametric surfaces are both a means to complexity and the way out of its mystifying embrace. They are, in other words, the ultimate objects of knowledge. ⌂

Notes
1. See George Liaropoulos-Legendre, *IJP: The Book of Surfaces*, AA Publications (London), 2003, pp 2, 8.

Foster + Partners, Al Raha Beach, Plot 801, Abu Dhabi, 2007
The seemingly intuitive form of the building is in fact based on a sustainable environmental strategy that relies on a series of passive controls, permitting for natural ventilation cooling and minimisation of solar gains while allowing views out.

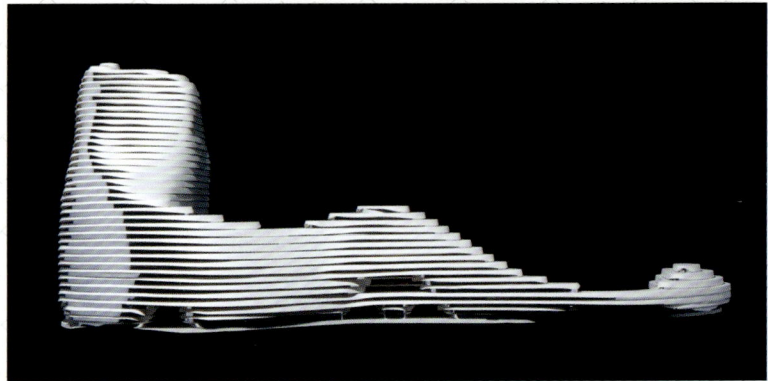

The wavy forms of the louvres wrapping around the building are shaped to reduce solar radiation on the facade depending on orientation. The exposure of the more vulnerable east and west facades is therefore reduced by minimising the shading devices' angle based on year-round insolation measurements.

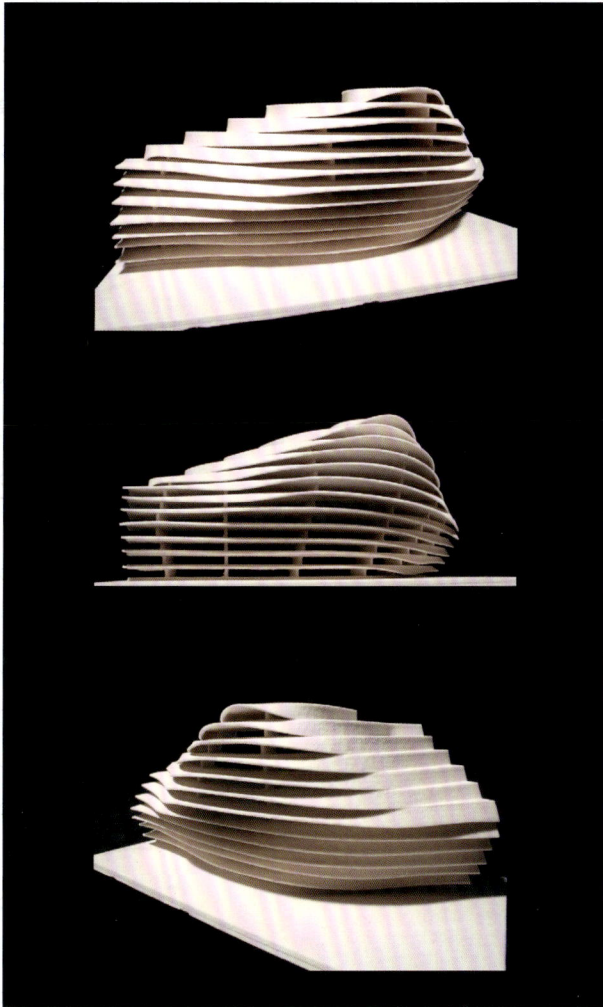

Close-up of the angular variation of the louvres, as seen from different viewpoints.

A SENSE OF PURPOSE

MATHEMATICS AND PERFORMANCE IN ENVIRONMENTAL DESIGN

SPECIALIST MODELLING GROUP, FOSTER + PARTNERS

Mathematics in design is most often associated with its visual manifestation in geometrical surfaces and elements. The finely tuned ambient qualities of a space, necessary for environmental performance, may not be so apparent, but can involve the application of many branches of mathematics. **Martha Tsigkari, Adam Davis and Francis Aish** of Foster + Partners' Specialist Modelling Group bring this to the fore by describing how at Al Raha Beach development in Abu Dhabi and the City of Justice in Madrid environmental considerations were interpreted through analytical numerical data.

Discussions of mathematics in architecture often concern the perception of numeric and geometric relationships as embodied in patterns of structure and material. A similar dialogue within environmental design suggests maths is the means of logically elucidating our perception of what we unconsciously sense as optimum performance, rather than a driving force directly and visibly discernible to us through the form of things.

Where design follows environmental considerations, perception becomes a very small part of sensible interaction with architecture. Building occupants are seldom aware of the various complex factors affecting their comfort and what they might do to improve or otherwise manipulate it. Of all the ambient qualities which affect our occupation of architecture – temperature, air flow, lighting – only some rise to the level of conscious awareness. When these qualities are given priority in design, the performance of architecture is less perceptible because it is operating more directly on our senses; this is also the way mathematics is experienced in the context of the natural environment. Patterns and forms found in the natural world are understood more in terms of experience than in the logic or principles by which they were created. Beauty in nature is largely driven by mathematics that do not necessarily have a direct visual manifestation in the form

itself, but rather in the way that form performs within its context.

The manipulation of the environment through design involves many branches of mathematics: the projective geometry of light transmission, the chaotic and probabilistic maths of weather patterns, and the statistical algorithms required to make analysis legible and obtain discrete building components from continuous distributions. Such an approach always favours pragmatism over mathematical 'purity'. Yet the results thus produced have a profound effect on the experience of architecture precisely because of the fundamental sensory experiences concerned.

This indirect employment of mathematical analysis in design promotes a spatial experience in which any visually recognisable effects of an analytical process are subordinate to an unconscious perception of comfort. Where entasis in the classical orders employs geometry in a subtle way to make things appear as they should be, environmental design employs mathematics to produce a similar sense of fitness for purpose. Both of these applications rely on commonalities of perception. However, where the former is an analytic approach to visual aptness, the latter – because of contingencies of site, climate and culture – is necessarily differentiated and synthetic. While the visceral sense of comfort produced

through this approach will be similar between designs, the visual and physical manifestations may vary considerably. Situated along the continuum between pure and applied mathematics, this approach could be conceived as the application of analytical mathematical processes as an exact science, distorted to provide a responsive synthetic solution. The selection of significant weather data, for instance, may be a probabilistic function, while the embodiment of an environmental mediator based on this data may take the form of an optimisation algorithm, approximating a continuous distribution through discrete iterations.

The Al Raha Beach development in Abu Dhabi is a characteristic example of a building driven by environmental considerations which, interpreted through analytical numerical data, inform its shape. The interaction of the elements (sun and wind) with the parametric model began a form-finding exercise that sought to balance performance-driven optimisation with more intuitive aesthetic criteria. The building's undulating louvre system is an example of this process and is designed to minimise solar gain in response to facade orientation, while maximising views out. An optimisation problem at its core, the exercise varied the slope angle of constant-length louvres around the facade to allow no more than a maximum amount of radiation to hit the building. The derived

Foster + Partners, City of Justice, Madrid, 2007
The facades of both court buildings bear shading devices optimised to balance solar performance with views to the exterior.

script sorted the resulting angles based on set theory and morphed the shading system accordingly.

A study for the facades of the City of Justice in Madrid produced a dramatically different appearance to the Al Raha Beach development, yet was based on very similar underlying principles. As with that project, the facades of the court buildings minimise incident solar radiation on the facade, above a threshold value based on historical weather data. Instead of a single-dimensional optimisation, the City of Justice facades have a three-dimensional solution space: edges of the pyramidal shading device were tested for possible degrees of aperture along three independent axes. The optimal shading device would offer the best ratio of shading performance to the area of opening, in order to promote views out from the judicial offices behind.

Despite the obvious differences of appearance between the two projects, each responds to the continuity of the sun's path over the days and seasons as continuity of transition across neighbouring bays of the facade. The numerical relationships governing the cycle of the sun's travel and the intensity of its rays underlie the sensible experience of the buildings. ⌂

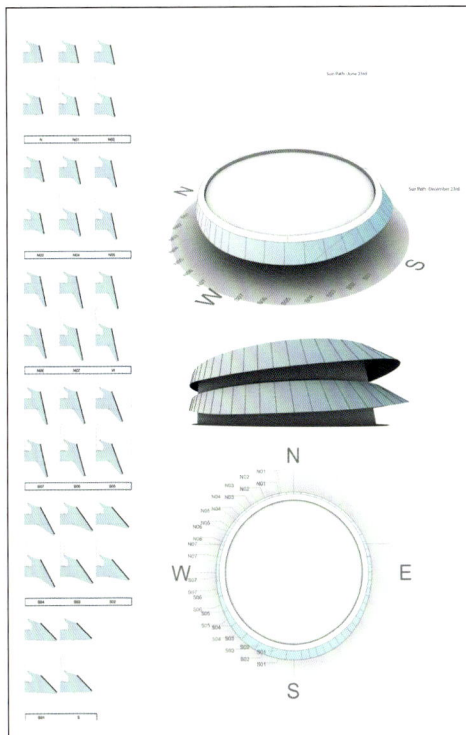

Sample points around the facade evaluate the range of different sun directions and intensities throughout the year and use the results to drive the louvres' slope angle.

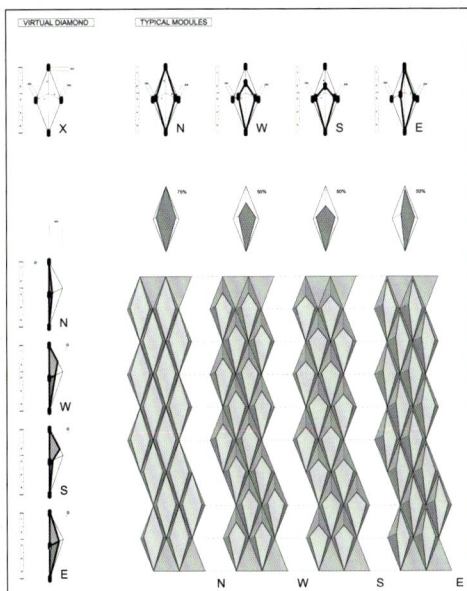

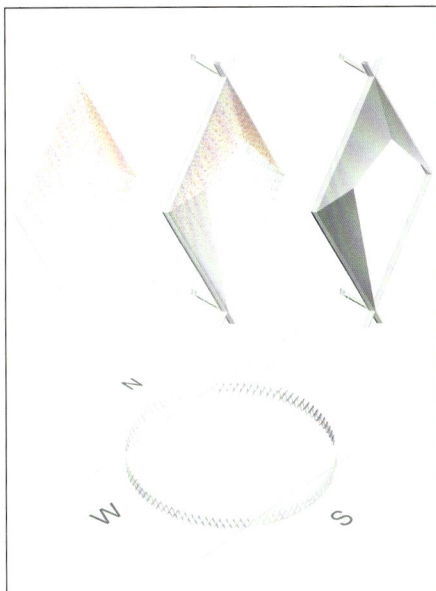

far left: Each orientation requires a different shading configuration, according to the optimisation algorithm used. The west-facing and east-facing shades are asymmetrical due to the intended hours of occupation and the differences between morning and evening solar radiation, as obtained from historical weather data.

left: Shading is optimised for each bay in a three-step process. First, sample points on the facade directly behind each shade are projected onto a virtual pyramidal shade across each month, day and hour as required by occupancy. Historical weather data is used, associating each point of solar incidence with a radiation value. Second, different apertures are tested along three axes. Each aperture's fitness is determined by the total radiation blocked, factored against the visible area through the aperture. Finally, the aperture which provides the optimal ratio of radiation blocked to obscured area is selected as the louvre for that bay.

Daniel Bosia

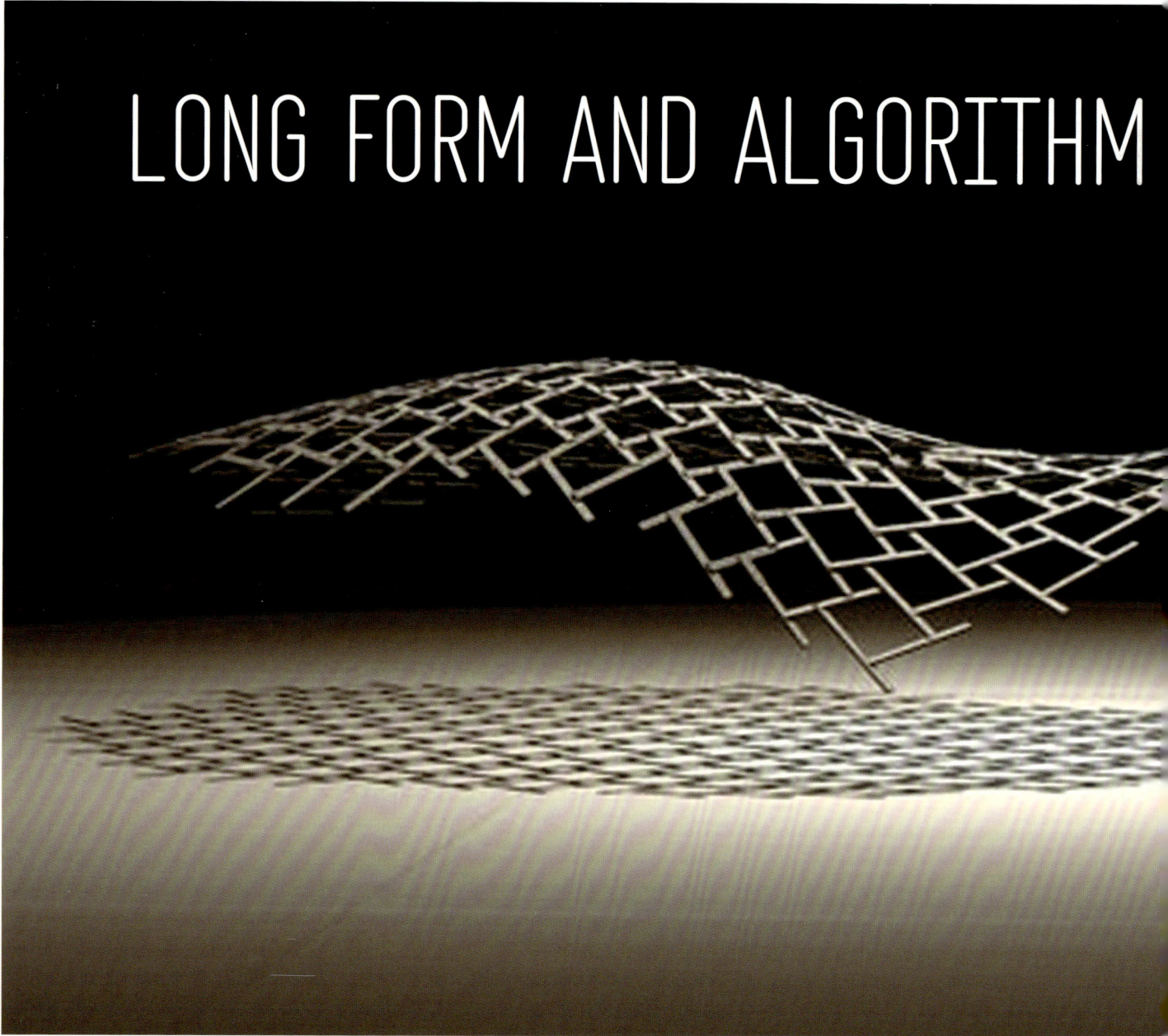

LONG FORM AND ALGORITHM

Computer algorithms and scripting provide engineers and architects with the opportunities to design in a nonlinear way. This is a matter of learning from nature's evolutionary and nonlinear processes rather than mimicking them. **Daniel Bosia** describes how Arup's Advanced Geometry Group (AGU) has developed a method that uses abstract genetic algorithms to create rational and systematic organisations of space, which are structured and rational to construct and assemble.

Figure 1. Shigeru Ban and Arup AGU, Forest Park Pavilion, St Louis, Missouri, 2005
Form-found model of the pavilion showing synclastic and anticlastic curvature inversion of the reciprocal grid.

Pattern is deeply embedded in our very consciousness. It governs the rhythms of life from our own heartbeats to cosmological events such as the alternation of day and night and the succession of seasons.

Figure 2. Arup AGU, Weave Bridge, University of Philadelphia, Pennsylvania, 2009
Interior view of the Weave Bridge with its interlacing steel structure and timber and glazed infill panels.

Figure 3. Shigeru Ban and Arup AGU, Forest Park Pavilion, St Louis, Missouri, 2002
Physical model of the pavilion made of wooden plats and simple pin connections.

Figure 4. Alvaro Siza and Eduardo Souto
de Moura with Arup AGU (Cecil Balmond,
Daniel Bosia, Charles Walker and Lip Chiong),
Serpentine Gallery Pavilion, Kensington
Gardens, London, 2005
Interior of the 2005 pavilion with its reciprocal
'woven' pattern of flat timber beams.

Figure 5. Matthew Ritchie with Arup AGU
(Daniel Bosia and Nicolas Sterling) and
Aranda/Lasch, The Morning Line, Seville
Biennial of Contemporary Art, Seville, 2008
Fractal geometries of The Morning Line 'anti-
pavilion' at Seville.

Pattern can be found everywhere we look in the world, from our own molecular structure to the spiralling and branching forms of nature. Pattern is deeply embedded in our very consciousness. It governs the rhythms of life from our own heartbeats to cosmological events such as the alternation of day and night and the succession of seasons. From the origins of mankind, through civilisations, we have learned to recognise patterns in nature, their rhythms and hierarchies. We have learned to count, measure and abstract the archetypes of the forms we experience. This has helped us find order and structure within the chaotic complexities of the world around us.

However, a tendency towards variation and deviation from a condition of stability, regularity and constancy is at the very essence of our survival. We have learned that evolution of one pattern to the next, transition from a condition of stability to another, is what ensures the fitness of any system in space and time. We have learned to appreciate the non-linearity of nature's systems, based on recursion, cumulative processes of growth, evolution and feedback. We have understood that they are multilayered and multidimensional, because they contain the whole history of their genesis and transformation in time.

New Systems of Organisation and Tooling

In an era of new humanism, contemporary designers are faced with the opportunity of exploring new systems of organisation, far reaching beyond classical and static forms. The focus is on the processes that govern the genesis and transformation of these systems and the structure of their parts. Designing is organising space, establishing networks of programme and circulation, structuring of form from deep within. It is a nonlinear process like those that govern nature, but it does not mimic nature, it learns from it, promoting the emergence of new organisations. The starting point is often arbitrary and irrational, but the outcomes are structured and organised, providing surprising new answers. What emerge are not static forms but dynamic systems, expressions of simple and rigorous

recursive processes. They are complex not complicated, rich in their varied ramifications and intrinsic patterns. Non-linearity produces multiple outcomes, not single answers, requiring a more critical and selective evaluation than in the traditional approach. Evolution is at the core of this forensic research where the answers are not locked into stylistic mindsets, but selected on the basis of their fitness.

The power of computers has enabled us to articulate new organisations and configurations of space based on simple rules, properties and proportional relationships where complexity is generated by the recursive repetition of simple processes. We have crafted our own working tools, scripting them from basic principles, compiling them from numeric recipes that we call computer algorithms. We have been able to generate what commercial software could not offer: forms that are based on different conceptual processes. We have coded routines that simulate growth, subdivision, erosion in their basic form and crossbred them to create hybrid recipes. In doing this we have multiplied the outcomes and discovered new worlds of different solutions. We have combined generative algorithms with procedures that test for efficiency so that engineering is no longer a process of post-rationalisation, and the intelligence of new solutions is inherent in their very creation.

Manifestation of the Process

Arup's Advanced Geometry Unit (AGU) was set up as a research-based design group striving to create exciting new built architectural forms and solutions by examining the structural dynamics of everything from geometric shapes and patterns to naturally occurring phenomena. The following examples of the group's work demonstrate a process taking from abstract geometric algorithms to rational and systematic organisations of space that are structured and rational to construct and assemble. It is apparent from these projects how simple geometric constructs find rational applications, how geometric symmetries, hierarchies and proportions present advantages in

Figure 6. Anish Kapoor with Arup AGU, Tall Tree and the Eye, Royal Academy of Arts, London, 2009
Fractal reflections of the Royal Academy courtyard into the Tall Tree and the Eye installation.

Figure 7. Arup AGU, Torre Reforma, Mexico City, 2007
View from below of the Torre Reforma with its aperiodic three-dimensional glazing pattern that forms the external facade and also internal atria.

Figure 8. Anish Kapoor with Arup AGU, Tall Tree and the Eye, Royal Academy of Arts, London, 2009
The 70-sphere installation in the courtyard of the Royal Academy.

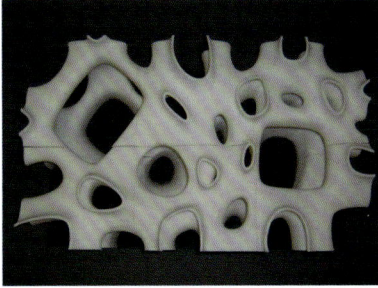

Figure 9. Toyo Ito & Associates with Arup AGU, Taichung Opera House, Taiwan, 2007
Rapid prototype model of the Taichung Opera House concrete structure.

Figure 10. Arup AGU, Pedro and Inês Bridge, Coimbra, Portugal, 2007
View of the central 'floating' square with the folded balustrade pattern.

the construction of real structures. As lines become steel beams and surfaces materialise into glass and aluminium cladding panels, the rigours of geometry translate in highly structured and efficient constructions. The outcomes are often unexpected and new in their appearance, sometimes even revolutionary in setting new trends. Although every project is unique, all are derived using a common method based on the rigorous application of algorithmic processes of space and form-making.

Woven Networks
The Weave Bridge at the University of Pennsylvania in Philadelphia (2009) is a coiling in space of six strands of steel interlocking to form a rigid three-dimensional braided structure which unwinds into the landscape forming paths, balustrades and bleachers around the university sports fields. Differing from traditional warren trusses which linearly span enclosing space, the structure of the Weave Bridge spirals around a square cross-section without corner members. The result is a dematerialisation of the prismatic envelope of the bridge and the opening of the view towards the fields and the city beyond.

The Forest Park Pavilion in St Louis, Missouri, designed with Shigeru Ban (2002), is a structural weave of straight timber elements interwoven in what is known as a 'reciprocal network'. This allows the creation of a large span with relatively short transportable beams and simple, economic, overlapping connections. It is a simple geometric pattern where every element of the grid spans onto another until the perimeter is reached. The order in which the beams are overlapped determines whether the curvature of the grid is synclastic or anticlastic, and the point at which the beams meet and their thickness dictates the radius of curvature.

With a very different reading to the St Louis pavilion, the Serpentine Gallery Pavilion of 2005, designed by Alvaro Siza and Eduardo Souto de Moura with Arup AGU (Cecil Balmond, Daniel Bosia, Charles Walker and Lip Chiong), is also a reciprocal grid. Located in Kensington Gardens,

London, here the reciprocal nature of the grid is expressed in the timber beams never lining up axially, but passing each other in an interlocking, weaving pattern. The mortice and tenon joint adopted produces a constantly moving cascading effect which ripples across the structure, breaking the linearity of the Cartesian grid and expressing its reciprocal non-linear nature.

Tiled Networks
The Morning Line installation (Seville Biennial of Contemporary Art, 2008), designed with Matthew Ritchie and Aranda/Lasch, is a structure that is simultaneously expandable and reducible to a series of modular units. It can evolve in space and time as it travels through different venues. It is based on the tetrahedron, the simplest and most rigid solid in nature, which, if truncated at its vertices generates the basic unit of a fractal geometric system. By mapping two-dimensional drawings onto the surface of the truncated tetrahedron, the unit transforms from a solid to a structural 'knot' in space, which, tiled, produces a complex network in space, a 'three-dimensional drawing'.

A scheme for Torre Reforma, designed by AGU (2007), is a three-dimensional aperiodic tiling system used to generate the basic framework of a 200-metre (660-feet) tall tower in Mexico City. Based on four tetrahedral tiles, capable of subdividing in self-similar copies of themselves, this particular tiling system displays fractal properties that establish a hierarchy of primary, secondary structure and tertiary cladding pattern. The tiling is also aperiodic, such that the order of the same four basic tiles never repeats, ensuring a continuous variation of the patterns across the facades. Because of its three-dimensional nature, the tiling also creates the geometry of the internal atria and floors.

Packed Networks
In the Tall Tree and the Eye at the Royal Academy of Arts, London (2009), designed with Anish Kapoor, 70 mirror polished spheres, each with a thickness of 1.5 millimetres (0.06 inches) and a diameter of 1 metre (3 feet), are stacked

Figure 11. Arup AGU, Pedro and Inês Bridge, Coimbra, Portugal, 2007
View of the bridge from below, showing the 'cut-and-shift' forming the 'floating' square.

Figure 12. Toyo Ito & Associates with Arup AGU, Serpentine Gallery Pavilion, Kensington Gardens, London, 2002
Interior of the pavilion showing the dynamism of the algorithmic pattern.

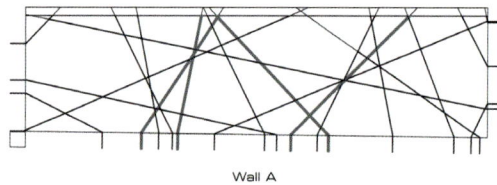

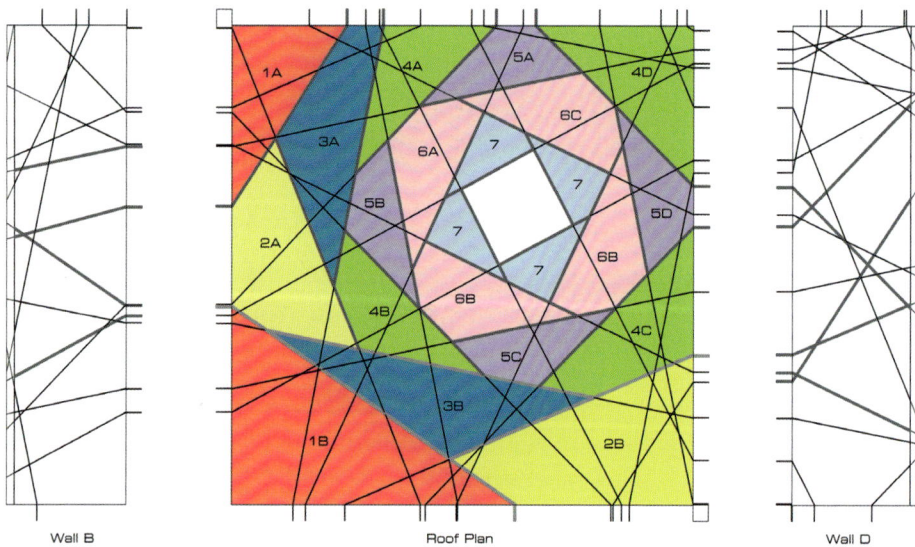

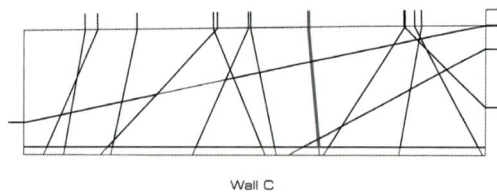

Figure 13. Toyo Ito & Associates with Arup AGU, Serpentine Gallery Pavilion, Kensington Gardens, London, 2002
Interlocking pattern of panels forming the pavilion deriving from geometric construction.

Wall A

Wall B

Roof Plan

Wall D

Wall C

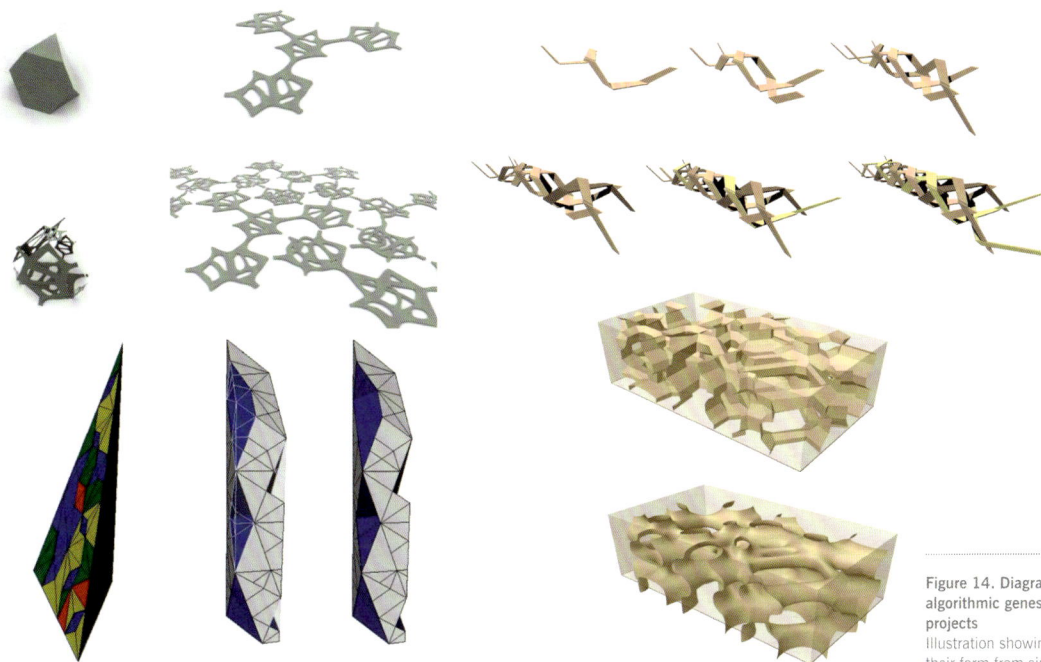

Figure 14. Diagrams illustrating the algorithmic genesis of the different projects
Illustration showing how the projects take their form from simple recursive processes.

to a height of 14 metres (46 feet). The piece is based on the observation that the reflection of perfectly reflective tangent spheres into each other generates infinite fractal patterns (a tetrahedron of spheres, for example, creates a Sierpinski-type gasket). The reflection becomes increasingly complex and rich when people and surrounding buildings are introduced into the space and when the packing is carried out in an irregular form.

Smooth Surface Networks

The Taichung Opera House, designed with Toyo Ito & Associates (2007), consists of a single smooth concrete surface dividing space in two regions A and B, never connecting, but constantly flowing into each other. Organised in a three-dimensional chequerboard of alternating A and B voids, the surface is the structure to a three-storey building where vertical support seamlessly merges into horizontal diaphragms. The surface is also a grid of seamlessly smooth lines flowing from one end of the building to the other, providing the underlying grid of its reinforcement and shuttering patterns.

Folded Networks

The Pedro and Inês Bridge in Coimbra, Portugal (2007) questions the traditional concept of crossing a river in a straight linear trajectory, subverting the two-dimensional balance of forces typical of classical arching bridge structures. It does this through the introduction of a disruption at its midspan, a 'cut-and-shift' move which splits the deck into two, pushing the supports towards the outer edges of the bridge. The structure remains perfectly balanced in its three-dimensional form, acquiring lateral stability through the spreading of its supports. Spatially the cut-and-shift move generates an unexpected event at the midspan; a 'floating' square hangs suspended over

the water where people meander and pause. The balustrade is a three-dimensional folding of four shapes of coloured glass animating the bridge with reflections and shades of light.

Proportional Networks

The Serpentine Gallery Pavilion of 2002, designed with Toyo Ito & Associates, is based on a network of lines that originates from connecting the half point to the third point of each side of the square plan. The recursion and extension of this rule generates a complete network which folds from the roof of the pavilion to the walls to form a rigid structure. The pattern of the facade is a simple polygonal chequerboard of glass and aluminium panels. The hierarchies and regularities of the geometric pattern facilitate the segmenting of the structure in panels that are easily transportable and buildable on site like interlocking pieces of a puzzle. It is also apparent that within the chaotic array of lines in space there is an underlying order of simple proportions, a dynamic pattern that follows the concentric lines of its geometric genesis.

In the past few years the AGU has demonstrated, through built projects, that new spaces and structures can be formed by the introduction of systems of organisation not previously explored in architecture or engineering. By employing a mathematically rigorous method, recursive algorithms have been coded in computer applications as the new tools of the designer and used to promote the emergence of a rich world of new spatial networks where habitable space, circulation, structure and pattern can be found. ⌀

Heatherwick Studio, British Pavilion, Shanghai, China, 2010
Close-up of the spike distribution.

INTUITIVE MATERIAL DISTRIBUTIONS

PANAGIOTIS
MICHALATOS AND
SAWAKO KAIJIMA,
*ADAMS KARA
TAYLOR (AKT)*

Panagiotis Michalatos and Sawako Kaijima describe how the Optimisation Design team at *Adams Kara Taylor (AKT)* work with mathematical algorithms to develop interactive software applicatons that help inform structural behaviour in the early parts of the design process. This is exemplified by the project-specific software they developed for Thomas Heatherwick's British Pavilion at the 2010 Shanghai Expo.

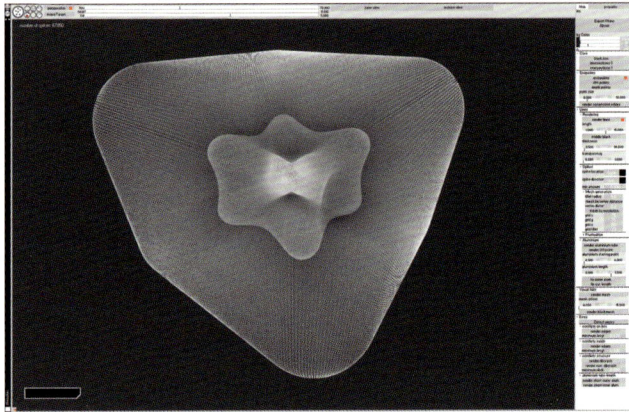

Heatherwick Studio, British Pavilion, Shanghai, China, 2010
Screen captures from software made for a spike distribution study at AKT for the British Pavilion at the Shanghai Expo.

The pavilion is constructed from 60,000 7.5-metre (24.6-foot) long acrylic rods suspended in a timber frame structure.

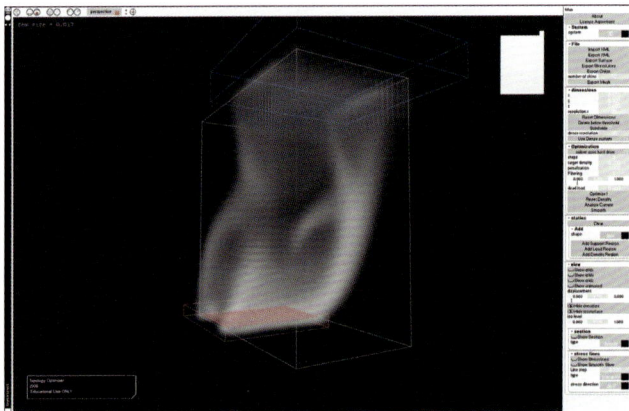

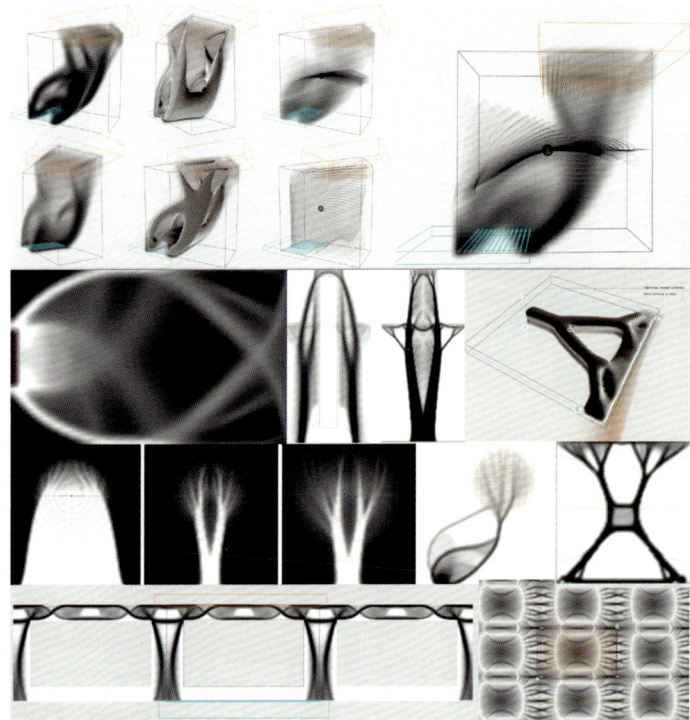

Panagiotis Michalatos and Sawako Kaijima (Adams Kara Taylor/AKT), TopoStruct software, 2008
Screen capture of the TopoStruct software for structural optimisation.

Different combinations of boundary conditions and forces give rise to a variety of structural forms and patterns, some familiar from living organisms or typical steel structures and others more unexpected.

The applied research of the Optimisation Design team at Adams Kara Taylor (AKT) focuses on the development of interactive software applications that induce intuition towards specific counter-intuitive design problems, often related but not limited to the understanding of structural behaviour. Intuition is considered as insights gained by practice (play) and feedback (observation) which makes possible informed decisions in the context of a specific design problem.

The process involves effective abstraction of the problem, development and implementation of mathematical algorithms in order to extract a set of pre-solutions; that is, semi-determinate results that operate as design hints in the early stages of the design process rather than definite outcomes. In addition, close attention to interface design enhances the accessibility of often-complicated algorithms as well as the intuitive understanding of their inner workings. Hence more than any specific algorithms used, the controls and observables that make up the digital design environment constitute the ingredients for an intuitive approach to the problematic of structure.

One aspect of architectural design that is often opaque to many architects, especially during the early stages of development, is the question of structural behaviour, because in many cases it is difficult to think of structure without definite geometry. With the aim of achieving a closer and yet not super-determined relationship between design and structure, the work seeks to describe the structural aspects of design as continuous material distributions in space.

TopoStruct is one application that has been developed based on the theory of topology optimisation (by Martin Philip Bendsøe and Ole Sigmund), a methodology that produces optimal geometric and material distributions in space with respect to structural behaviours. The application allows those with little prior knowledge of engineering to acquire some understanding of the physics of structure. In fact, after interacting with the software for some time, users tend to anticipate the results as if they have gained this intuitive understanding of the underlying principle.

However, the importance of the software does not lie only in the particular method itself but in its potential to alter an architect's perception of material and structure.

Design is often seen as an articulation of solid elements within an empty space or a manipulation of clear-cut boundaries in the form of surfaces. A more abstract concept of structure and material is instead introduced here where some regions of space are solid and some empty, but the boundaries between them are diffused. In this case materiality gradients traverse the design space, carrying material information and endowing space with some structural behaviour, although of a very exotic 'could observe and discuss' kind. These properties are encoded in scalar and tensor fields which act on the design and give hints about material density and directionality without imposing a specific formal expression. The latter, the interpretation of the material fields, will be part of the designer's decision-making process. Here, the question of what to design is transformed into what are the properties of the space itself in which we embed a design artefact. Such a conceptual shift can be useful in the early stages of design as it gives clues about the behaviour of material distributions and the structural patterns that emerge within them.

A similar line of thought is followed in the research by AKT's optimisation design team on the discretisation of surfaces using tensor fields that are related to material and structural information. Here, rather than the distribution of material density, the quest is the abstraction of a patterning exercise to one of controlling vector fields and hence directionalities in space.

All of these methods often require a statistical intuition of the design domain properties. This was the case with the development at AKT of project-specific software for several design problems. For example, for Thomas Heatherwick's British Pavilion at the 2010 Shanghai Expo, an interface was created for the early stages of design through which could be observed and discussed the properties and problems of different distribution methods for the pavilion's 60,000 spikes, seen both as individual elements and as a continuum with statistical and smoothly varying aspects. This ability to operate intuitively at the borderline of the discrete and the continuum is critical for projects that are geometrically hyper-fragmented and work at multiple scales. ◮

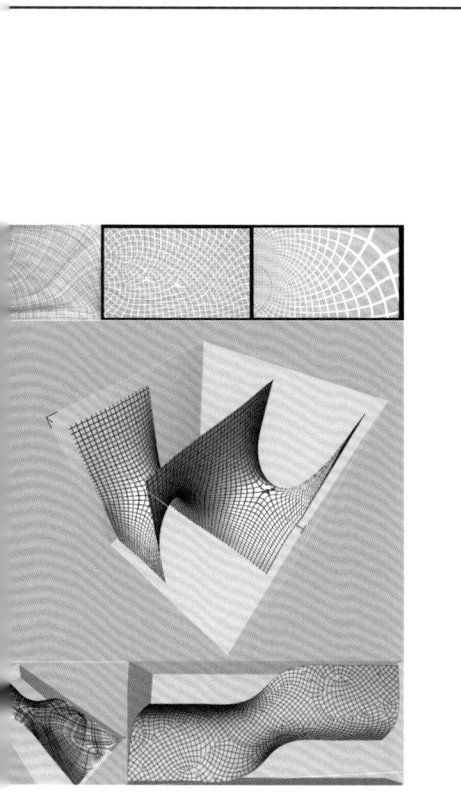

Generation of structural patterns over plates and shells, driven by material and structural properties.

Text © 2011 John Wiley & Sons Ltd. Images: pp 66-7, 68(tr) © Hufton + Crow; p 68(tl) © AKT; p 68(b), 69 © Sawako Kaijima / Panagiotis Michalatos

Fabian Scheurer
Hanno Stehling

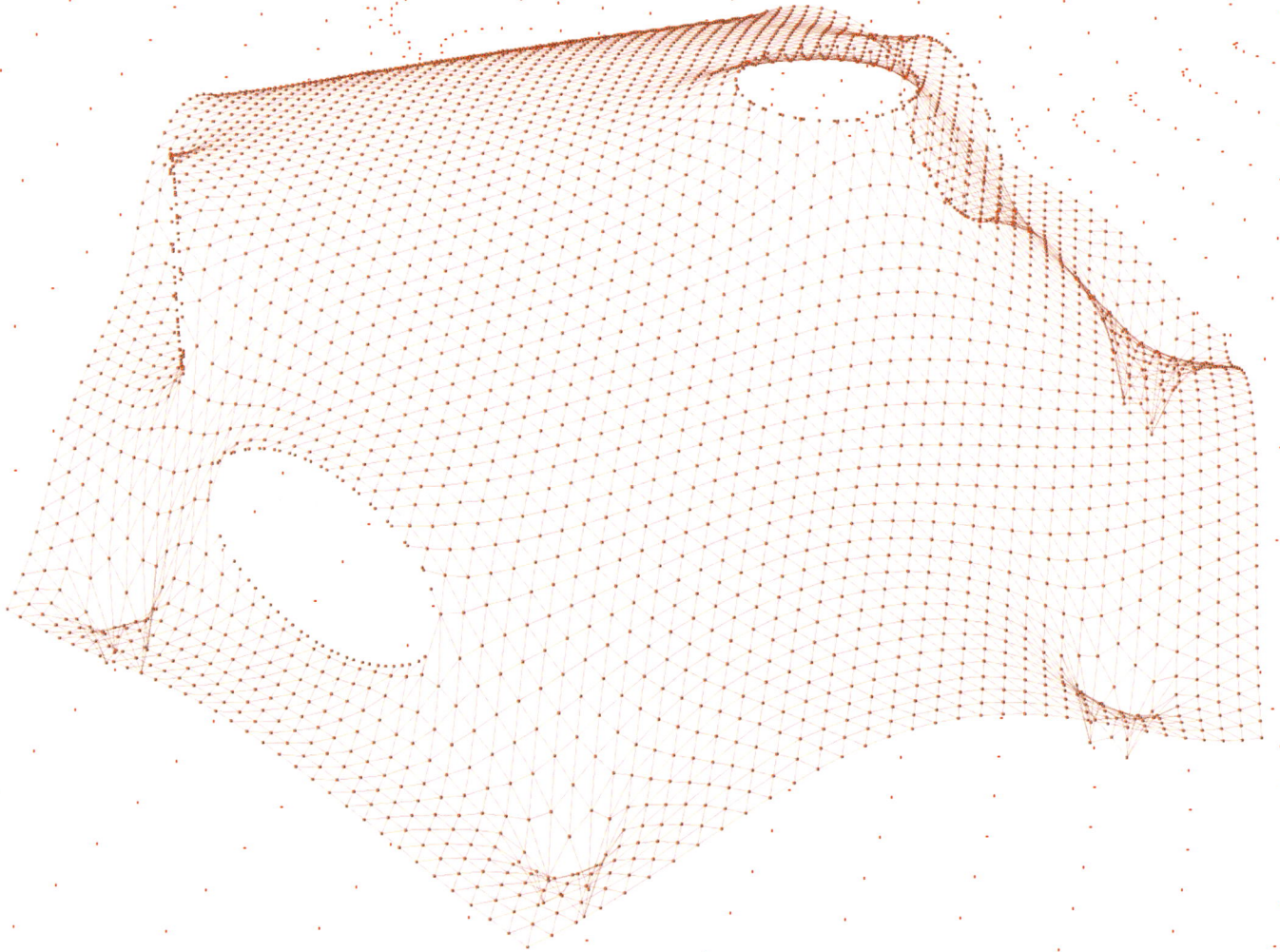

LOST IN PARAMETER SPACE?

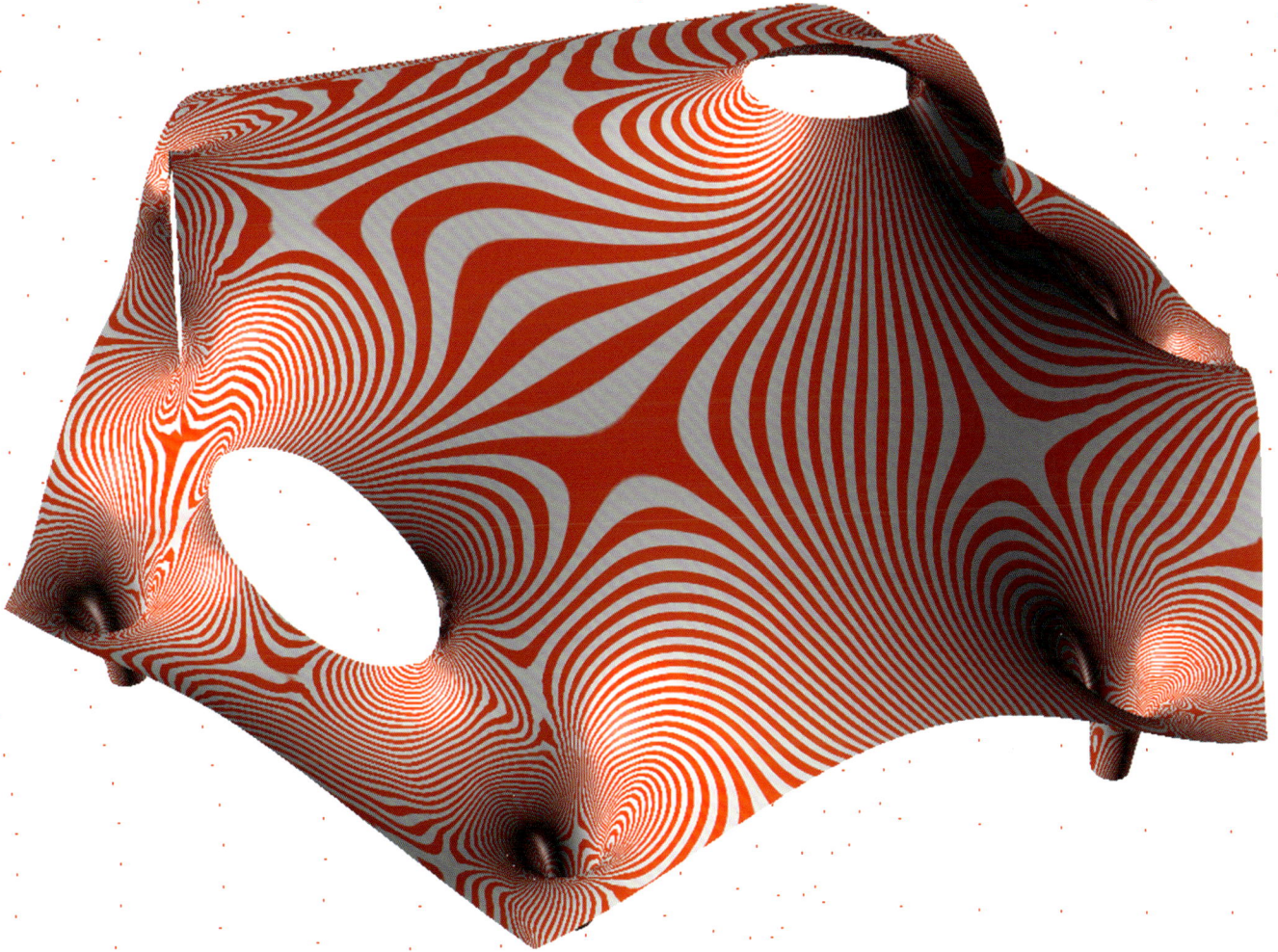

Rather than eradicating the need for mathematics in architectural practice, computation has intensified it. As **Fabian Scheurer and Hanno Stehling** of designtoproduction explain, the uneven flow of a complex design from computer-aided design (CAD) to computer-aided engineering (CAE) and through to computer-aided manufacturing (CAM) necessitates an understanding of abstract mathematical concepts that facilitate communication, precision and an accurate assessment of quality throughout the process.

Figure 1. Shigeru Ban, Centre Pompidou, Metz, France, 2010
The roof surface as triangle mesh (left) and as NURBS surface (right). Only the latter allowed for the fabrication of smoothly curved girders, but its definition took some help from specialists who usually work for the automotive industry.

A few years ago the introduction of ever more powerful computer-aided design (CAD) systems seemed to have almost eradicated mathematics from architectural practice. At least when looking at the curricula of architecture schools one could have the impression that this subject – anyway unloved due to its 'uncreative' formal rigidity – was happily replaced by CAD courses and the belief that somewhere in the background the software would take care of all the calculations. Under this cover, even highly sophisticated mathematical concepts like non-uniform rational b-splines (NURBS) managed to sneak into architecture, understood by very few but happily applied nevertheless.

Recently this seems to have changed again. Architects have suddenly shown an increasing interest in mathematics[1] and its abstract concepts. Surprisingly at first glance, the very same process of digitalisation that once marginalised mathematics in architecture now actuates its re-establishment. On closer inspection, however, this is a consequent progression: it turned out that the complex shapes unleashed by digital design tools did not smoothly flow down the process chain from CAD to computer-aided engineering (CAE) to computer-aided manufacturing (CAM) until automatically materialising inside some digital fabrication machines, and that the implementation of a passably seamless digital workflow requires more than the flick of a button in the designer's CAD software. To understand why this is the case we need to take a look at mathematics and the closely related theory of computation.

First of all, architectural design is a process of communication. It is a long way from the designer's initial idea to the built result, necessitating means to describe a design in ways that give sufficient and unambiguous instructions to the builders.

Traditionally and despite all digitalisation, this is still achieved mainly by 2-D drawings. Mathematically speaking, the projection of a three-dimensional object onto a two-dimensional sheet of paper is a mapping transformation that must be set up carefully in order to deliver not only correct but also meaningful results. Ideally, a projection plane is defined so that most of the object's edges keep their length and inscribed angles, allowing measurements in the drawing to give valid information about the real thing.

Unfortunately, such a projection plane does not now exist for a complex shape with no planar faces. Subsequently, any 2-D plan might transport parts of the topology (how certain features are related to each other) but no reliable metrics any more (how far those features are from each other). This loss of information, in the end, makes it impossible to reconstruct the 3-D object based on a set of 2-D drawings – the traditional language of architecture becomes insufficient.

Luckily, CAD systems have evolved from a stage where they merely were simulating 2-D drawing boards.

Nowadays CAD models can – contrary to a sheet of paper – unambiguously store the actual 3-D information of an object. Consistent 2-D plans can then be derived from those 3-D models on request. So complex designs consequently have to be modelled in three dimensions before they are flattened to drawings; the model becomes the core of communication.

Abstraction

A model, by definition, is always an abstraction of reality. Building a model means reducing the infinite complexity of the real world to a level where it can be described with manageable effort. What is obvious in the workshop of a model builder sometimes gets forgotten when almost infinite digital storage space is at hand: a perfect model does not contain as much information as possible, but as little as necessary to describe the properties of an object unambiguously. Any extra bit would be meaningless for the given purpose and only impede comprehensibility. In information theory, this is known as 'Kolmogorov complexity' or 'descriptive complexity': the complexity of an object is defined by the length of the shortest possible description. While modelling starts with gathering data, it is far more important to then throw away everything that turns out to be superficial. This task requires quite some (human!) intelligence, because it involves finding patterns and defining general cases.

This is easily done for planar faces and regular grids: details can be defined once and then multiplied; local changes do not induce re-evaluations of the whole structure. But again, the fun stops as soon as the shapes get curvy.

Abstracting Shape

A straightforward approach to describe a non-planar shape would be to define a large number of points – for instance by laser-scanning a physical model – and connect them by straight lines to form a mesh. Meshes are an easy way to define complex shapes, but they have a severe disadvantage: the planar facets of a mesh can only approximate a curved shape, which is usually acceptable for rendering an image, but certainly is not for digital fabrication as the approximation errors quickly exceed the machine precision (typically some 1/10 millimetre for large-scale fabrication equipment) and are duly and visibly reproduced.

Fortunately, there is a mathematical model for precisely describing curved surfaces. Developed in the 1950s and 1960s, the computational complexity of NURBS meant it took almost 50 years until they started their impressive career in architecture. NURBS allow the precise definition of complex shapes through control points. When used properly, significantly fewer control points are needed for a NURBS surface than vertices for a similar mesh, while at the same time NURBS allow the precise calculation of all in-between points on the

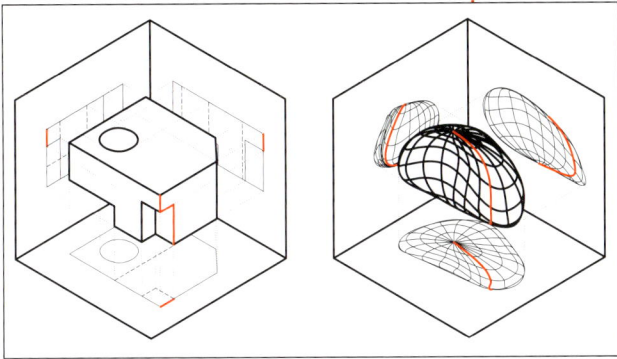

Figure 2. Planar projection
Simple 3-D objects with planar faces (left) can be unambiguously described by a small set of 2-D plans preserving lengths and angles for all edges running parallel to the projection planes. For curved surfaces (right), this approach fails because no projection plane would preserve the metrics.

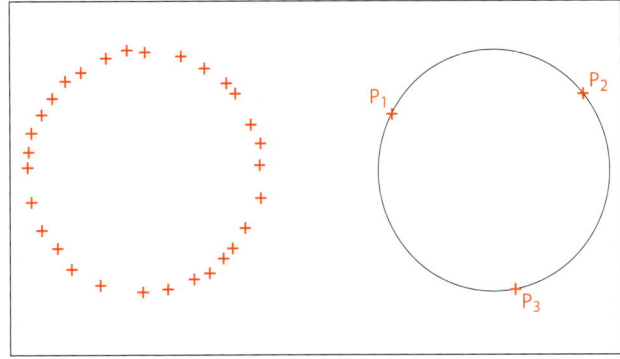

Figure 3. Abstracting a circle
A circle is unambiguously defined by only three points. After discovering the shape behind those 30 points we can throw away 27 of them (90 per cent of the data) and still have the same figure defined in the drawing. Additionally, the geometric definition of a circle lets us now identify the exact location of infinitely many more points than the 30 we started with.

Figure 4. Shigeru Ban, Centre Pompidou, Metz, France, 2010
The roof during erection. The structure is composed of six layers of double-curved girders that were precisely pre-cut on a computer-controlled machine.

Figure 5. ALA Arkitekter AS, Kilden Performing Arts Center, Kristiansand, Norway, due for completion 2012
The facade towards the waterfront is clad by straight oak boards, only twisted around their longitudinal axis.

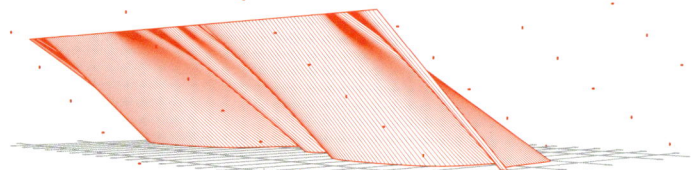

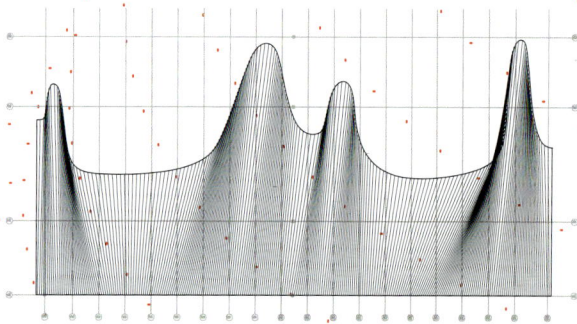

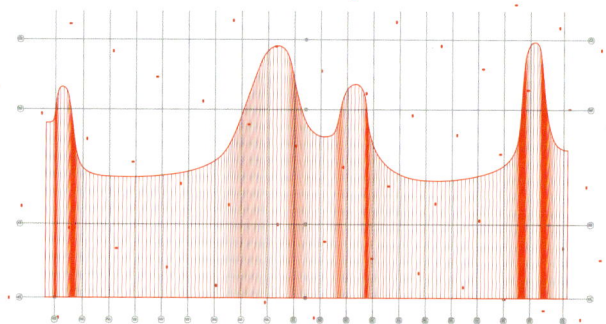

Figure 6. ALA Arkitekter AS, Kilden Performing Arts Center, Kristiansand, Norway, due for completion 2012
The facade's shape is defined by a ruled surface with a straight upper and a curved lower edge. For the intended prefabrication concept all generatrices had to be aligned with the building axes, a demand that could not be met with the default 'loft' method found in standard CAD packages (left), but needed a custom NURBS-definition (right).

surface. In this respect, a mesh can be abstracted by a NURBS surface like a polygon can be abstracted by a circle. But finding a proper NURBS representation for a given mesh or point-cloud requires quite a bit of knowledge of the underlying mathematical methods.

So it is more efficient to work with NURBS from the beginning, which is exactly what modern 3-D modelling software offers. But modelling a free-form surface means more than just tweaking control points; in order to come up with something buildable in the end, it means understanding the mathematical concepts behind those surfaces and relating them to the material world.

Abstracting Material

Curved surfaces have many geometrical properties that directly influence the options to actually build them (like developability and curvature radii). Most CAD programs can visualise those surface properties, but the designer has to interpret the colourful images and either match the design to the available material or find a suitable material for the given design. Speaking from experience, the latter approach is chosen far too often, frequently resulting in awkward and inefficient solutions.

For the development of smart solutions, the properties of both shape and material have to be known in detail. And, in order to precisely describe them in a 3-D model, the mathematics behind their physical behaviour have to be known too. If, for example, a curved surface is to be clad with thin strips of wood, it is easy to map a 'pinstripe' texture to the respective NURBS model and render a realistic looking but physically wrong image. In order to find out what really happens, one needs to base the stripe pattern on the bending characteristics of real-world wood strips. Only with this knowledge is it possible to create a valid geometry for all the slats on the surface and tell a fabricator how many to order and how to pre-cut them. Also, it enables the designer to optimise both surface and pattern for fabrication as well as for visual impression.

Abstracting Detail

Architectural design does not stop at defining an overall shape; a large number of components have to be joined to create a building. And, as soon as the underlying grid becomes non-regular, both components and joints must be adjusted to the geometrical situation at every grid position, rendering every piece unique. To save designers from manually modelling thousands of components, the concept of 'parametric modelling' was introduced: instead of describing the final result as a model, the process of modelling itself is described. A sequence of instructions (an algorithm) generates output (a detailed model) based on input (a set of parameters). By varying the input values, different output can be generated.

Abstraction in this context means to systematically develop a general solution suiting all individual components. This usually starts with finding the extreme cases – for example, the joints with extreme angles or the members with highest loads – and developing a parametric solution that can handle those as well as all intermediate cases. But since the (conflicting) requirements usually define a multidimensional solution space it is not always obvious whether all occurring cases are within the boundaries. Verifying the validity of a parametric solution might still require testing every single case. So, the challenge of building a parametric model is to untangle the interdependencies created by different requirements and find a set of rules that is as simple as possible while remaining flexible enough to accommodate every occurring case. In other words: to pinpoint the view to the exact level of abstraction where no important point is lost and no one gets distracted by unnecessary detail.

Reduction

Reduction, in contrast to abstraction, is not about reducing the amount of information but rather about finding the optimal way to transport it, hence rewriting the description without altering the content.

In the CAD domain, reduction can happen on different levels. Low-level reduction is about optimal descriptions of single geometric entities that save resources such as memory and disk space.

Fortunately, reduction on this level happens deep within the CAD system. It is higher-level reduction that is more interesting to the designer. Here we are mainly talking about two different procedures: elimination of redundancies and optimisation of descriptions and processes.

Normalisation

Redundancies (information that is present more than once) increase the weight of the model without adding detail and, more importantly, lead to update anomalies: the model can become inconsistent if only parts are updated. In database theory, the process of eliminating such anomalies is called normalisation. But it comes at a price: while changing information (writing) is made safer and quicker, extracting information (reading) becomes more complicated and generally slower, because it must be compiled from several spots throughout the dataset. Therefore, databases that are significantly more read than written are often kept partly redundant on purpose.

Carried over to CAD, this means that when creating 1,000 parametric components on one reference surface it could be sufficient to save one single point per entity and define a set of geometric operations to re-create its actual shape. However, this might render the model unusable as those operations have to be repeated on every information request. So the shortest possible description is not necessarily the best one. It might be worthwhile to keep some redundancies while carefully respecting update consistency.

Parametric modellers like McNeel's Grasshopper generally produce largely normalised models. When setting up a model, the user builds a hierarchical graph rooted in the input geometry. Grasshopper achieves a great deal, representing the graph visually and letting the user interact with it in a fairly intuitive way. Still, designers should be aware that the resulting geometry at every stage is volatile and immediately dependent on the input. While this eliminates the risk of update anomalies it also suppresses the possibility of deliberate redundancies or manual intervention.

Refactoring

The second flavour of high-level reduction could be described as cleaning up a model. Again, it can be rooted in computer science, where it is known as refactoring; that is, changing the source code of a program without changing its functionality in order to ensure maintainability and extensibility. This can be mapped directly to CAD: by throwing away superficial parts and simplifying parametric dependencies, a model can be kept sleek and efficient. This is especially important when it is used by more than one party.

However, it is important to note that reduction is irreversible: once we reduce a circle's description from three points to centre and radius, there is no way to get our initial points back – the information is retained, but not its history. This means that designers have to make sure the parts they eliminate are truly superficial; otherwise reduction becomes further abstraction that affects the functionality of the model.

Algorithms

Theoretical computer science is definitely unlisted on the average architecture student's agenda. But when parts of the design are delegated to computer programs (as in computational optimisation) or new computational tools are developed within a design process (as in parametric modelling), some knowledge about algorithms becomes key to understanding their influence both on the process and its result.

Determinism

First and foremost, contrary to a design problem, an algorithm has to be well defined. Since computers cannot guess based on experience and intuition, every step in a computer program has to be completely and unambiguously determined by the previous steps. Any decision making on how to proceed has to be already embedded in the program, and randomness is only simulated by numerical methods. Even computer programs that seem to exhibit experience (like expert

systems) or random behaviour (like evolutionary systems) are running on deterministic hardware that can only switch currents on or off in a silicon chip (non-deterministic algorithms do exist, but they are mainly of interest for computational theory due to the lack of appropriate non-deterministic hardware).

Thus, defining an algorithm to solve a class of problems means to already know a general solution for those problems and describe a step-by-step process to derive an output from the given input. The first step usually is to assert that the input matches the problem specifications and can be processed (so the range of allowed inputs – the so-called 'parameter space' – has to be already well defined). From there on, the algorithm deterministically proceeds step by step, until it presents always the same final result for the same given input. Incidentally, evolutionary methods are no exception to this rule; they merely lift it to a different level of abstraction. The evolutionary method as such has to be well defined and deterministic, only the results are probabilistic.

Termination

Unfortunately it is not at all given that even a deterministic algorithm will eventually deliver a result. As soon as an algorithm contains some sort of loop it becomes hard to prove that it never gets lost in perpetual orbit for any given input. Consequently, parametric modellers like Grasshopper do not allow loops in their models. The data-flow diagram set up by the user always forms a directed loop-free graph assuring that data passes through without ever reaching the same point twice. On the other hand, iteratively executing the same step many times or even recursively calling an algorithm from within itself are very powerful and indispensable methods for efficient programs. And as a matter of fact, loops are used in parametric models, albeit only within the encapsulated components provided by the modeller and carefully hidden from the user to rule out infinite loops.

Computational Complexity

Sometimes even finite loops are too much. There are problems that can be solved by perfectly well-defined and provably terminating algorithms – only it takes far too long to wait for the result. A striking example is the so-called 'Travelling Salesman Problem' of finding the shortest route through all cities on a given list. An algorithm just has to generate all possible permutations of the listed cities, calculate the respective route lengths and find the shortest one. Since the number of cities is finite, so is the number of routes that can therefore be tested in finite time by a deterministic algorithm. The only problem is that for n cities the number of permutations accounts to $\frac{1}{2} \times (n-1)!$, a term that grows by the factorial (that is, the product of all positive integers

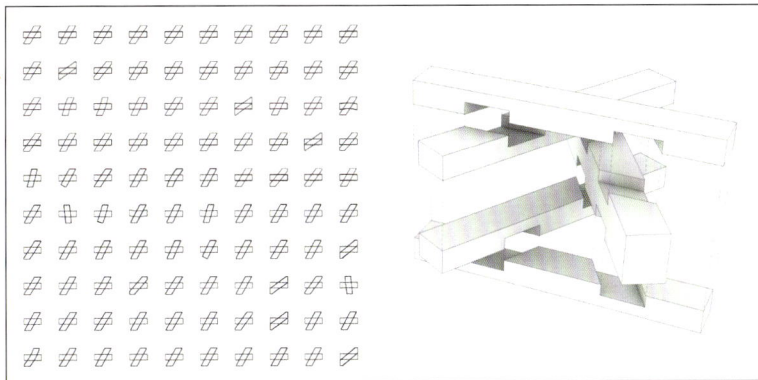

Figure 7. Shigeru Ban, Heasly Nine Bridges Golf Club, Yeoju, South Korea, 2010
To allow for continuous girders in all three directions, they are split into five layers with two lap joints at every crossing. The complete roof contains some 3,500 curved timber components with almost 15,000 lap joints. Even though many parts are similar, 467 individual components with over 2,000 different joints had to be described in detail. This was only possible by formally describing the whole structure in a parametric system that automatically generated the detailed models from a reference surface and some numerical parameters.

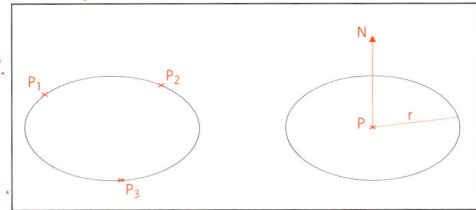

Figure 8. Reducing a circle
A circle can be unambiguously described by three points. However, if the notation is changed into one centre point plus normal vector and radius, the description size can be reduced from nine values (three points at three coordinates each) to seven values (two points and a number), saving 22 per cent.

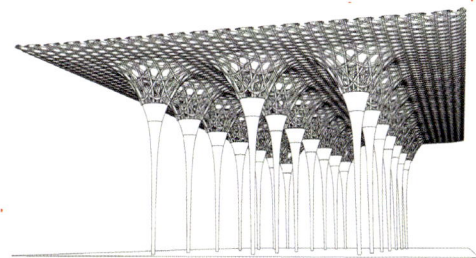

Figure 9. Shigeru Ban, Heasly Nine Bridges Golf Club, Yeoju, South Korea, 2010
The timber roof structure is defined by a regular tri-fold grid that is vertically projected to a curved surface. Girders are created on every projected grid line. Their orientation follows the surface, rendering them curved and twisted. The girders intersect at almost 7,500 crossing points.

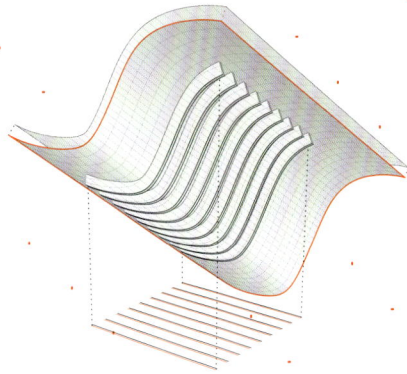

Figure 10. Curved beams in the Kilden facade
All timber beams are derived by projecting straight lines onto offsets from the same reference surface. The shortest possible description of each beam would therefore only contain one line, a width, a surface offset distance and a reference to the original surface. But the laborious offset and projection operations would have to be repeated whenever information about the beam geometry is needed. So it is reasonable to save the projected beam edges in the model, as long as they are updated when the reference surface changes.

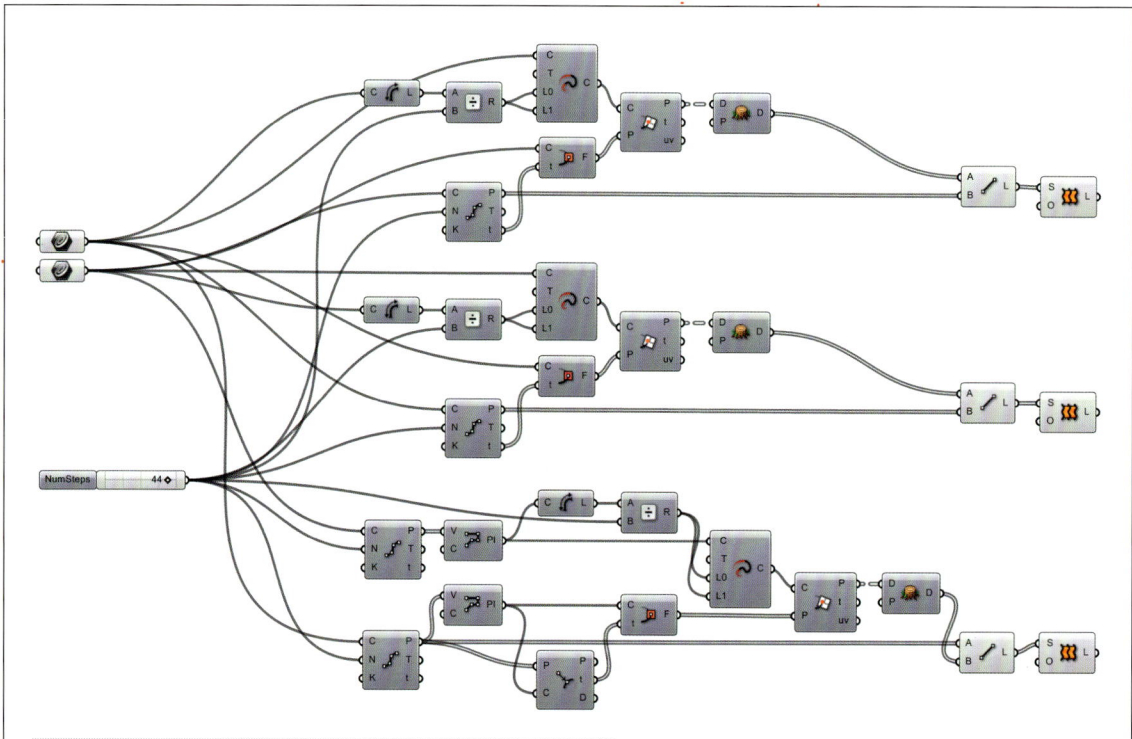

Figure 11. Parametric Grasshopper model
Parametric models describe the relations between different parts of a model as a graph where each node defines a (geometric) entity. The properties of one entity can be passed on to dependent entities, influencing their behaviour. This visually explains the flow of data and the hierarchy of entities in the model. Shown here is a parametric model that takes two curves and a number and generates three different NURBS surfaces.

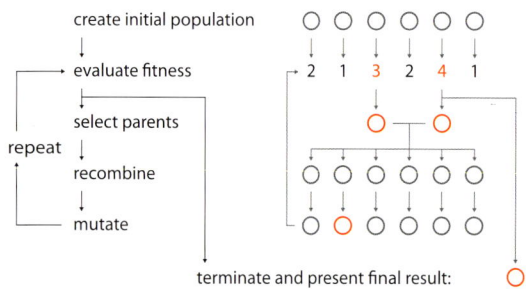

Figure 12. Schematic view of a genetic algorithm (GA)
Evolutionary methods seem to find surprisingly good results in vast solution spaces by chance, but they are based on completely deterministic algorithms. Notably the encoding of an individual's properties into a genome, the recombination of genomes during reproduction, and the selection based on a quantifiable fitness measure have to be formally well defined and unambiguous. Virtual dice are tossed at some steps of the algorithm to draw decisions, but this is also part of the predefined recipe.

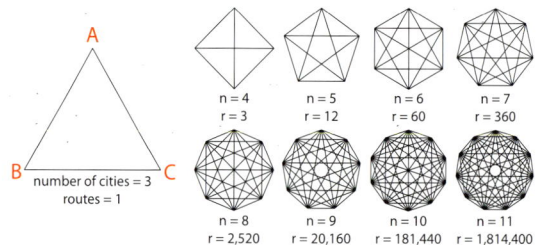

Figure 13. The Travelling Salesman Problem
For three cities A, B and C, the six permutations would be [ABC], [ACB], [BCA], [BAC], [CBA] and [CAB]. If we assume that neither starting city nor travelling direction matter, those three routes are effectively the same. So for three cities, there is only one possible route. But that changes quickly for n>3.

less than or equal to a number) of the list length. For n=16 there already are ½×1×2×3×4×5×6×7×8×9×10×11×12×13×14×15 = 653,837,184,000 alternatives to check, which at a rate of one million routes per second takes about 7.5 days; and one single extra city would raise the waiting time to four months.

The amount of resources consumed by an algorithm in relation to the number of inputs is called 'computational complexity'. As the travelling salesman problem shows, the computational complexity of most problems does not scale linearly with the number of inputs. In particular, computational simulations like finite element analysis (FEA) and computational fluid dynamics (CFD) are not easily scalable, which makes it practically impossible to simulate large models in reasonable time, for example to use the results as fitness measures for evolutionary optimisation. Buying faster processors will only help momentarily; building leaner models and applying smarter methods is a much more sustainable approach.

Precision

It is a still common misconception that digital models are infinitely precise. Truth is that every computational operation on real numbers is subject to slight errors due to the fact that those numbers are stored as a combination of a whole number and an exponent, with finite precision (this is called 'floating point' to illustrate that the position of the radix point depends on the variable exponent). While these imprecisions can be neglected in most cases, they can add up and become relevant especially in complex geometric operations. Because of the finite number of digits available for both integral and fractional part, floating point errors are also dependent on the operands' magnitudes, which is why the exact same operation might succeed at the model origin [0,0,0] but fail at [$10^{15}, 10^{15}, 10^{15}$].

Furthermore, many fundamental geometric operations – like finding the intersection of two NURBS surfaces – utilise numerical approximation, which ultimately destroys the notion of infinitely precise CAD models. This is also the reason for CAD modellers to provide a tolerance setting. Increasing the tolerance can help working with imprecise input geometry, but will also lower the resulting quality. While decreasing it raises precision, it also elevates the barrier for geometric operations to succeed and boosts computation time.

While this impreciseness is inherent to geometric operations, it is notably not so to their formal description; formally defined models are precise until they are rendered into geometry. So the transition from formal relations to geometric operations is an important one that should be commenced carefully.

Of course, error-bound geometric operations are impossible to avoid in CAD modelling, but knowing when and why these errors occur can help to improve the construction sequence instead of just readjusting the tolerance settings when Boolean intersection fails again.

Quality

As we have seen, complex shapes can only be handled if digital or even parametric models are an integral part of the architectural design and communication process. Digital models, which aim at describing and simulating aspects of real objects, need to be set up carefully, with the right focus and the appropriate level of abstraction to deliver meaningful results. Especially when using parametric models, the hierarchic dependencies within complex structures have to be thoroughly untangled and precisely described in formal algorithmic and mathematic notations; only then can the output be rebuilt automatically upon changing the input parameters. But when a specific design is just one out of a myriad of possible instances a parametric machine can produce, what is the appropriate level to discuss the quality of design? Clearly, meaningful evaluation cannot stop at the skin-deep layer of the output's visible appearance. Nevertheless, today's architectural discourse rarely dives below this level, even though designers are gradually becoming programmers who design their own, highly sophisticated tools.

We think it is about time to discuss the quality of the processes instead of merely reviewing the end results that can be generated in endless variations. If we do not want to get lost in parameter space, we need to assess and understand the quality of the algorithmic machines we design, not the designs they produce. Which are the defining parameters of a model? Where and how does abstraction strike and why are certain things included and others left out? How are algorithms conceived and rules defined? What are the quantifiable – and therefore optimisable – measures for the quality of a design and how are they weighed against each other? What defines the quality of an algorithm and how does it reflect in its output? And finally, how can we communicate and discuss complex architectural structures in a meaningful way – not between digital machines but between the human minds assembled in a project team? Because in the end 'designing' means drawing decisions and taking the responsibility, not delegating them to a machine. Only this prevents algorithmic design, which is largely based on formal descriptions, from itself becoming formalistic. ∆

Note
1. See, for example, Helmut Pottmann, Andreas Asperl, Michael Hofer and Axel Kilian, *Architectural Geometry*, Bentley Institute Press (Exton), 2007. Also Jane Burry and Mark Burry, *The New Mathematics of Architecture*, Thames & Hudson (London), 2010.

Mark Burry

GEOMETRY WORKING BEYOND EFFECT

With the onset of fully fledged file-to-factory design techniques, why should architects want to restrict themselves to the prescribed limits of descriptive geometry? In this article **Mark Burry** looks at a specific set of geometries – doubly ruled surfaces – that have been most explicitly developed by 'structural artists' Antoni Gaudí, Vladimir Shukhov and Félix Candela. He asks whether the application of doubly ruled surfaces like these might help us to make a significant distinction between architecture and sculpture.

Figure 1. Félix Candela's use of several hyperbolic paraboloids used in combination
The development of four intersecting 'hypars' with curved edges. Candela used this process for engineering his structural shells made from relatively lightly reinforced concrete. He was the first to determine through calculation that the entire shell was in compression: in ordinary circumstances hyperbolic paraboloid roof forms do not experience significant tensile stress.

Plastic arts traditionally describe the work of the sculptor and the way they manage material through shaping or modelling. Shaping implies a reductive process: from a block of stone, for example, material is chiselled roughly, finely, and abraded to release the artifice. Modelling implies the reverse: lumps of pliable material are cajoled and caressed to the satisfaction of the artist. Were both processes to lead to an identical outcome – same shape and form – the critical nuances around the creative route taken, the haptic and tactile qualities of the resulting artefact, and the meanings ascribed to the choice of material would ultimately influence their relative levels of appreciation.

For the sculptor, the role of mathematics such as descriptive geometry would most likely be seen as a highly deliberate gesture not necessarily occasioned around thoughts of facilitating the object's making, nor as a means to provide a greater economy of means. Sculpture is typically smaller than the scale of architecture and the sculptor has not been presented with the quandary that architects have been faced with since the primitive hut: a means to understand their design and communicate it to others, not least the builder in order to realise the project.

Up until the end of the 19th century, descriptive geometry typically engaged students for a sixth of their architectural training. The emphasis on geometry as part of the architect's skill set became more sophisticated from the Renaissance up until the modern epoch of iron and steel construction: the earlier congruence between architecture and engineering design thinking fell away as each profession charted quite different paths to practice. Typically, it is the engineer who is called upon to engage with the mathematics of architecture.

Descriptive geometry from the 16th century onwards was especially stimulated by the need to fragment increasingly complex overall design composition into pieces of stone sized to be practical as much for the needs of the quarry master and the stonemason as for the capability of the contractor to raise each worked piece perfectly into place. Descriptive geometry allows the general description of the composition to be more readily templated so that individual components could be worked without physical reference to each other.

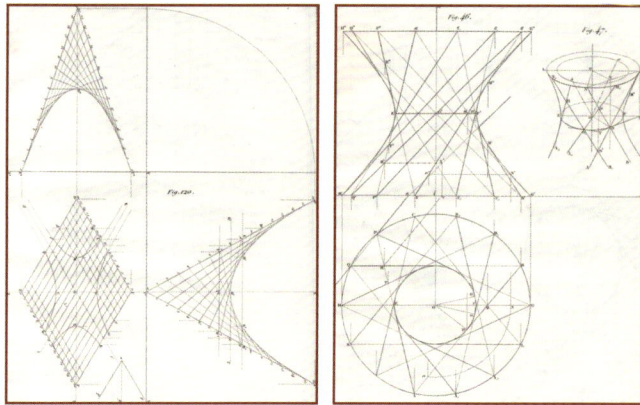

Figure 2. Parameters of a
hyperbolic paraboloid
A hyperbolic paraboloid is a
saddle-shaped doubly ruled
surface that has a convex curve
as a section across one axis and
a concave curve in the other.

This particular skill, stereotomy (from the Greek words for stone and cutting), would have been a principal point of difference between how Michelangelo would have approached sculpting the *Pietà* in St Peter's, Rome (1499), and crafting the Medicean-Laurentian Library in Florence (commenced in 1523). With the exceptions of a relatively few schools of architecture worldwide, since early in the 20th century most have reduced any emphasis on descriptive geometry in their curricula due to a combination of the increased technical specialisation away from the hands-on involvement of the architect, two generations of rationalist ideology favouring the orthogonal, vertical and planar, and the advent of advanced computation especially for engineers. As a force of destiny, together they have further distanced the designer from any role as stereotomer.

Where there is evidence of a healthy presence of descriptive geometry retained in departments (for example in certain schools in Spain and in Budapest), far from being defended from any unspoken accusation of being an anachronism, its role is actively promoted as an enabler of different types of conversations around spatiality, as a tool to cement a strong sense of the architectural tradition in the emerging architect, and as a philosophical link back to the Greeks. This exception is not the rule, however, so the almost palpable contemporary interest in a return to the mathematics of architecture begs many questions, for whereas once there may have been an overriding pragmatic advantage for geometry to help colour the description of architectural components, there is not that need today. With the quest for machines that will print full-scale buildings well advanced at the time of writing, and computer numerically controlled (CNC) robot cutters and routers already capable of making any shape or form to order directly from the designer's computer file, why would any architect bother to restrict themself to a protocol based on particular sets of geometries?

This article looks at one set of geometries – doubly ruled surfaces, and proposes that their attendant facilitation for construction purposes, even if obviated by file to factory production may yet point to a useful distinction between the fundamentals of architecture (Vitruvian trinity) and the aesthetic priorities of sculpture. In making this claim it will self-contradict, showing how taking up such geometries has

thus far blurred the distinction between architects, engineers and sculptors. The emergence of the term 'structural artists' to describe engineers such as Pier Luigi Nervi (1891–1979), Félix Candela (1910–97), Frei Otto (1925–), Heinz Isler (1926–2009) and Peter Rice (1935–92) points to a more common outcome, one where consideration of particular geometries signals a rethink of rather artificial professional boundaries.[1]

Ruled Surfaces and Developable Surfaces

Ruled surfaces can be considered as a principal component of a particular definition of the mathematics of space. For any ruled surface, a single straight line lying on that surface will pass through a given point also lying on that surface. Every point on that surface will have at least one line passing through it that lies on the surface. Ruled surfaces include the plane, cones and cylinders as well as hyperbolic paraboloids and hyperboloids of revolution. Some ruled surfaces such as cones and cylinders are also described as developable surfaces; that is, surfaces that can be flattened out onto a plane without distortion or stretching of any kind, although cutting may be required. As children we recall making conical wizards' hats starting out from a sheet of paper by removing a sector from a cut-out disc. Making a cone in this way is possibly the most haptic means of all to manifest the conceptual spatial leap from two to three dimensions. And examining the stiffness of the cone made in this way relative to the flaccidity of the paper disc is a perfect lesson in imbuing materials with greater strength through the application of geometry – more with no more.

In three-dimensional space, all developable surfaces are ruled surfaces, but not all ruled surfaces are developable surfaces. Doubly ruled surfaces, a subset of ruled surfaces, have at once a geometrical simplicity and a visual sophistication: they have two straight lines lying on the surface passing through any point on the surface, and the surfaces are doubly curved. They are not commonly used in architecture, and usually in the role performing more engineering-oriented tasks than from purely visual motivation, but their aesthetic ranges from the subtle way they direct light across their surfaces to their ready describability, both in terms of representation and fabrication. Used well they point to an intellectual scope that re-engages curious minds with the compositional power of geometry. 'Used

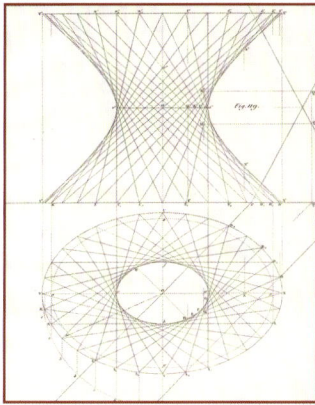

Figure 3. Geometric description of hyperboloids
At its simplest, a hyperboloid of revolution of one sheet can be circular, obtained by revolving a hyperbola around a central axis. An elliptical hyperboloid is a non-uniformly scaled circular hyperboloid – it cannot be obtained by rotating a hyperbola.

Figure 4. Model of hyperbolic paraboloid
A parametrically variable analogue model of a hyperbolic paraboloid.

Figure 5. Model of hyperboloid of revolution
A parametrically variable analogue model of a hyperboloid of revolution. The most recognisable hyperboloids of revolution are cooling towers of power stations.

well' here refers to the language implicit in their use extending beyond their practical advantages, which will be spelt out in more detail further on. The three doubly ruled surfaces are not mathematically complex. In terms of parametricisation for hyperboloids of revolution and hyperbolic paraboloids via their mathematical formulae these are respectively:

Hyperboloid of revolution

$$\frac{x^2}{a^2} + \frac{y^2}{a^2} - \frac{z^2}{c^2} = 1,$$

Hyperbolic paraboloid

$$z = \frac{y^2}{b^2} - \frac{x^2}{a^2}$$

Who has Used Doubly Ruled Surfaces Architecturally and How Well?

Given their structural advantages remarkably few architects and engineers have made the use of doubly ruled surfaces as prominent elements within their compositional repertoire. I will identify three who have done so with aplomb in the order of their application: Catalan architect Antoni Gaudí (1852–1926), Russian polymath engineer Vladimir Shukhov (1853–1939) and Spanish/Mexican architect-engineer Félix Candela. Their uses of doubly ruled surfaces were very singular relative to each other, but all have important points in common that are summarised at the end of this article.

Antoni Gaudí

With one minor exception, Gaudí first applied doubly ruled surfaces to his design for the Colònia Güell Chapel near Barcelona based on his renowned hanging model (developed 1898–1906) from which only the crypt went on to be constructed (1906–12/14), at which point the project was abandoned. The crypt is a remarkable space despite its minor role for what should have eventuated as an extraordinary chapel towering above amid the pine trees surrounding it. In addition to the hanging model used as an analogue parametric performance design tool, there were many other innovations.

Figure 6. Geometry of an amalgam of doubly ruled surfaces

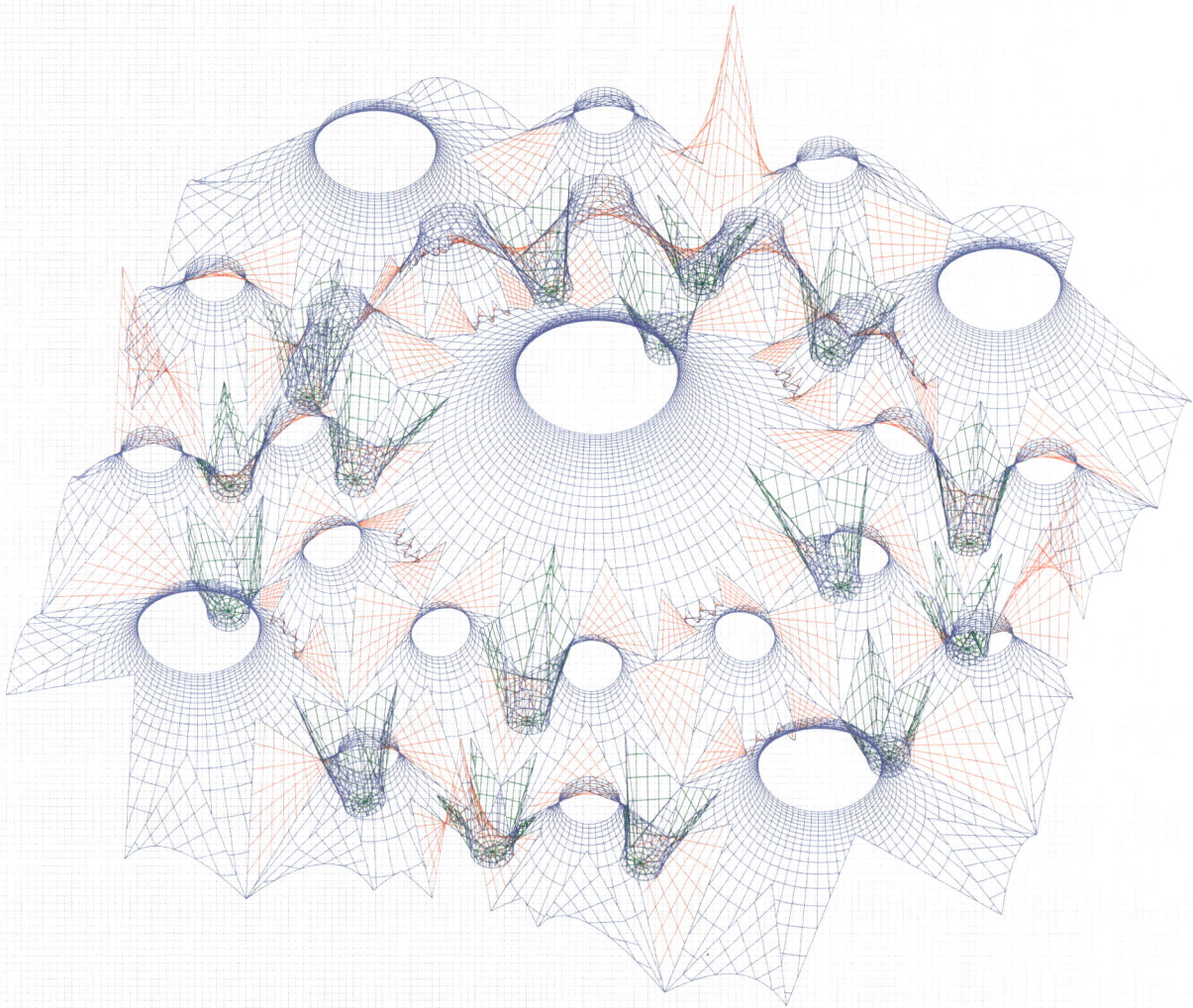

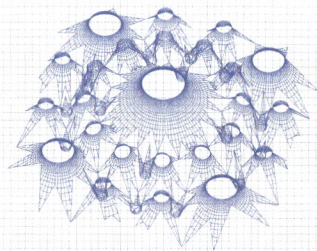

Hyperboloids of revolution of one sheet

Hyperbolic paraboloids

Planar elements

Figure 6. Geometry of an amalgam of doubly ruled surfaces
Diagram indicating the geometry of an amalgam of all three doubly ruled surfaces: hyperboloids of revolution, hyperbolic paraboloids and planar fragments. Gaudí used them exclusively for the Sagrada Família Church ceiling vaults and windows, which are supported by helicoidal columns.

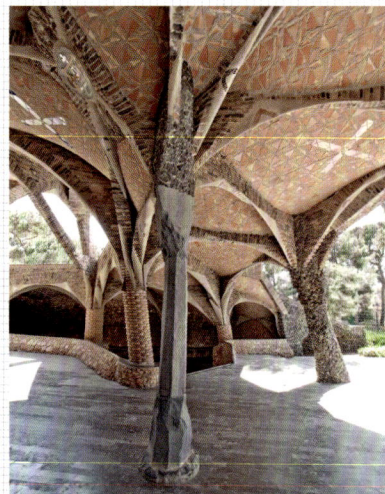

Figure 7. Antoni Gaudí, Colònia Güell Chapel porch undercroft, Santa Coloma de Cervelló, Catalonia, Spain, construction 1906–1912/14
In terms of doubly ruled surfaces, this building, at the middle stage of Gaudí's career, was his launching point. He uses singly ruled surfaces such as helicoids and hyperbolic paraboloids for both structural wall elements and decorative elements that assert the muscularity of the rib vaulting supporting the main staircase landing above and so forming the crypt's porch.

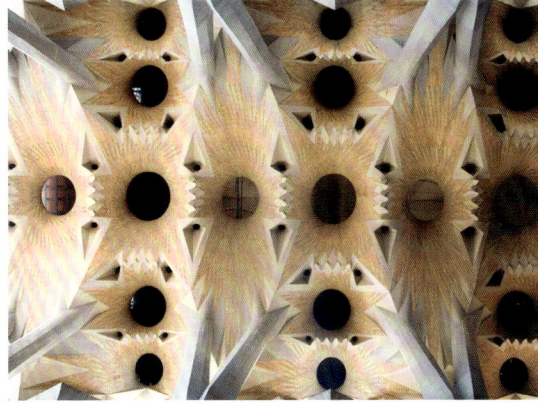

Figures 8 and 9. Antoni Gaudí, Temple
Sagrada Família, Barcelona, 1883–ongoing
The ceiling of Temple Sagrada Família, fully completed in 2010.

Despite the spatial complexity of the space, Gaudí employed an absolute minimum of materials both in quantity and selection. Principally, there are only five: naturally occurring hexagonal basalt prisms for the main columns, brick in various grades, cement, glass and recycled steel. Even if reinforced concrete had been used invisibly, the bravado of the structural outcome would still command awe. That it was executed entirely in Catalan vaulting (sandwich layers of structural tiles and special cement) held aloft by twisting helicoidal columns axially aligned off the vertical to correspond with the forces calculated from the hanging model all helps make this such a timeless building, despite missing the church it was designed to support. High-quality brick is used only at points of structurally critical performance, with a series of material downgrades to the level of clinkered waste from over baking at the brick kilns used as infill.

In terms of doubly ruled surfaces this building, at the middle stage of Gaudí's career, was his launching point. He used singly ruled surfaces such as helicoids and doubly ruled hyperbolic paraboloids for both structural walls and decorative elements that assert the muscularity of the rib vaulting supporting the main staircase landing above and so forming the crypt's porch.

With the inauguration of the Sagrada Família Church as a consecrated basilica on 7 November 2010, for the first time visitors could see the amalgam of hyperboloids of revolution, hyperbolic paraboloids and planar fragments that form the ceiling vaults and windows supported by helicoidal columns. All that Gaudí designed during his last 12 years is composed of the three doubly ruled surfaces (planes used to the minimum) with the helicoid being the sole representative of singly ruled surfaces.

As Gaudí wrote nothing of significance about his architecture during his career that spanned almost half a century, we do not know exactly why he devoted himself to doubly ruled surfaces to the virtual exclusion of all other geometry. With their implementation as core to the description and production of the building we can cite them as evidence of the holism of Gaudí's design approach. We have seen their description facilitated by the straight lines describing the surfaces in two directions, we have seen the reinforcement rods aligned to the same straight paths allowing them to perform optimally, and now we have seen their effect

on light which Gaudí describes as gliding along the surfaces. Though untested technically, it seems that the reverberation of the giant interior is positively enhanced by their presence on over 90 per cent of the surfaces.

Vladimir Shukhov

Unlike Gaudí, Shukhov is a relatively obscure figure despite his extraordinary range of talents that include being the first engineer to understand structural shells sufficiently well to calculate their performance. He was a prolific inventor and many of his structures survive today. He was responsible for the first ocean-going oil tanker and indeed designed tanks to contain liquids using half the material used previously. He also produced the world's first doubly curved steel lattice roof structure for the pavilions at the 'All Russia' exhibition in Nizhny Novgorod (1897). A search for material about him reveals articles on 'Shukhov the engineer', 'Shukhov the architect' and 'Shukhov the photographer'. He was the genuine polymath for his time.

What he is probably best known for are his various communication towers and pylons made from a series of hyperboloids of revolution stacked on top of each other. By selecting directrices that are not equidistant with respect to the collar he was able to taper the towers as they rose in height. This is to say the directrix above the collar is closer to the collar than the one below it, such that the diameter of the top collar is proportionally smaller than the one below. At first sight they are improbable structures, with their diaphanous appearance seeming far too delicate for the task in hand. Although hyperboloids of revolution are inefficient spaces at an architectural scale (Gaudí used them at a component scale), they are superbly efficient structural systems with every element working at its optimum. All the vertical elements are in straight lines, taking load transfers axially, while the horizontal rings – some of which are also grid shell trussed – are obviously optimised through being circular. His most famous is the Shukhov Tower in Moscow (1922) that still stands 160 metres (525 feet) in height. We are more familiar with thin-wall concrete cooling towers, which are also hyperboloids of revolution exploiting the same properties that Shukhov had been the first to identify.

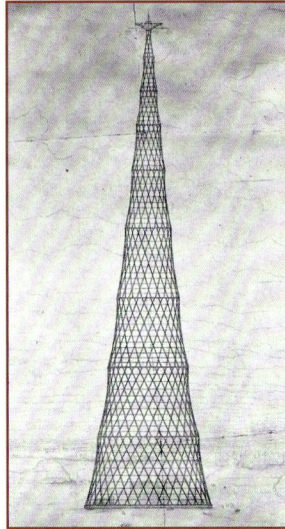

Figure 10. Vladimir Shukhov, Shabololvka (Shukhov) Tower drawing, Moscow, 1919
A series of truncated hyperboloids of revolution that stack up on each other; each element could be made at ground level and be hoisted-up into position.

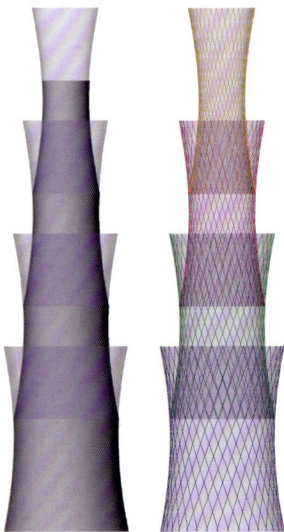

Félix Candela

Candela's story is also a fascinating one, but relative to the contribution he made, he too has less written about him than one might expect. He was born in Spain but exiled to Mexico at the age of 26 at the conclusion of the Spanish Civil War (1936–9) having worked as a military engineer for the Republicans. The first half of his professional career was in Mexico where he established himself as an architect–engineer–builder, and for the second half he was based in the US.

Principally he is known for the form that many of his structures take: one or more hyperbolic paraboloids, remembered for their beauty and economy of means, and not so much for their actual geometry. Publications on Candela have an engineering bias and it is through those resources that we gain an insight into Candela's favourable disposition to the 'hypars', as they have become known. It seems quite clear that Candela sought a rich mixture of constructional logic, extraordinary structural performance and a compelling aesthetic that seems to work at any scale. Many of his pioneering structures were made only centimetres thick as he was the first to exhaustively calculate that the entire shell was in compression: in ordinary circumstances hyperbolic paraboloid roof forms do not experience significant tensile stress.

According to David Billington, Candela wrote that the hyperbolic paraboloid 'is the only warped surface whose equation is simple enough to permit stress calculation by elementary mathematics'.[2] In terms of structural shells made from relatively unreinforced concrete, Candela was a key member of the first echelon. He found his niche as a mathematician while studying architecture in Madrid, and this talent provided his route.

Developability

Developable surfaces present fascinating opportunities for architects and engineers interested in 'affordable complexity of form'. Their mathematical appeal and their practical benefits may seem at odds with an equivalent postulation around doubly ruled surfaces, however. Let us consider the practical advantage that makes full use of their geometry, such as a conical roof.

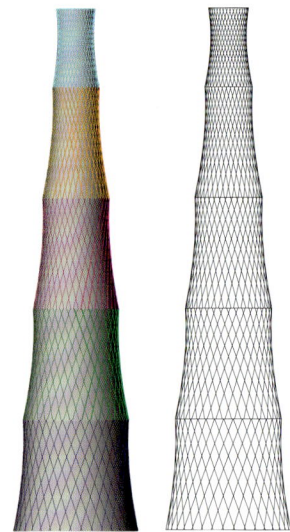

Figure 11. Vladimir Shukhov, Shabololvka (Shukhov) Tower drawing, Moscow, 1919
By selecting directrices that are not equidistant with respect to the collar, Shukhov was able to taper his towers as they rose in height. This is to say the directrix above the collar is closer to the collar than the one below it, such that the diameter of the top collar is proportionally smaller than the one below.

Figure 12. Vladimir Shukhov, Shabololvka (Shukhov) Tower, Moscow, 1922
Interior view showing a series of hyperboloids of revolution stacked on top of each other.

It is unlikely that a conical roof clad in copper will be made from a single giant disc of copper, sector removed, and wound round the conical substrate in a single operation. The advantage of developability is that subsections of the whole retain the geometrical qualities of the parent. From the parent template, child templates of individual pieces can be appropriately sized to match practical copper-sheet size or maximum size for practical on-site manipulation by the plumber, whichever is the major constraint.

Were the roof to be clad with copper over a hyperbolic paraboloid substrate the advantages of developability are apparently lost; by definition any child of the parent geometry will have a degree of double curvature, however small. This can be appreciated by holding a piece of cardboard in our hands. With a simple manipulation it can be curled around a circular template so that opposite edges come together to make a cylinder, demonstrably a developable surface. Trying to make a hyperbolic paraboloid from the same sheet requires two sets of hands. If Actor A passively supports a sheet of card by holding it by diametrically opposite corners, while Actor B pulls down on both the opposite corners the sheet is curved cylindrically. Taken to its limit the sheet will eventually fold diagonally across to form two triangles hinged along the crease. Imagine the same sheet with both actors active in their role – in the example given above Actor A simply holds their corners in position while Actor B translates their two corners downwards, inducing the curved cylindrical surface. If Actor A pulls their corners up while Actor B pulls theirs down with equal force, the stiffness of the sheet prevents the double curvature from taking place; the sheet stays resolutely planar. The geometrical construct in this case is not especially demanding, but the mathematics is potentially rather more sophisticated.

Let us extend this experiment a little further. Imagine that the sheet of cardboard used in our experiment above was soaked in water before attempting to form a hyperbolic paraboloid. Whereas our dry sheet would not conform even with uniformly applied pressure and the aid of a relatively unexaggerated hyperbolic paraboloid former (a 'mould' to press a material against to make it change geometrical form) as it would crease, in contrast the wet cardboard sheet would 'relax' into the former. The reason for the difference is obvious, of course, as the soaking allows the cellulose fibres to stretch as well as displace spatially (to a limited degree).

This material quality of flexibility is available in all sheet materials, even the most brittle when applied carefully. For a roof built with a substantially robust substrate any metal other than lead will not be formed easily, especially in regions where the curvature becomes exaggerated – unless it is developable or highly flexible. It is very likely to crease, as anyone gift-wrapping a soccer ball will attest to. Needless to say, our copper cladding example needs to be refined a little, as copper, like all metals, is malleable, and in fact is one of the most malleable of all – hence its traditional use for making cooking vessels. To take advantage of the malleability, a former has to be provided, and is a major cost if metal is to be stretched into a new form. Steel for making car bodies, which is far less malleable compared with copper, can also be 'stretched' into shape by stamping sheet steel over formers, the cost of which is eye-wateringly significant but afforded by the large number of repeats that the vehicle industry strives for. This is not a practical arrangement for the building industry, but let us not forget the intrinsic flexibility of rigid sheets of material, including steel, within the limits of its molecular structure.

The physics of these material properties were described for the first time in the 17th century. Hooke's law (1660) states that all materials may deform elastically to a limit.[3] The following century this was defined by Thomas Young (1773–1829) as the 'modulus of elasticity' which, when passed, means that the metal will not spring back to its original state once the applied load has been removed.[4] The yield point in a ductile material such as copper allows it to be formed easily compared with steel. A material such as glass, notwithstanding its debatable property as a super-cooled liquid, has a brittleness that leads to snapping immediately once it is pushed beyond its modulus of elasticity. The unexpected flexibility of glass is first witnessed in the school laboratory when a long glass rod is shown to be bendable to a surprising degree, and if left to droop between two supports eventually will assume the catenary curve. Fibre optics provide the ultimate evidence of extreme flexibility of an otherwise brittle material. This is where computation enters the arena at an exciting level.

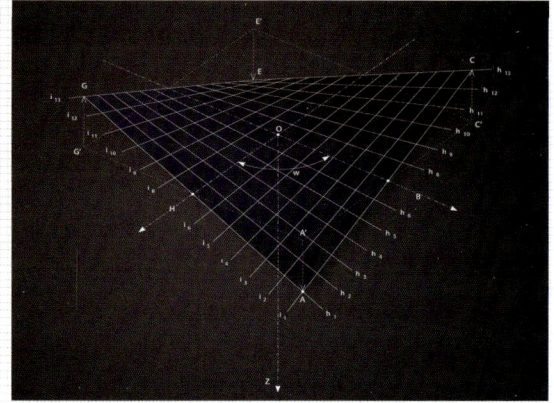

Figure 14. Generic hyperbolic paraboloid as Candela would have seen it geometrically (referred to as 'hypars')
A hyperbolic paraboloid with straight edges (directrices) and rulings (generatrices).

Figure 13. Félix Candela, L'Oceanogràfic, Valencia, Spain, 1998
A rich mixture of constructional logic, extraordinary structural performance and a compelling aesthetic that seems to work at any scale.

Any given material has a modulus of elasticity and a limit. If the flexibility of a sheet metal of a particular thickness and its elastic limits are built in as a parameter of flexion over length, algorithmically, a surface can be tiled with pieces of the chosen cladding that will conform to double curvature without creasing or snapping. Mathematically this is a demanding optimisation task. As a process, the region of greatest curvature has to be identified, and a shape calculated that will assume the double curvature within its own elastic limits yet be as large as possible to limit the overall number of pieces required for the entire surface. To make the computation task more demanding still, criteria such as searching for a shape as regularly polygonal as possible can be added along with a nesting requirement that minimises wastage. If the underlying geometry is mathematical such as a hyperbolic paraboloid, there is a greater possibility for a tessellation to be derived that looks more organised than would be the case were this approach to be applied to an extravagantly expressive freeform surface, especially one with folds and creases. The aesthetic would therefore be the difference between a tortoiseshell pattern organised principally around the hexagon, for example, conforming to a doubly curved ruled surface, and the ordered chaos of a Voronoi diagram which would most likely result from tackling a freeform in this way. The designer would no doubt appreciate being able to try this in real time, but this has yet to be put to test as the computation aspects are still to be resolved in terms of performance.

The Natural Calculator Route

Within the blurred boundaries of the discipline, there are several practitioners who have sought to establish optimal form through inverting their models and allowing gravity to assist directly. In this regard, Gaudí's Colònia Güell Chapel has been referred to earlier, and Otto's work in this field, beginning in 1925, is especially well known. The Swiss 'structural artist' engineer Heinz Isler (1926-2009), almost a contemporary of Candela, Otto and Nervi, but unlike Candela, felt impelled to calculate the geometries that come from the material response under gravity; he was the first person to derive the formulae for gravity-induced curvature in 3-D. He was a fascinating inventor, and based on a chance observation of draped material on site,

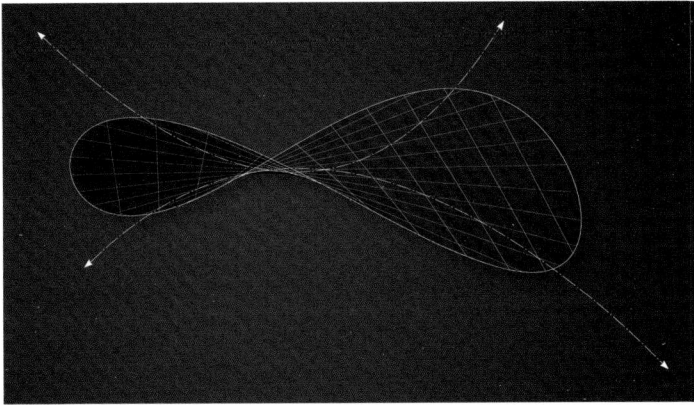

Figure 15. Hyberbolic paraboloid 'region'
In actual use, Candela saw the value of trimming the hyperbolic paraboloid with curved edges as a rich architectural opportunity.

hung a wet piece of hemp sackcloth between poles arranged in a 4-metre (13-foot) square out in his office yard on a day with sub-zero temperatures and, once frozen, inverted the resultant stiffened funicular 'cupola' and measured it accurately. By his own account, using this means of form-finding and a more exact effort to measure a pneumatic pillow of latex inflated between cramps to each side of the scaled quadrilateral, he was able to convert the minute measurements to usable formulae for full-sized structures.[5] By 'minute measurement' he claimed that his own body heat was inducing otherwise inexplicable distortions to his results, obliging him to wear a thick winter coat regardless of ambient temperature.

Critical Engagement: Ruled Surfaces Versus Freeform
This article delves into the apparent positive advantages of using certain geometries as principal architectural compositional strategies, yet fails to explain why architects should bother with them in their work today beyond an aesthetic predilection. It has shown how doubly ruled surfaces exhibit a more expansive set of values relative to singly ruled surfaces and certain developable surfaces. Yet despite these qualities, including their unique aesthetic appeal, their limited general take-up refers us to a particular professional grouping: structural artists. The first part presented the enigmatic aspects behind geometrically describing doubly ruled surfaces and developable surfaces, examining their architectonic suitability. Examples of their use in built work demonstrate the relevance of their particular benefits in pre-digitally represented architecture, when the representational issues of complex architecture placed tough challenges for the builder several orders of magnitude above those faced by post-digital constructors today. Referring to structural artists' work, using these surfaces has shown them to have aesthetic, structural and constructional advantages that distinguish them from other 'useful' geometries. The selection here inadvertently identifies a professional group neither purely architect, nor engineer, nor sculptor.

The dilemma of 'why bother with geometrical describability when machines can cut/rout/extrude/print freeform surfaces with equal facility' is probably a false one. A case might be defensible that postulates that projective geometry has mathematical and philosophical value extending well into our era of digital design, regardless of automation. In avoiding the mathematical consideration of geometry, architects might be 'fiddling' as sculptors regardless of the spatial sophistication, but the maths may afford different levels of conversation especially between architect and engineer. The burgeoning computational tools for the next generation of architects offer all sorts of advantages, such as real-time design optimisation alluded to above. Perhaps there is a tacit acknowledgement of these advantages already, hence the apparent reawakening within the avant-garde. Tomorrow's architects might more likely resemble yesterday's structural artists. ᴆ

Notes
1. See DP Billington, *The Tower and the Bridge: The New Art of Structural Engineering*, Princeton University Press (Princeton, NJ), 1983 for his discussion on the art of engineering.
2. M Moreyra Garlock and D Billington, *Félix Candela: Engineer, Builder, Structural Artist*, Yale University Press (New Haven, CT), 2008, p 76.
3. Hooke's law, law of elasticity discovered by the English scientist Robert Hooke in 1660, which states that, for relatively small deformations of an object, the displacement or size of the deformation is directly proportional to the deforming force or load. Under these conditions the object returns to its original shape and size upon removal of the load. Elastic behaviour of solids according to Hooke's law can be explained by the fact that small displacements of their constituent molecules, atoms or ions from normal positions is also proportional to the force that causes the displacement. Retrieved from www.britannica.com/EBchecked/topic/271336/Hookes-law.
4. Young's modulus, numerical constant, named after the 18th-century English physician and physicist Thomas Young, that describes the elastic properties of a solid undergoing tension or compression in only one direction, as in the case of a metal rod that after being stretched or compressed lengthwise returns to its original length. Young's modulus is a measure of the ability of a material to withstand changes in length when under lengthwise tension or compression. Sometimes referred to as the modulus of elasticity, it is equal to the longitudinal stress divided by the strain. Retrieved from www.britannica.com/EBchecked/topic/654186/Youngs-modulus
5. G Nordenson and T Riley (eds), *Seven Structural Engineers: The Félix Candela Lectures*, Museum of Modern Art (New York), 2008, p 90.

DESARGUES AND LEIBNIZ: IN THE BLACK BOX

A MATHEMATICAL MODEL OF THE LEIBNIZIAN MONAD

Here **Bernard Cache** provides a detailed analysis of a paper written in 1636 by the French mathematician, architect and engineer, Girard Desargues. Desargues is best known as the founder of projective geometry. Cache explains how he initally developed this significant concept in response to the very practical problems of producing a perspectival drawing. The introduction of projective geometry, though, had potentially more far-reaching implications on philosophical thought, informing the theory of monads developed by the German philosopher and mathematician Gottfried Leibniz in 1714 to explain the metaphysics of simple substances.

Strangely, the short essay on perspective published by Girard Desargues in 1636 makes no mention of any notion of projective geometry, explicitly at least, before reaching its rather contemplative conclusion. This remarkably curious text consists of a commentary of a single engraving presumed accessible enough for the knowing reader to apply its premises to any practical situation, a drawing expressing a 'universal way', in other words – as stated by the title of the essay itself: 'A Sample of the Universal Way of SGDL:[1] On the Practice of Perspective Without the Assistance of a Third Point, Distance Measurement Or Any Other Expedient External to the Task at Hand' (*Exemple de l'une des manières universelles du SGDL. Touchant la pratique de la perspective sans employer aucun tiers point, de distance ni d'autre nature qui soit hors du champ de l'ouvrage*).[2]

The absence of any reference to projective geometry confirms the author's intent to address the material constraints of daily practice, primarily the fixed size of the board or sheet on which the drawing is laid out. The need to resort to 'third points' lying beyond the surface of the sheet, such as vanishing points, or those mapped from a transversal section onto the drawing plane (*rabattement*), was a frequent problem in practice – hence Leon Battista Alberti's famous recommendation that an extra sheet of paper be deployed next to the drawing itself.[3]

To address these two constraints, Desargues advocates a new method: 'The agent, in this instance, is a cage made simply of lines,'[4] he writes in a rather surprising comment, followed by the description of the plan and location of the cage, as well as a statement to the effect that 'the engraving itself is like a wood plank, a stone wall, or something like it' – seemingly turning on its head the accepted interplay between transparency and opacity advocated by most theoreticians of perspective before him.

In lieu of a solid and opaque body, such as the Baptistery of Florence depicted on Filippo Brunelleschi's experimental tablets (1415), Desargues presents the reader with a transparent cage.

Compare this to the very edifice that Flemish mathematician and military engineer Simon Stevin

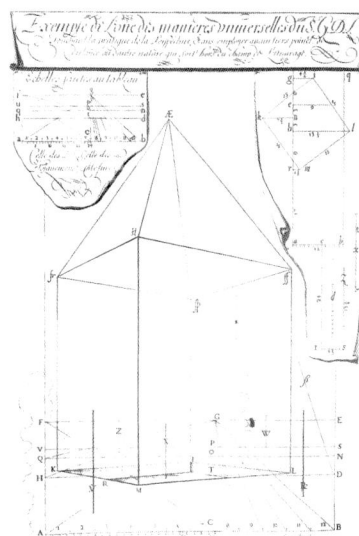

Figure 1. Girard Desargues, Exemple de l'une des manières universelles du SGDL (A Sample of the Universal Way of SGDL: On the Practice of Perspective Without the Assistance of a Third Point, Distance Measurement Or Any Other Expedient External to the Task at Hand'), 1636
The original 17th-century engraving.

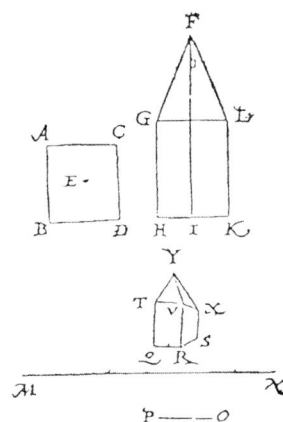

Figure 2. Simon Stevin, A Study in Perspective: top and front orthographic views and perspective projection of a solid modelled on the Baptistery of Florence
J Tuning's edition (1605), Vol III, Book I, prop Xi, problem V.

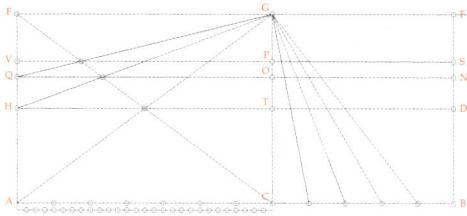

Figure 3. Reproduction of Desargues's original
layout for the geometric demonstration
On this diagram (culled from the upper-left corner
of the original engraving), three separate geometric
constructions overlap onto a single space, and three
sets of diagonal lines converge towards a single point.

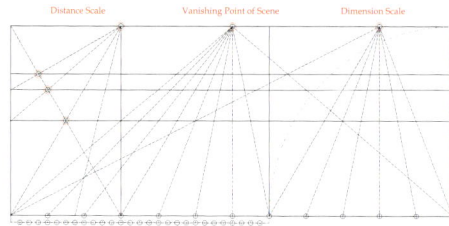

Figure 4. Graphical reorganisation of
Desargues's original diagram
The reorganisation lays out the three separate
geometric constructions side by side, revealing
distinct points of convergence for each
construction.

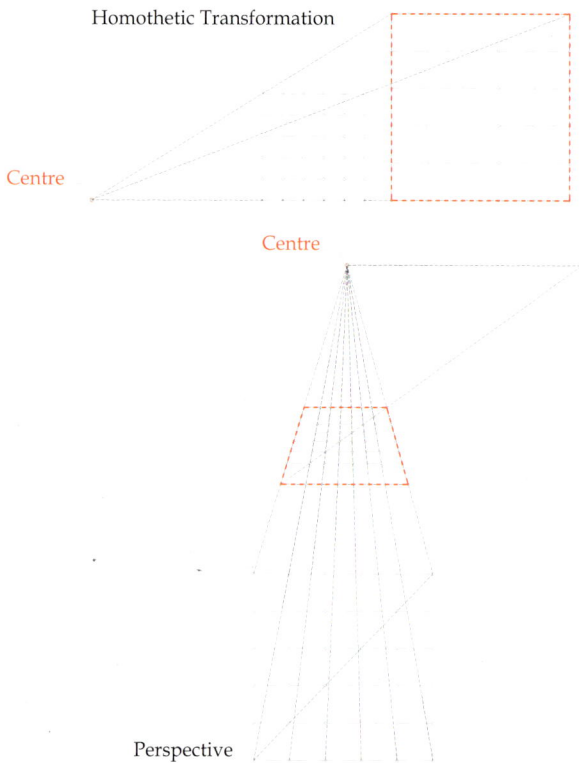

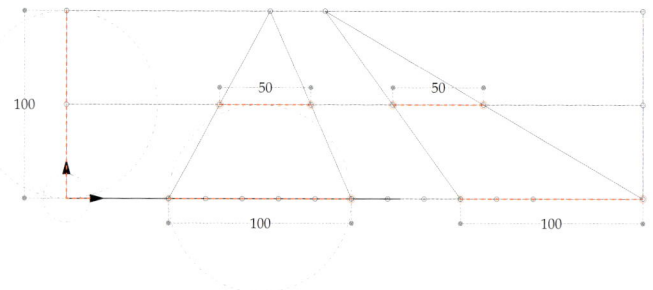

Homothetic Transformation

Centre

Figure 5. The Dimension Scale
(*above*) Diagram demonstrating the use of the
Dimension Scale to figure out a length on the
projection on the picture plane of a line parallel
to the picture plane, assuming we know its
elevation (in this instance, halfway up the Y
axis of the Dimension Scale).

Centre

Perspective

Figure 6. Homothetical (scaling) transformation
and conic projection (perspective)
(*left*) Top: The small square maps onto the large
one relative to a fixed point on the plane. The
transformation alters the measurements of the
original figure, but preserves its angles. Bottom:
The transformation alters the measurements
as well as the angles of the original figure, but
preserves some given dimensional ratios.

(1548–1620) chose to illustrate his own take on the problem: the two volumes are nearly identical, with the difference that Desargues proposes a wireframe, whereas Stevin does not even bother to dot in the hidden edges of the solid. Rather than opening a window onto the world, Desargues walls us into a windowless black box, reminiscent of Gottfried Leibniz's monad.[5] Let us examine what this means in practice.

The engraving commented on by Desargues features several parts. In the upper left corner we find a greatly simplified plan view, consisting of a few simple strokes and annotated with measurements (such drawings used to be known as *géometral*, or orthographic, projections). In the middle of the engraving we find the perspectival view of the cage, drawn over some sort of diagram reproduced, at a smaller scale, in the upper left corner of the sheet.

Desargues's overlapping of three separate geometric constructions onto a single diagram is most certainly confusing, hence the importance of pulling this diagram apart in order to analyse it. The interpretation of it lays out the three constructions side by side, rather than on top of one another. Desargues's method seems to work just as well, if not better, with this alternative layout, where, unlike what is shown on the original engraving of Sieur Girard Desargues de Lyon, the three sets of diagonal lines do not converge towards a single point – each construction has a distinct point of convergence.

Let us begin with the central part of the diagram, where Desargues hardly innovates at all. Here the lines normal to the picture plane converge towards a single vanishing point, illustrating the orthogonal projection of the gaze on the picture. Desargues says no more than Alberti did on the same subject – nothing, that is.

Desargues's method is based on the commonly known (at the time) expedient of transferring points from one grid to another, traditionally deployed for the purpose of scaling figures (now known as a homothetic transformation).[6] By extension, applying the same method to map a point from an orthogonal grid to another kind of grid resulted in a projective transformation. To configure

Desargues's method is based on the commonly known (at the time) expedient of transferring points from one grid to another, traditionally deployed for the purpose of scaling figures (now known as a homothetic transformation).

Figure 7. Desargues's Black Box
(*right*) Lateral view indicating the position of
the ideal observer G (which determines the
vantage point of the perspective construction),
the edge of a transversal line in space T_1, and
the profile of the picture plane FF_0.

Figure 8
(*below*) Lateral view demonstrating the
application of the three geometric expedients
available to Desargues: internalisation (point
G_0 stays inside the box, left); swapping (points
F_1 and G_1 are interchangeable, middle); and
drawing diagonals (point H_1 is obtained by
intersecting diagonals FG_0 and GF_0, right).

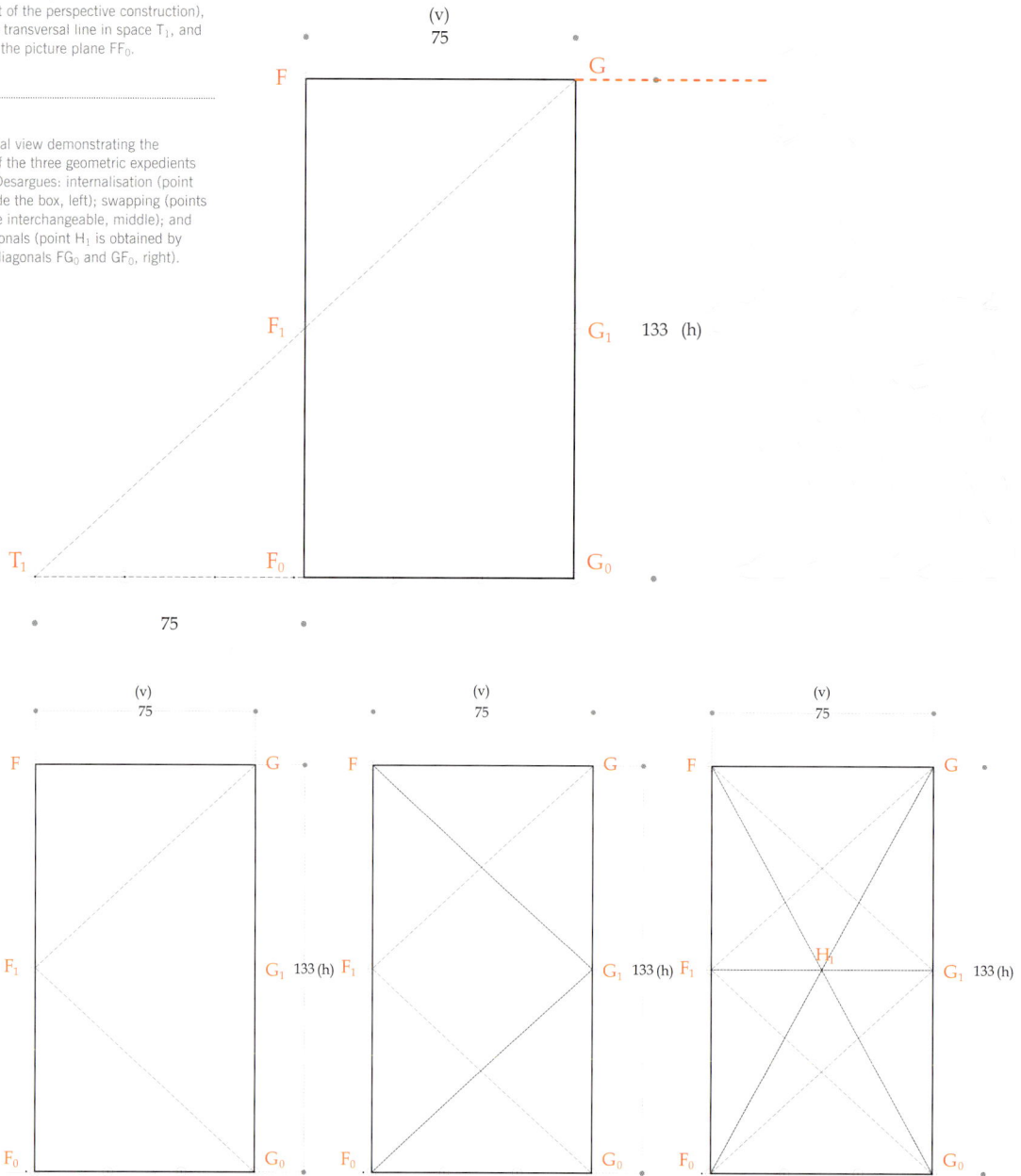

(v)
75

F   G

F_1 G_1 133   (h)

T_1 F_0 G_0

75

(v)   (v)   (v)
75   75   75

F   G   F   G   F   G

F_1 G_1 133 (h) F_1 G_1 133 (h) F_1 H_1 G_1 133 (h)

F_0 G_0 F_0 G_0 F_0 G_0

this new grid, Desargues needs to locate the vanishing point of all lines normal to the picture plane (on a separate note, the method does not guarantee that the said lines will converge within the extents of the page – especially where oblique projection is concerned).

Once the 'converging lines' (those lines normal to the picture plane) have been drawn, we need to establish dimensions along the 'transversal lines', or 'transversals' (those lines parallel to the picture plane), which Desargues calls the 'Dimension Scale'.

To figure out a length on the image of a given transversal, assuming of course we know its elevation on the picture plane, we will report in true length the segment of reference on the base of the Dimension Scale, then draw two convergent projectors from its endpoints. The intersections of these projectors with the image of the transversal at the given elevation will give us two points – and the distance between these two points, the desired length. It is critical to note that the point where these projectors come to a focus is not the same as the central point where converging lines meet. In other words, the focal point of the Dimension Scale does not have to coincide with the vanishing point of the scene. The two points must be located at the same elevation, but the former will move laterally by any amount without altering the reported measurements from one transversal line to the next.

Why insist on this particular aspect of Desargues's strategy? Because this is the crux of the originality of Desargues's perspectival method, which implies that the Distance Scale[7] cannot be understood unless it is radically distinguished from those lines converging towards the vanishing point of the scene. How does Desargues determine the elevation of the image of a transversal line then? What exactly is going on here?

Let us recall Alberti's *Construzione Legittima* and his section of a tapering cone of vision. For the sake of the demonstration, let us imagine that the eye, notated G, lies at a distance d from the picture, the section of which determines the vertical line FF_0. The elevation of observer G relative to the ground line is equal to h.

Desargues cunningly prioritises the determination of the image of the transversal line T_1, a line located in the ground plane at a distance d from the section FF_0, but on the side opposite to observer G. Since line T_1 and eye G lie on two vertical planes symmetrically disposed about section FF_0, the ray of vision GT_1 will interest section FF_0 at its midpoint, notated F_1. This point will remain the midpoint of section FF_0 regardless of any fluctuations of distance d taken between eye G and the picture F, provided of course that the distance between the transversal line T_1 and the picture is adjusted accordingly. Prefiguring in some way the projective method of homogeneous coordinates, the transversal lines of Desargues are located at a distance equal to a multiple of the distance separating the eye G from the picture F. Following, the position of these transversal lines can vary arbitrarily, provided the elevation of observer G relative to the ground line remains equal to h.

This is the first benefit of Desargues's method. Notwithstanding the risk of proposing something most historians of descriptive geometry would regard as an anachronism, we will refer to Desargues's system as a system of homogeneous coordinates. Assuming that height h of rectangle GG_0F_0F is correct, the width of this rectangle may vary arbitrarily, given that T_1 will always remain symmetrical to G about the axis FF_0. The maintenance of the symmetry between the eye G and any transversal line T_1 opens up three more potential configurations, which, taken in tandem, make it possible to determine the height F_0F_1 of the image of line T_1 relative to G without using a point located outside the rectangle itself. These three provisions may be summarised as follows:

(a) Internalising Moves

All geometric moves will take place within rectangle GG_0F_0F. So long as $T_1F_0=F_0G_0=d$, the width of the rectangle (and the correlative position of any transversal line in space) will vary as needed, but from now on everything takes place indoors. Like an inward reflection, the lines meeting the boundaries of the back box will bounce back

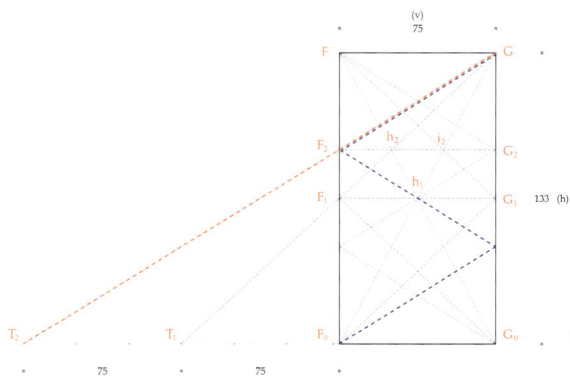

Figure 9. Desargues's use of the Black Box
Desargues's use of the Black Box (and the three geometric expedients shown in Figure 8) to determine the image (projection) of a line T_2 located two times further than the observer from the picture plane (but on the opposite side). The length of the red dotted line is equal to that of the blue one, providing a vivid and accurate visual account of the folding of outer space within the confines of the Black Box.

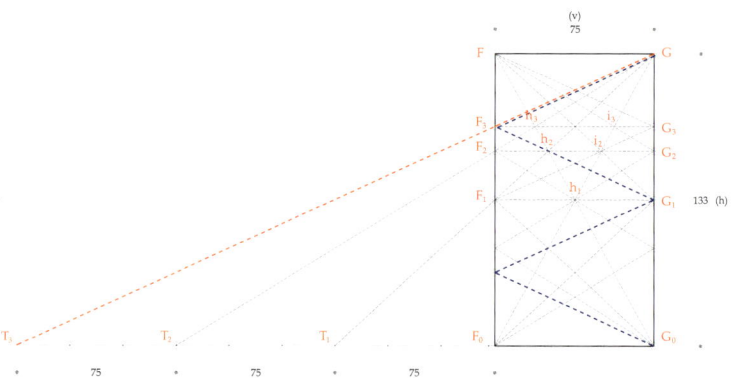

Figure 10
The same operation as in Figure 9, assuming that the transversal line is now located three times further than the observer from the picture plane. Here too the length of the red dotted line is equal to the length of the blue one.

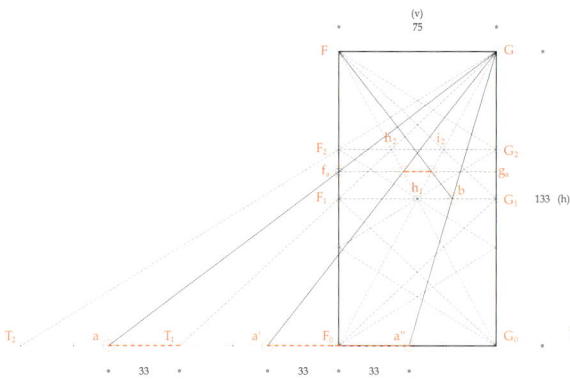

Figure 11
The same operation as in Figures 9 and 10, assuming now that the transversal line is located at a random distance from the picture plane (somewhere between lines T_2 and T_1). The same metrical equivalence between red and blue dotted lines applies, and space folds like an accordion.

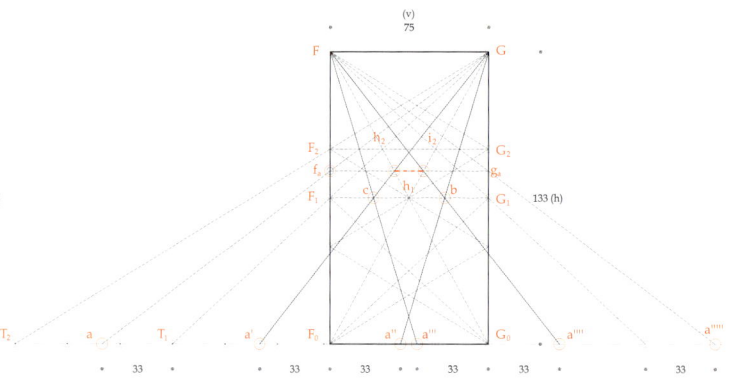

Figure 12
The full deployment of internalisation, swapping and extra diagonals helps determine the image of any transversal line in space thanks to a bevy of auxiliary points, two of which are strategically located within the Black Box (a'' and a''').

in, and their image will be determined without reference to any external points.

(b) Swapping Points

Since all moves now take place within the box, points F and G are equivalent. The reflected image F_1 of G_0 relative to G is equivalent to the reflected image G_1 of F_0 relative to F. Points F and G may therefore be swapped at will, something Desargues himself does repeatedly in the course of his explanation on how to determine the image of a given point, invariably losing his reader who labours under the double misapprehension that G represents the vanishing point of the scene, and F some kind of distance point – or at least an accessory vanishing point of sorts. This is why it is critical to distinguish G from the vanishing point, as well as to move point F away from the left border of the picture. For the essential raison d'être of the Distance Scale is to fold and unfold itself at will, accordion-like, admittedly not the easiest of procedures when it comes to the wooden engravings of Desargues's time, but a mere trifle for today's parametric software routines.

(c) Drawing Diagonals

Since our goal is to determine from within the elevation of the image of transversal line T_1, which happens to coincide with the midpoint of the box's vertical edge, is it not simpler to look for the intersection of the box's two diagonals, leaving aside all reflections in F_1 or G_1? This final provision will prove essential when it comes to determining not only the image of a given transversal line T_1 located at distance d from the picture, but that of any transversal line in space.

To figure out the image of a line located two times further than transversal T_1 (n=2) from the plane of the picture, Desargues methodically generalises his application. First he takes into account the image of a transversal line T_n located n

times further than transversal T_1 from the plane of the picture, at a distance dn = n • d. The diagrams reproduced here should provide enough evidence to shore up the conclusion that the four provisions outlined in the case of the transversal line T_1 apply equally to lines T_2 and T_3, and by extension, to any line T_n. When it comes to multiple transversal lines, we note that, if G is the eye of the observer, any transversal line T_n located beyond the confines of the box will map internally to either F_0 or G_0, depending on the parity of integer n (if n is odd, it will be G_0; otherwise F_0). If F is posited as the eye of the observer, the reasoning is precisely reversed.

The same applies to determining the image of a line T_3 located three times further than transversal T_1 (n=3) from the plane of the picture.

It is important to note the key role diagonals play in the general case where a transversal line T_n is located at a random distance from the plane of the picture (this distance no longer being a multiple of d). Let us for instance determine the elevation of the image of transversal line T_2. The elevation is set by point h_2, located on a horizontal line going through point F_2, itself the intersection of lines GT_2 and F_0F. Point h_2 is also the intersection of line GT_1 and diagonal FG_0. The elevation of the image of point a, randomly located between T_1 and T_2, will be found within the diagonal segment h_1h_2, at the intersection with a line passing through eye G and a new point a', located between F_0 and T_1, at a distance equal to the distance between a and T_1.

To remain 'within the box', as it were, we will simply swap vantage points and look for the elevations of the images of any point a between T_1 and T_2 on the opposite diagonal segment GF_0, between h_1 and i_2. Starting with point a", located directly opposite point a' about F_0, we can trace a line a"G intersecting the horizontal F_1G_1 in point b, from which we can draw another line to point F. This line meets segment h_1i_2 at the desired elevation, notated f_a. Moreover, the line connecting F and b implies that b lies on a sight line originating in F and ending in a'''', a new point located directly opposite a' about a vertical axis through h_1, halfway across rectangle GG_0F_0F. In the end, the inclusion of this vertical axis of symmetry brings the number of points available to help us determine the image of a transversal line passing through T_1 and T_2 to a staggering six. Critically for Desargues, two of these points, a and a', are located inside the black box.

At this juncture of our demonstration, the reader will probably be subject to mixed emotions of shock and awe. Let us dispense with shock first. In essence, none of the elementary steps described here is truly complicated. The whole thing may perhaps be a little more complex than the 'enchanted description of a palace in a novel' which, upon reading the author's draft *Brouillon Project Sur les Coniques*,[8] Descartes had admonished Desargues to pursue. But let's face it; this is the stuff of elementary geometry: a few lines and their intersections here and there, some scaling applications, some symmetry. Yet this is where a 17th-century reader might have struggled a bit, lest we forget that the term 'symmetry' had other meanings before 1794, when Adrien-Marie Legendre recovered the moniker to designate an inversion of spatial orientation, whereby the right-handed becomes left-handed.[9]

We can think of at least one reader of Desargues who must have fully appreciated the awe and power of this perspective method – Leibniz himself, who indeed might have been surprised to find here something akin to his own preoccupations. Leibniz's monads are some kind of individuated atoms,[10] combining in nature to produce a complete and optimal set of bodies, under God's coordination.[11] Monads aggregate into bodies under the aegis of a higher monad, vested with the power of soulfulness. Given that 'it has no windows through which to come and go',[12] each monad is solely determined by itself. On the basis of this purely internal principle,[13] a given monad will be the locus of changing perceptions,[14] independent of any other source. When one looks at a moving body, suggests Leibniz, God has tuned one's internal principles of perception in harmony with the movement of the moving body, while

> Leibniz's monads are some kind of individuated atoms, combining in nature to produce a complete and optimal set of bodies, under God's coordination. Monads aggregate into bodies under the aegis of a higher monad, vested with the power of soulfulness.

blocking all communications between the two monads governing the body and the moving body.

At this juncture, Leibniz calls upon the higher authority of perspective: 'Just like a city considered from different vantage points looks different every time, seemingly multiplied by perspective; likewise it so happens that an infinite multitude of simple substances will produce many distinct universes, which are nothing but alternative perspectives of a single universe, taken from the vantage point of each individual Monad.'[15]

How did Leibniz devise the notion of a perception ordinated internally by closed, windowless and individuated monads, moving independently from one another yet highly coherent as a whole? It is precisely on such a double regimen of interiority/exteriority that Desargues's Distance Scale is based. It is on a purely internal basis that the vertical boundary F_0G_0 determines the reflected image taken from G. Whether the perceived object is located outside in T_1, or inside in F_0, the internal and external procedures will yield the same image in F_1. Critically, the multiple reflections determine how the boundary F_0G_0 will allow us to calculate the image of any point, however remote, or even infinite, by folding space over and over. And as for the swapping of the viewing points F and G, this expedient cannot fail to remind us of Leibniz's fundamental distinction between perception and apperception.

No model is equivalent to the theory it is meant to subtend. Undoubtedly, Leibniz will have devised the monad from a multiplicity of models, later surveyed by the philosopher Michel Serres.[16] Naturally our own conjecture ought to account, upfront, for Leibniz's vague use of perspective in his philosophic writings at large. This is a tough question indeed, a question requiring us to precisely analyse the full extent of the many mathematical domains into which Leibniz wandered, specifically as well as relatively to one another. Yet moving on from Desargues's perspective to differential calculus, Leibniz may have simply laid to rest the precise workings of the practical application of the Distance Scale in the safe knowledge that his conception of the monad had been properly grounded. ◪

Notes

1. Sieur Girard Desargues de Lyon.
2. The essay first appeared in English in JV Field and JJ Gray, *The Geometrical Work of Girard Desargues*, Springer (New York, Berlin, Heidelberg, London, Paris, Tokyo), 1987, pp 147–60.
3. Leon Battista Alberti, *De Pictura* I, 20, 1485. 'I take a small surface …', specified in Italian as *'prendo un piccolo spazio'*, or in Latin as *'habeo areolam'*.
4. See Field and Gray, op cit, p 147. Desargues reverses the accepted interplay between opacity and transparency that perspective is based on: for him the represented object is a wireframe, and his picture plane a screen. Alberti's picture plane, on the other hand, is like a window – or a light veil – and the object a solid and opaque mass.
5. The idea of the monad was first published in his *La Monadologie* (The Monadology) of 1714.
6. In this Desargues is among other things heir to Ptolemy, and his use of different coordinate systems in each of his three cartography mappings.
7. The Dimension Scale (*échelle des mesures*) unfolds *parallel* to the picture plane, and its base (the edge along which the Dimension Scale meets the ground) offers a ground line. The Distance Scale (*échelle des éloignements*) unfolds *perpendicularly* to the picture plane and records measurements extending in depth. Determining exact metric correspondences on the Distance Scale using only the Dimension Scale and a few elementary planar geometric operations, such as bisecting or mirroring a line, is the great innovation of Desargues, who manages to determine the exact foreshortening of distances in depth without resorting to perspective – as claimed in the subtitle of the *Universal Way* (translator's note).
8. Descartes, Letter to Desargues dated 19 June 1639. See Field and Gray, op cit, pp 176–7.
9. Giora Hon and Bernard R Goldstein, *From Summetria to Symmetry : The Making of a Revolutionary Scientific Concept*, Springer (New York), 2008.
10. Leibniz, *La Monadologie*, article 3.
11. Ibid, article 55.
12. Ibid, article 7.
13. Ibid, article 11.
14. Ibid, article 14.
15. Ibid, article 13.
16. Michel Serres, *Le système de Leibniz et ses modèles mathématiques*, PUF (Paris), 1968.

Article translated from the original French by George L Legendre

PASTA BY DESIGN

GEORGE L LEGENDRE, IJP

Guest-editor **George L Legendre** has taken the parametric surface model that he developed for buildings through his practice, IJP Corporation, and applied it to pasta. The result is *Pasta by Design*, publishing in September 2011 by Thames & Hudson, which classifies this *primo piatto* into 92 basic topological types.

IJP uses mathematics to design anything from pedestrian bridges to contemporary art museums. When a neighbour and London-based colleague from Italy suggested (over a steaming pile of *spaghetti all'olio, aglio e peperoncino*) that the practice look at something like food, the blurry outline of a book on pasta gradually came into focus. Its concept is simple: to figure out the mathematical formulas of one of the most popular foods on earth and to use them to produce an inventory, guide and culinary resource on the subject.

Pasta by Design explores in depth some mathematical aspects of molecular gastronomy. Specifically, it offers a magnified view of the forming stage of the pasta-making process (the mechanical extrusion of a mix of durum wheat flour and water into the familiar edible shape). Mechanically mass-producing pasta is a process dependent on pressure, viscosity, precise temperatures, pressure differentials and airflow: all these factors determine the material properties of the product – as well as its market value. Leaving aside the thermodynamic issues involved and using a parametric surface model originally developed by IJP to model building structures, the book explores the geometry of pasta through the deployment of algebraic equation sets.

Classifying pasta is a particularly difficult task, however *Pasta by Design* pares down the puzzling variety of pasta to 92 types based on their unique morphological features. In a technical mathematical sense, the criteria of differentiation are topological invariants involving the edges and surface of each sample (such simple properties are common to widely different shapes and help understand accidental differences), which is described by its parametric algebraic equations and illustrated with a line diagram and specially commissioned photograph.[1] △

Note

1. *Pasta by Design* by George L Legendre, with photographs by Stefano Graziani and a foreword by Paola Antonelli is due to be published by Thames & Hudson in September 2011. The project was completed by IJP in 2009–10. Text, phylogenetic chart and mathematics by George L Legendre and Jean-Aimé Shu for IJP. Photography by Stefano Graziani. Additional illustration by Woonyin Mo Wong for IJP. Layouts by Niccolo Marini for KGA. Based on an idea by Marco Guarnieri. Original book design by IJP.

FAGOTTINI

A paid-up member of the *pasta ripiena* family, the Fagottini ('purses') are made of round, durum-wheat based dough gathered into ball-shaped bundles and stuffed with ricotta and fresh pear. These square filled dumplings are in fact similar to ravioli, only larger and easier to make.

< Pinched Longitudinal Profile

< Hollow Cross-Section

< Smooth Surface

< Smooth Edges

ranges

$$i := 0, 1 .. 200$$
$$j := 0, 1 .. 50$$

equations

$$\alpha_{i,j} := \left[\left(0.8 + \sin\left(\frac{i}{100} \cdot \pi\right)^8 - 0.8 \cdot \cos\left(\frac{i}{25} \cdot \pi\right) \right)^{1.5} + 0.2 + 0.2 \cdot \sin\left(\frac{i}{100} \cdot \pi\right) \right]$$

$$\beta_{i,j} := \left[\left(0.9 + \cos\left(\frac{i}{100} \cdot \pi\right)^8 - 0.9 \cdot \cos\left(\frac{i}{25} \cdot \pi + 0.03 \cdot \pi\right) \right)^{1.5} + 0.3 \cdot \left(\cos\left(\frac{i}{100} \cdot \pi\right) \right) \right]$$

$$\gamma_{i,j} := 4 - \frac{4 \cdot j}{500} \cdot \left(1 + \cos\left(\frac{i}{100} \cdot \pi\right)^8 - 0.8 \cos\left(\frac{i}{25} \cdot \pi\right) \right)^{1.5}$$

$$\Pi_{i,j} := \cos\left(\frac{i}{100} \cdot \pi\right) \cdot \left[\alpha_{i,j} \cdot \sin\left(\frac{i}{100} \cdot \pi\right)^8 + 0.6 \cdot \left(2 + \sin\left(\frac{i}{100} \cdot \pi\right)^2 \right) \cdot \sin\left(\frac{j}{50} \cdot \pi\right)^2 \right]$$

$$\Theta_{i,j} := \sin\left(\frac{i}{100} \cdot \pi\right) \cdot \left[\beta_{i,j} \cdot \sin\left(\frac{j}{100} \cdot \pi\right)^8 + 0.6 \cdot \left(2 + \cos\left(\frac{i}{100} \cdot \pi\right)^2 \right) \cdot \sin\left(\frac{j}{50} \cdot \pi\right)^2 \right]$$

$$K_{i,j} := \left(1 + \sin\left(\frac{j}{100} \cdot \pi - 0.5 \cdot \pi\right) \right) \cdot \left[\gamma_{i,j} - \frac{4 \cdot j}{500} \left(1 + \sin\left(\frac{i}{100} \cdot \pi\right)^8 - 0.8 \cos\left(\frac{i}{25} \cdot \pi\right) \right)^{1.5} \right]$$

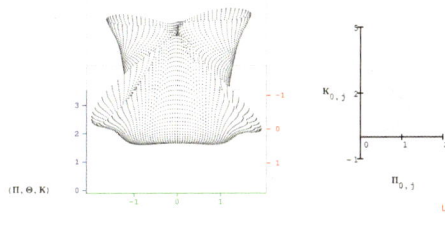

(Π, Θ, K)

$K_{0,j}$

$\Pi_{0,j}$

Length: 30 mm | Width: 30 mm
Boiling Time: 4 min

above: A notable member of the *pasta ripiena* (filled pasta) family, fagottini (little purses) are made from circles of durum-wheat dough. A spoonful of ricotta, steamed vegetables or even stewed fruit is placed on the dough, and the corners are then pinched together to form a bundle. These packed dumplings are similar to ravioli, only larger.

left: Typical spread from *Pasta by Design*. Top to bottom: Name and phylogenetic address of the form, dimensional information, ranges of the calculation, parametric equations, surface plot, two parametric graphs (function graphed against another function) and a short note on regional provenance and cuisine.

left: The Pasta Table. IJP used real samples to develop the mathematics of the project and hence had to purchase kilos of common (and less common) pasta from vendors worldwide. For ease of use, these samples were placed in test-tube-like glassware, labelled, and laid out on a long table. Eventually, the team decided to create a permanent installation for the workbench. The 'tablecloth' of the Pasta Table, a 4-metre (13-feet) long graph of overlapping topological relationships between shapes, is included in the book under the title 'The Pasta Family Reunion, Seating Plan'.

above: Detail of the Pasta Table.

Michael Weinstock

THE METABOLISM OF THE CITY
THE MATHEMATICS OF NETWORKS AND URBAN SURFACES

The anthropologist Claude Lévi-Strauss described the city as 'a congregation of animals who enclose their biological history within its boundaries and at the same time through their every conscious action mould and shape it. By both its development and its form, it belongs simultaneously to biological procreation, organic evolution, and aesthetic creation. It is at one and the same time an object of nature and a subject of culture; an individual and a group; something lived and something dreamed; the supreme human achievement.'[1] Half of all humans alive today live in cities, although the geographical pattern is uneven; in Europe and North America, four out of every five people live in cities. As the world population continues to grow, existing cities are expanding and new cities are being built, connected and integrated into the world system. The urbanisation of the world is accelerating, and it is thought that within less than two generations there will be an additional 2 billion urban dwellers, most of whom will be located in Southeast Asia, China, India and Africa.[2]

The expansion of existing cities and the creation of new cities to meet this demand is a daunting task. Cities are the largest and most complex material forms constructed by humans, but they are far more than an immensely extended artefact. They are dynamic, spatial and material arrays of buildings that are constructed, reworked and rebuilt over time, decaying, collapsing and expanding in irregular episodes of growth and incorporation. As they grow and develop, their systems for the movement of food, material, water, people and manufactured artefacts must grow and extend with them.

From this perspective, cities are not static arrays of material structures, but are regarded as analogous to living beings, as they consume energy, food, water and other materials, excrete wastes and maintain themselves down through the generations.

Contemporary mathematical studies of cities that are derived from the historical development of the studies of metabolism in biology have been focused either on the 'allometric'[3] relations of the physical forms of the urban morphology such as the overall shape, compactness and density,

Figure 1. Shanghai
The city covers more than 6,000 square kilometers and a metropolitan population is approaching 20 million, making it one of the largest and most densely populated cities on earth. The velocity and quantities of urban metabolism are producing environmental problems of great complexity.

How might we best track the accelerating demands of global urbanisation? **Michael Weinstock**, Director of Research and Development at the Architectural Association (AA) in London, proposes a mathematical approach to uncovering the dynamics of cities. He advocates a dual method that reveals any city's particular metabolism by simultaneously mapping its physical shape – its compactness and densities – and its flows of energy, information and materials.

or on the relations of energy, information and material flows and their networks[4] with the spatial patterns of the city. The hypothesis of this article is that the unification of these two approaches, combining the studies of flows through networks in relation to the physical forms of the city, and how each acts upon the other over time, will be a significant step towards understanding of the dynamics of cities.

Networks and Scaling Phenomena

In all living beings, the morphology of the species and their metabolism are intricately linked through the flow of energy and materials. Metabolism is the 'fire of life', the system of all living forms that captures energy and materials from their environment, transforms it and transports it in fluids to every cell, and excretes changed materials as waste back into the environment. Biological metabolism operates through surfaces and branching networks that exhibit identical mathematical parameters in all living forms, from the smallest microbes to giant sequoias, from mice to mammoths. The common

metabolic characteristics are exhibited in the relations between the geometry and overall size of the body plan, the internal operating temperature and the mode of existence in the environment. Metabolism also determines the relations of individuals and populations of forms with their local environment. Higher levels of biological organisation emerge from metabolic processes, in the relations between species, and in the density and patterns of distribution of species across the surface of the earth.[5]

As all biological networks tend to evolve over time, an architectural form that maximises flow under the constraints specific to it,[6] it follows that similar scaling effects may also be demonstrated in the networks of urban systems, cities and conurbations. For example, just as the cardiovascular network distributes energy and materials to cells in a living form, so it seems that urban traffic networks distribute energy, materials and people through a city.[7] Biological metabolism functions through surfaces and branching networks, and there has been a century or more of research into the mathematical parameters common to all living forms. In cities too the operation of metabolism occurs through urban surfaces and urban networks, and there is a remarkable similarity between the mathematics of biological metabolism and urban metabolism.

Although there is wide variation in their individual components and chemical processes, the metabolic branching networks of all living forms, from the smallest of microbes to the very largest blue whale, exhibit the same topological scaling properties. Networks for information distribution exhibit many similar parameters to the hierarchical branching metabolic networks of living forms, and a great variety of other culturally produced networks also exhibit comparable 'scale free' power law characteristics. Scaling is an invariant property of a dynamic system in general, most likely to be produced by the way in which the systems grow. Both biological and cultural networks grow continuously by the addition of new nodes or hubs, but these new nodes preferentially attach to nodes that are already well connected. In consequence, the topology of the whole network has only a few nodes with a high number of connections that link to all of the other nodes that have progressively smaller numbers of connections.

Flow patterns are dominated by the highly connected nodes, through which the maximum volume and velocity of energy, information or material flow. These properties characterise the evolution of biological systems and of culturally produced metabolic systems.[8]

Most known scaling phenomena observed in biological organisms have a relation to body mass – efficient fluid energy transportation in particular is an essential determinant of biological body plan and overall morphology, and the size of elements in the metabolic networks of aortas and blood vessels, lung branches and tissues, tree trunks and branches, even lifespan and heart beats, all of which scale in relation to body mass. The scaling is simply expressed as a power law: $Y = Y_0 M^b$

where Y is an observable magnitude, Y_0 a constant, and M is the mass of the organism. The metabolic exponent b $\approx 3/4$ is found across nearly 27 orders of magnitude in life, from molecular levels up to the largest organisms,[9] in the differing metabolisms of ectotherms and endotherms,[10] and in the photosynthetic metabolisms of plants.[11]

Scaling phenomena are also evident in cities,[12] significantly in relation to the number of inhabitants rather than to the material mass of the built fabric. Analysis of the large multi-decade data sets of mature Western cities reveals the space per person decreases as the population size increases; with greater densities and greater flows through transport infrastructures, there is a greater diversity of economic and cultural activities and the pace of all activities increases accordingly, including individual consumption and waste, crimes, pollution and diseases. There is also dramatically reduced access to open green spaces in high-density cities that correlates to city area more strongly than to population size; and in Europe to geographical location, in that green space per person increases proportionally with latitude, being greater in the northern latitudes than in southern-latitude cities.[13]

Scaling laws are exhibited by the distribution patterns found in many natural and cultural systems, and are considered fundamental to statistical physics. The linguist George Kingsley Zipf gave his name to the mathematical law that accounts for the frequency of occurrence of words within written texts[14] and is observed in the rank size distributions of the largest cities and metropolises of the world, and metropolitan areas of the US, which seem to be robust over time despite multiple economic and social fluctuations and perturbations. It is argued that as these patterns are also insensitive to topography and climate, it is likely that they are related to the flow and distribution of resources through ecological and urban networks.[15]

Figure 2. Aerial view at night of south Mumbai
The night image indicates the vehicle flow and energy use of one developed patch of a city that has a population that has doubled in only 20 years and now exceeds 20 million people. The extremely rapid growth is producing fragments of dense metropolitan development amongst extremely compromised urban environments and severe water shortages.

Morphology and Surfaces

The phrase 'urban metabolism' was in use almost 50 years ago[16] in reference to a hypothetical city of 1 million people, and elaborated in more recent studies of eight metropolitan cities across five continents,[17] although these studies are focused on the quantification and annual totals of flows rather than the network topology of their architecture and its relation to the morphology of the city. There are contemporary related analytical studies into the metabolism of discrete patches of a city.[18] This offers the potential to compare the annualised total flows of energy and material in and out of different urban patches, but without morphological analysis only generalised inferences may be made.

However, in all living forms, metabolism and morphology are intricately linked and operate through surfaces and networks. Mammalian metabolisms, for example, evolved their long intestinal tube with very large numbers of convolutions to increase the surface area, and use muscles to accelerate the passage of food. The evolution of greater surface areas for respiration, the intricate surface foldings of lungs in mammals and in birds, produces large surface areas for the exchange of gases packed into internal cavities. Enhanced circulatory systems were evolved by the development of more complex hearts and increased fluid pressures, as was the oxygen-carrying capacity of the blood being circulated. And within the cells, the evolution of increased mitochondrial surfaces through multiple foldings amplified the energy-processing capacity of cellular tissues. Morphology and metabolism are related in plants through the spatial organisation of large surface areas to capture light and for the exchange of gases, the structural system for the deployment of those surfaces, and the internal transportation systems for moving fluids.

This suggests the consideration of the physicality of the city as a porous surface, with buildings and spaces as folds

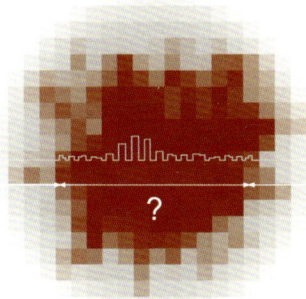

Figure 4. Ground drawings of cities
Traditional descriptive graphical technique depicting the solid–void relationships of a city, ascribed to the architect and surveyor Giambatistta Nolli,who made the famous map of Rome ('*La Pianta Grande di Roma*') in 1748 using this technique. In this diagram, nine urban patches depict urban figures of evolved and planned cities and reveal differences of building density and spatial continuity across the patch.

Rural
Urban

Figure 3. Gradient boundaries
The legal and regulatory boundary is often defined by the original core, so that cities are regarded as something quite separate from their surrounding territory. All cities have administrative boundaries, but cities are very rarely physically or energetically contained within those administrative boundaries. There is rarely a sharp morphological boundary distinction, rather an irregular gradation of density.

and cavities that together comprise the morphology. The relation of this porous material surface to its climate and environment, and thus to its energy consumption, is amenable to mathematical description, and may thus be used for analysis of the differentiated material and spatial conditions across the urban surface that influence and moderate the local urban microclimate[19] and consequently to its environmental performance and energy consumption. It has been argued that the urban surface may be modelled with nine parameters: the amplitude of the variations in height (rugosity); the proportion of open spaces to solid (porosity); the orientation of those open spaces to a particular axiality such as wind direction (sinuosity); the contained volume relative to surface (compacity); the closeness of buildings to each other (contiguity); the ratio of built perimeter to horizontal surface cuts (occlusivity); the surfaces exposed to the sun (solar admittance); the surface material that is not water or grass (mineralisation) and the built area proportion to unbuilt (density).[20]

This approach is coherent with a recent innovation in urban analysis used by urban climatologists: the division of the urban surface into strongly differentiated local climate zones, each defined by the surface cover (built fraction, soil moisture and albedo) and its structure (sky view factor and roughness), and human activities (*anthropogenic heat flux*). This extends the urban patch technique to a mathematical system that describes urban and natural landscapes in 19 morphologically and climatically differentiated surface 'zones' or patches.[21]

The urbanisation of the world is accelerating, and with it the complexity of the urban environment. Integrated and intelligent urban and infrastructural systems will be a critical component in the adaptation of expanded human societies to impending climatic and ecological changes. It is now widely accepted that urban morphology and density, and the evolution of transportation technology influence both

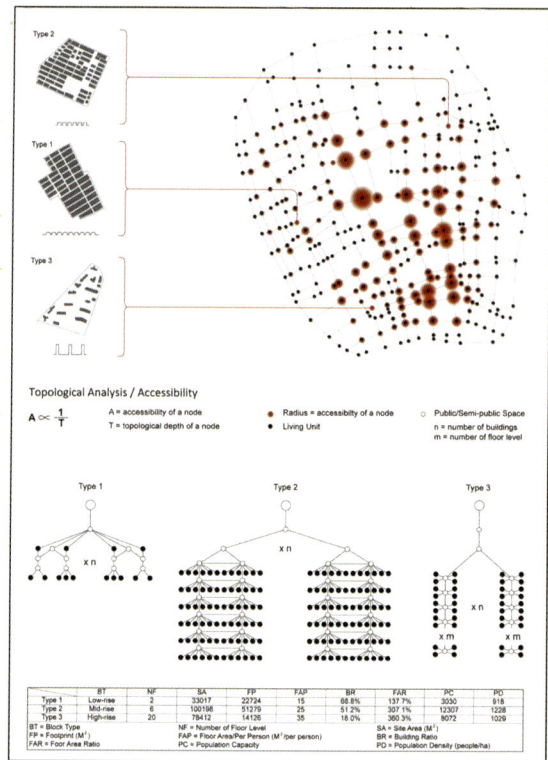

Figure 6. Topological analysis
above: This analysis of an urban patch in Shanghai reveals the connectivity in the network of spaces, from the private living space, the interior spatial organisation of buildings, the semi-public space of local context, and across the urban patch to its perimeter.

Figure 7. Nine parameters for modelling the surface of the city
below: These diagrams show the relation of the urban surface to climate and environment, and the mathematical description used for analysis of the differentiated material and spatial conditions; and when combined with urban climatology, for environmental performance and energy use.

Figure 5. Los Angeles
Massive highway infrastructure and the horizon-wide extension of low-density morphology characteristic of this city that extends over 10,000 square kilometers, with a population over 15 million.

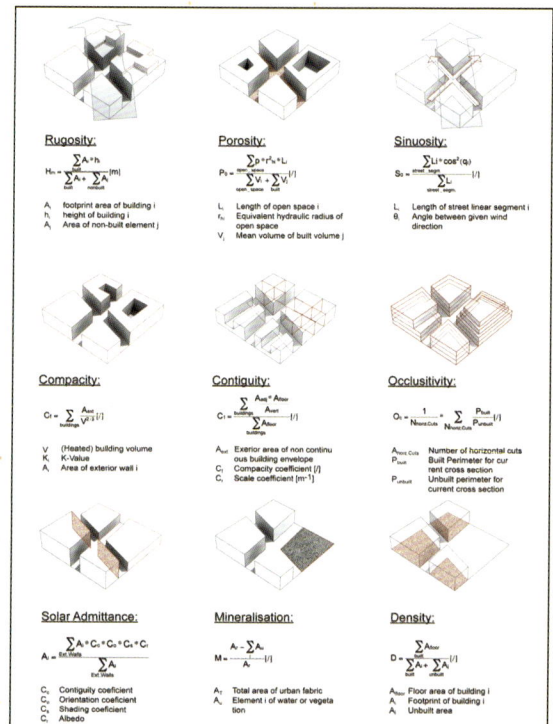

the energy and material flows through cities. The study and design of infrastructures is conventionally focused on the separate physical artefacts of the networks, and in recent times there has been strong focus on the architectural renewal and implementation of stations, bridges and terminals, but much less on the topology and physical architecture of the network systems themselves or on the interdependencies between differing infrastructural systems and even less on their integration. There are no known large-scale studies that couple the analysis of urban morphologies, the flows and capacities of their metabolic system, to the design of the physical geometries and engineering of material artefacts that comprise integrated urban metabolic systems within a regime of rapid climatic and ecological change, rising population and energetic constraints. The exponential acceleration of population growth and the projected proliferation of new cities requires the development of new 'flow' architectures, of 'metabolic' and intelligent inhabited urban infrastructural systems that harvest and distribute energy, water and materials, that intimately connects people and open urban green spaces, and that unites rather than divides urban and ecological systems. ∆

Notes

1. C Lévi-Strauss, *Tristes Tropiques*, Librarie Ploni (Paris), 1955, trans J Weightman and D Weightman, Jonathan Cape (London), 1973, p 155.
2. UN-Habitat. *State of the World's Cities 2010/2011, Cities for All: Bridging the Urban Divide (2010)*; see www.unhabitat.org/pmss/listItemDetails.aspx?publicationID=2917.
3. The relationship between size and shape, and of the differential growth of a part in relation to the whole.
4. M Batty, 'The Size, Scale and Shape of Cities', *Science* 5864, 2008, pp 769–71.
5. M Weinstock, 'Metabolism and Morphology', in *AD Versatility and Vicissitude*, Vol 78, No 2, 2008, pp 26–33; and M Weinstock, *The Architecture of Emergence: The Evolution of Form in Nature and Civilisation*, John Wiley & Sons (Chichester), 2010, pp 130–7.
6. AL Barabási and R Albert, 'Emergence of Scaling in Random Networks', *Science* 286, 1999, pp 509–12.
7. MA Changizi and M Destafano, 'Common Scaling Laws for City Highway Systems and the Mammalian Neocortex', *Complexity*, Wiley InterScience, 2009.
8. H Jeong, B Tombor, R Albert, ZN Oltvai and AL Barabási, 'The Large-Scale Organization of Metabolic Networks', *Nature* 407, 2000, pp 651–4.
9. GB West and JH Brown, 'The Origin of Allometric Scaling Laws in Biology from Genomes to Ecosystems: Towards a Quantitative Unifying Theory of Biological Structure and Organization', *The Journal of Experimental Biology* 208, 2005, pp 1575–92; BJ Enquist, 'Allometric Scaling of Plant Energetics and Population Density', *Nature* 395, September 1998, 163–5; and GB West, JH Brown and BJ Enquist, 'A General Model for the Origin of Allometric Scaling Laws in Biology', *Science* 276, 1997, pp 122–6.
10. RH Peters, *The Ecological Implications of Body Size*, Cambridge University Press (Cambridge), 1986.
11. KJ Niklas, *Plant Allometry*, University of Chicago Press (Chicago, IL), 1994.
12. LMA Bettencourt, J Lobo, D Helbing, C Kühnert and GB West, 'Growth, Innovation, Scaling and the Pace of Life in the City', *Proceedings of the National Academy of Science* 104, 2007, pp 7301–6; and M Batty, 'The Size, Scale, and Shape of Cities', *Science* 319, 2008, pp 769–71.
13. RA Fuller and KJ Gaston, 'The Scaling of Green Space Coverage in European Cities', *Royal Society Biological Letters* 5, 2009, pp 352–5.
14. GK Zipf, *Human Behavior and the Principle of Least Effort*, Addison-Wesley (Cambridge), 1949.
15. EH Decker, AJ Kerkhoff and ME Moses, 'Global Patterns of City Size Distributions and their Fundamental Drivers', *PLoS ONE* 2(9), 2007, p e934.
16. A Wolman, 'The Metabolism of the City', *Scientific American* 213, 1965, pp 179–90.
17. C Kennedy, J Cuddihy and J Engel-Yan, 'The Changing Metabolism of Cities', *Journal of Industrial Ecology*, Vol 11, 2008, pp 43–59.
18. N Codoban and CA Kennedy, 'The Metabolism of Neighborhoods', *Journal of Urban Planning and Development* 134, 2008, pp 21–31.
19. ID Stewart and T Oke, 'Newly Developed "Thermal Climate Zones" for Defining and Measuring Urban Heat Island Magnitude in the Canopy Layer', *Eighth Symposium on Urban Environment*, Phoenix, Arizona, 2009.
20. L Adolphe, 'A Simplified Model of Urban Morphology: Application to an Analysis of the Environmental Performance of Cities', *Environment and Planning B: Planning and Design* 28(2), 2001, pp 183–200.
21. ID Stewart and T Oke, 'Classifying Urban Climate Field Sites by "Local Climate Zones": The Case of Nagano, Japan', *Seventh International Conference on Urban Climate*, Yokohama, Japan, 2009.

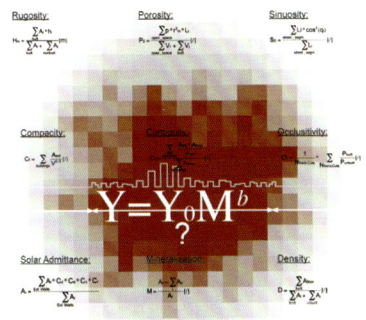

$$Y = Y_0 M^b_?$$

Figure 8. Mathematical hypothesis of this article
The combination of the mathematics of flows through networks and of the mathematics of surface modelling of the material forms of the city, and how each acts upon the other over time, provide a significant step towards modelling the dynamics of cities.

RISING MASSES, SINGAPORE

MAX
KAHLEN

Rising Masses, a year-long final design thesis undertaken at the Architectural Association (AA) School of Architecture, is for a high-rise building in the centre of Singapore's financial district. It is characterised by an extreme thinness that is intended to heighten the experience of working in such a dense urban context. As **Max Kahlen** of Dyvik & Kahlen, Architecture, explains, two mathematical-based methods were employed in order to aid the design of such a thin structure.

Max Kahlen, Rising
Masses, Singapore, 2008
Physical model of the
tower slabs and podium.
Scale 1:500.

The site for Rising Masses is located within the regimented grid of Singapore's booming office district. It was made available in 2008 with a tender package that included the provision of space for commercial, office and residential uses and which specified the project brief: a building structure capable of operating within the tight margins set by developers while aiming to maximise the efficiency of the building's performance ratios.

The articulation of the proposal challenges the phenomenon of thinness, the main desire at work here. Thinness is understood less as the ambition to reduce structural members to a minimum than it is the search for a spatial experience in an extra-thin building that intensifies the condition and atmosphere of working and living in an extreme urban context. The idea is not to scare the user, but to create a building of transparency, where minimum depth allows internal spaces to span from one facade to the other, opening up views on both sides. Being inside this space should trigger a feeling of floating between the pixellated facades of the neighbouring office towers.

Two approaches of mathematical nature were deployed to give distinct form to this desire. The first is a complex user interface that automatically calculates the building masses. A matrix processes the constraints given by the tendering package (such as plot size, floor height, number of floors, plot coverage, floor-to-ceiling height and floor area ratio) to determine dimensions of maximum efficiency. Additional parameters, such as the number of buildings and their proportion, as well as a periodic function that gradually arranges floor-to-floor heights, contribute to shaping a building mass of extreme dimensions. The final proportions determine two 180-metre (590-foot) high slab buildings of 6 x 40 metres (20 x 130 feet) each, sharing a common podium. The slabs face one another and are separated by only 24 metres (79 feet). They are staggered length-wise to create an in-between space serving as a vertical courtyard of private nature, in contrast to the open views onto the adjoining neighbourhood from the opposite side.

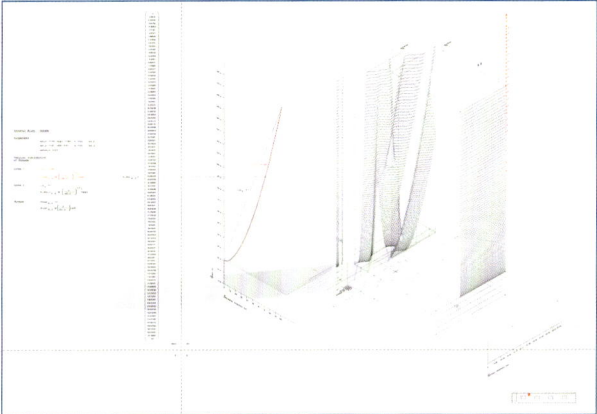

Fold-like deformations along the internal facades provide stability and space for vertical circulation.

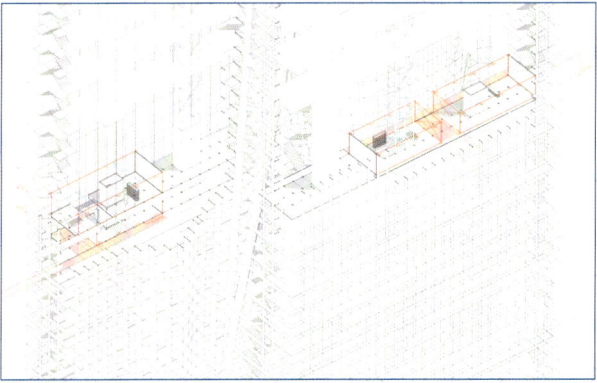

Detail showing two different types of residential units.

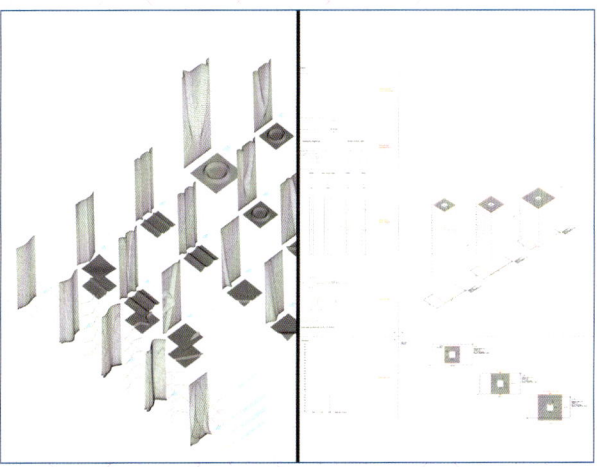

Left: Catalogue of forms - scaleless. Right: Calculation template to automate the building mass.

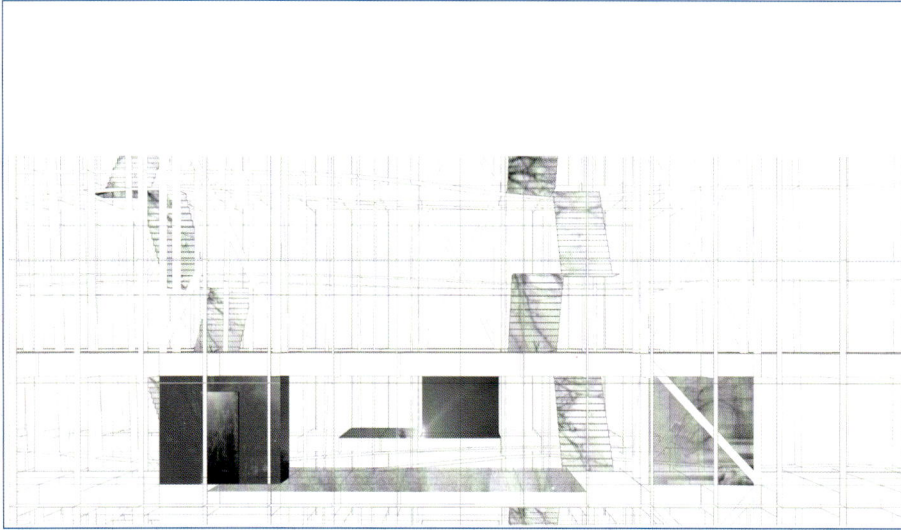

Perspective elevation looking through both tower slabs.

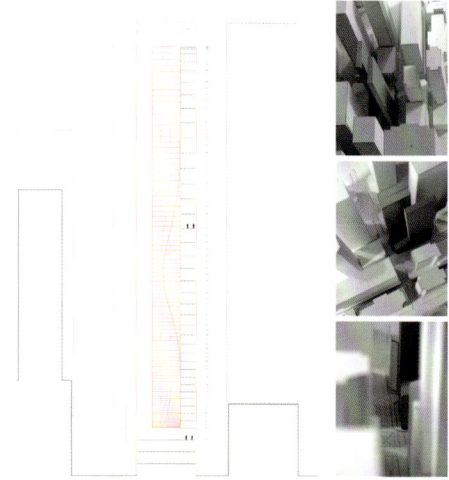

Vertical section exposing both 6-metre (20-foot) thin slabs in contrast to the in-between void and neighbouring buildings.

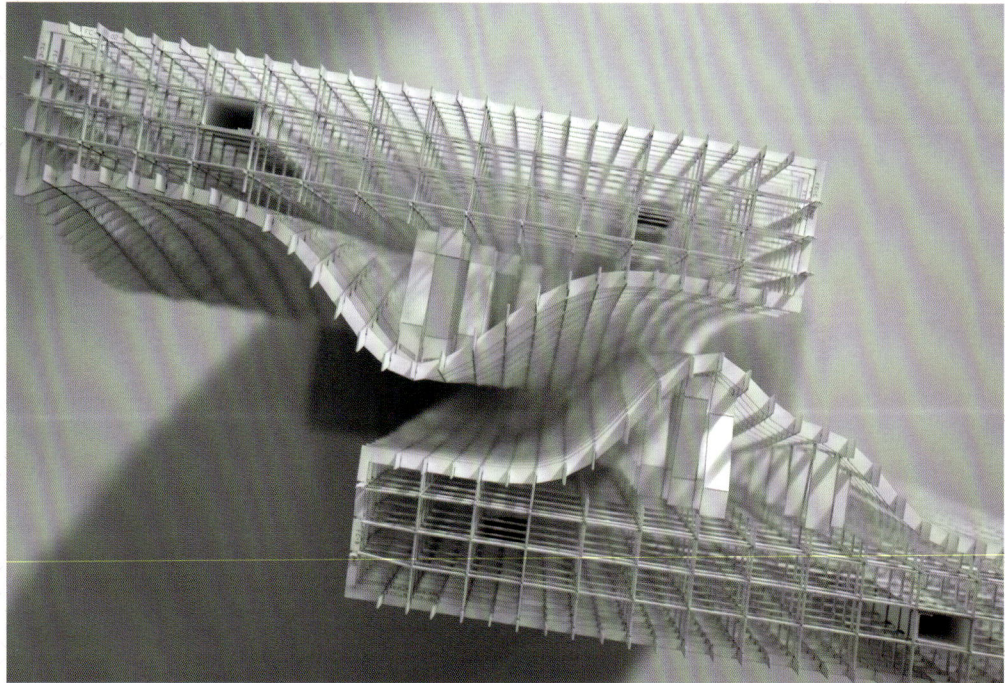

External staircases are placed between the vaulted facade grid and the straight inner slab. Both slabs connect at two points throughout the overall height.

Overview of the site within Singapore's office district.

Depending on the angle of view, the structure appears either solid or transparent, exposing the inner cores.

The second approach is based on a set of periodic functions that aggregate to define the gridded facades. Adjacent to the in-between courtyard, alongside the inner faces, several vertical sinus-shaped folds determine cavities with a structural role and enable vertical circulation. The outer faces of the slabs, on the other hand, remain flat. The gridded texture is kept independent of the floor arrangement, gradually distributing the horizontal members with increasing intervals towards the top, in keeping with the structural stress patterns of the facades.

The folds run diagonally on both building faces and intersect in two points to provide stability to the excessively slender slabs as well as to link the circulation paths. The cavities between the vaulted facade grids and the straight building slabs are open and accommodate external staircases. Walking along these stairs feels like stepping outside the building into the in-between courtyard, looking through a cloud of structure that hovers beyond the building limits. Commercial programmes are located in the podium. Offices and apartments occupy both slabs. The elevator cores are not clustered, but distributed equally throughout the length of each slab, providing direct access to the offices and flats, and external corridors alongside the courtyard connect to the external staircases to allow interim circulation and access of fresh air.

The project reconciles competing notions of 'automatic form' derived simply from the industry performance ratios, a personal desire, and the urge of continuity imposed by the periodic equations. What this struggle produces is a building structure appearing at times rigorously efficient and at others surprisingly excessive and redundant. The external facades reflect the monotony of the neighbouring buildings, while the discrete break between the two slabs offers a vertical territory that allows one to step out into an unresolved urban void. In this way, one never quite settles on whether the 'rising masses' are pragmatic or surreal. ⌂

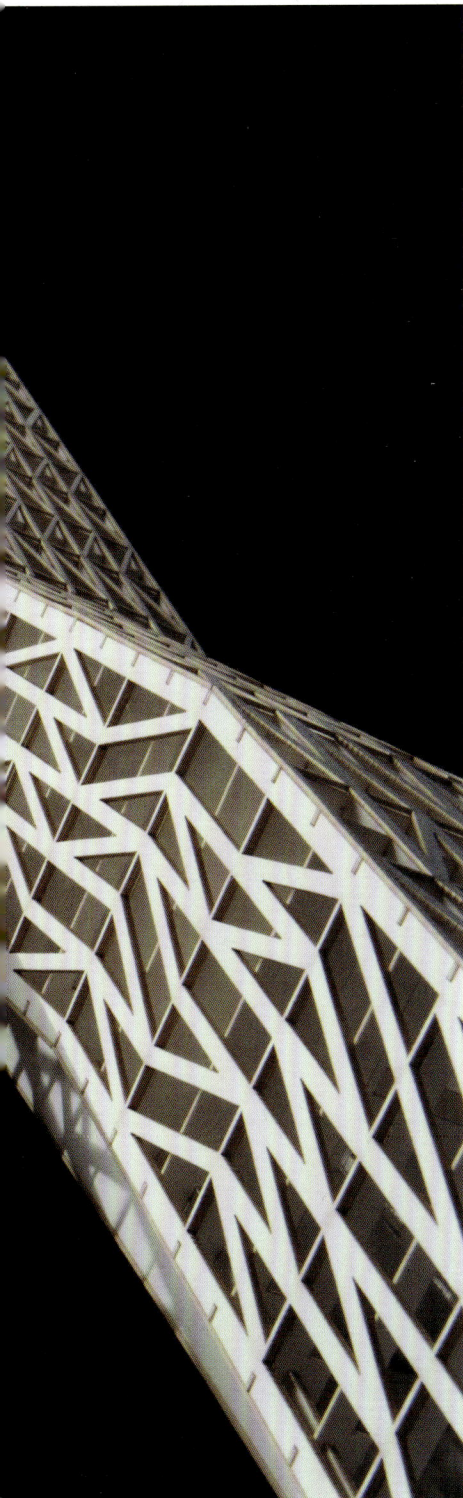

THE HINGING TOWER

ANA MARÍA FLOR ORTIZ
AND RODIA VALLADARES
SÁNCHEZ, RISING MASSES
STUDIO, HARVARD GRADUATE
SCHOOL OF DESIGN

For their project for a tower in downtown Singapore, which they undertook for the Rising Masses Studio at Harvard Graduate School of Design (GSD), **Ana María Flor Ortiz and Rodia Valladares Sánchez** adopted a mathematical approach. They explicitly used mathematical notation as a mechanism of controlling form, in a manner that could also harness the possibilities of more random and unanticipated influences.

Ana María Flor Ortiz and Rodia Valladares Sánchez, Hinging Tower, Rising Masses Studio, Harvard Graduate School of Design, Cambridge, Massachusetts, 2008
The Hinging Tower aims to challenge the ubiquitous skyscraper, characterised by mere extrusion and the stacking of floors.

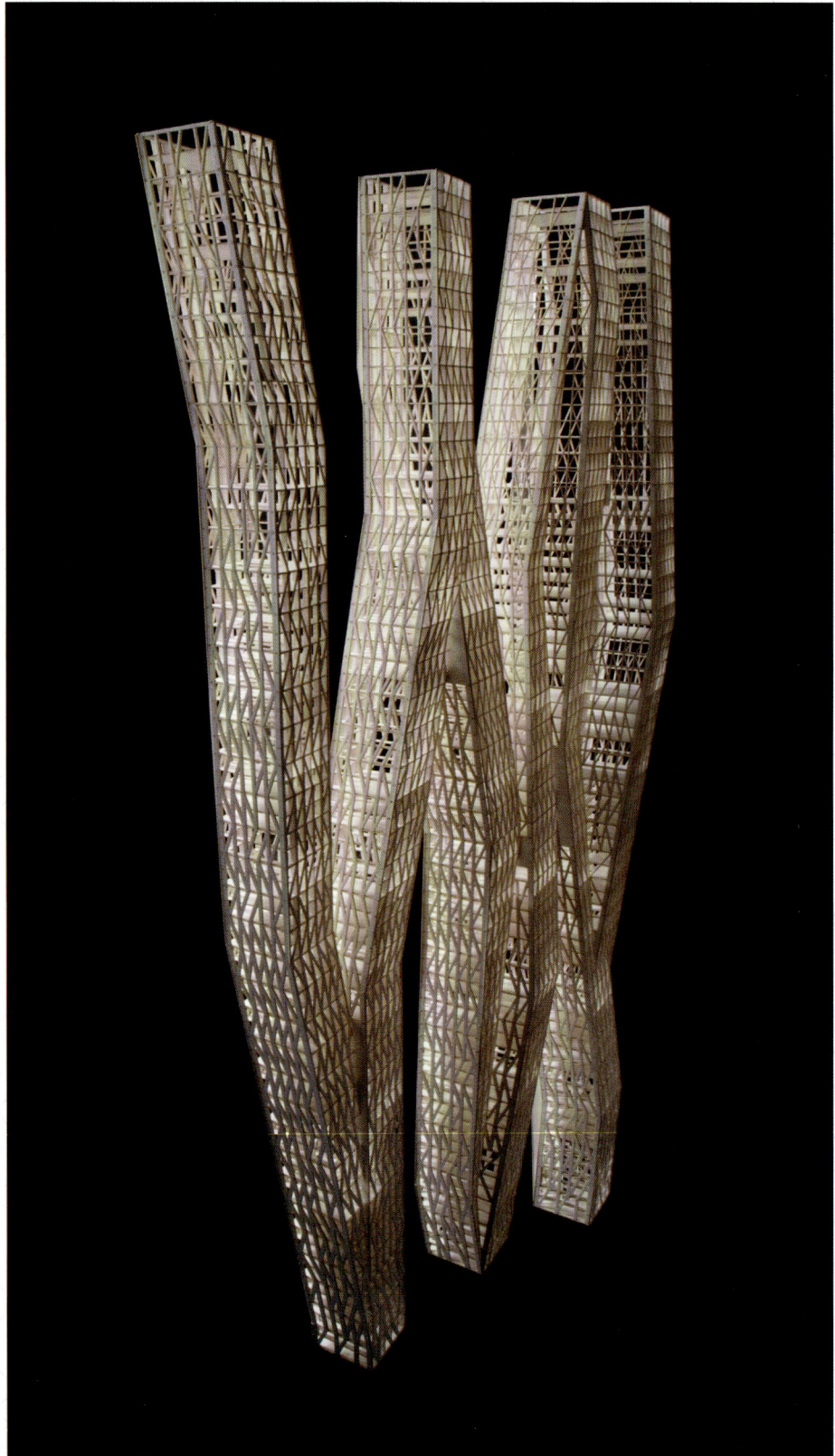

The architectural protocols defined by
mathematical notation celebrate the
potential of the unexpected as a way to
generate areas of opportunity.

The Hinging Tower, a high-rise development located on a Modernist corridor of downtown Singapore, explores mathematical notation as a mechanism to control form, while acknowledging the potential of the unexpected and the uncertain as key factors for finding novel formal solutions.

Through its language of functions, the mathematical apparatus becomes the ultimate tool that allows the generation of the 'proto-tower' diagram for the project. The combination of equations synthesises a system of geometric relations that contains the whole spectrum of possible differentiation (or variation). In this sense, the integration of multiple variables makes the final form (iteration) of the tower an organisation responsive to local conditions, as well as to site and programme specificities.

The programme requirements feature the mixture of residential apartments, offices and hotels so common to the urban landscape of modern Asian cities. Starting with this premise, the project constitutes an attempt to challenge the ubiquitous skyscraper, in which the form is achieved by a process of mere extrusion and stacking of floors.

The project began with a coiling diagram based on the combination of sinusoidal, continuous and periodic functions. This initial diagram was based on an equation originally developed by Myung Min Son, Claude Ballini and George L Legendre for the first Rising Masses studio at the Architectural Association (AA) in London. The next step was to introduce a series of 'deformers' that bring eccentricity and variation in size to the series of coils, resulting in a more complex scheme based on a three-dimensional curve.

The conceptual leap occurs when, in contrast with other parametric trends, the formal agenda of the Hinging Tower embraces a new 'coarseness' or

The morphology of the tower dictates the configuration of the circulation system and the programmatic pattern.

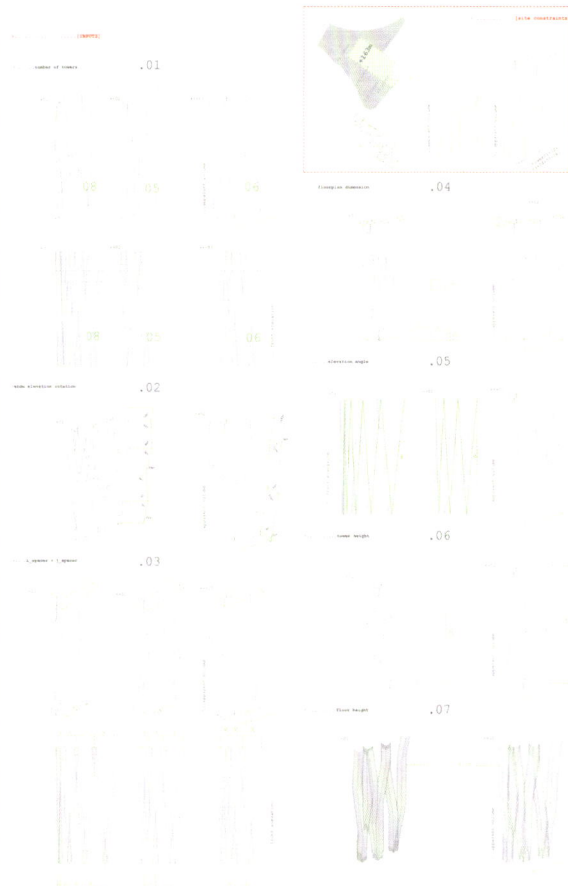

Within the infinite morphological variation that the diagram offers, the form of the tower is shaped by local conditions and the specificities of the site.

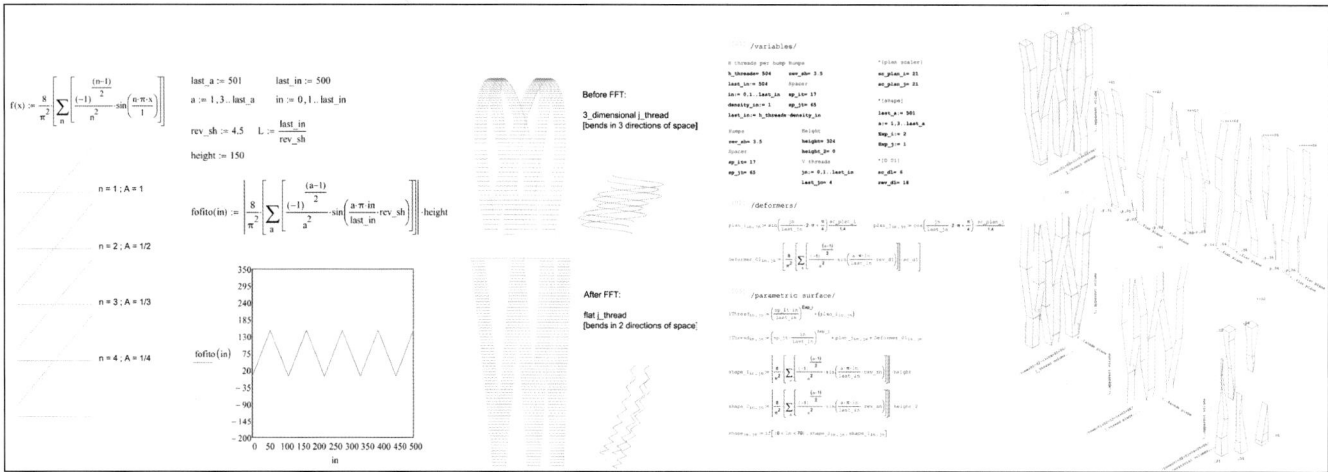

The application of fast Fourier transforms (FFTs) reduces discontinuous, complex three-dimensional geometries to simple/developable surfaces.

The tower's parametric surface description or diagram is constructed upon a number of variables that increase the spectrum of differentiation and at the same time make it more specific to site and programme conditions.

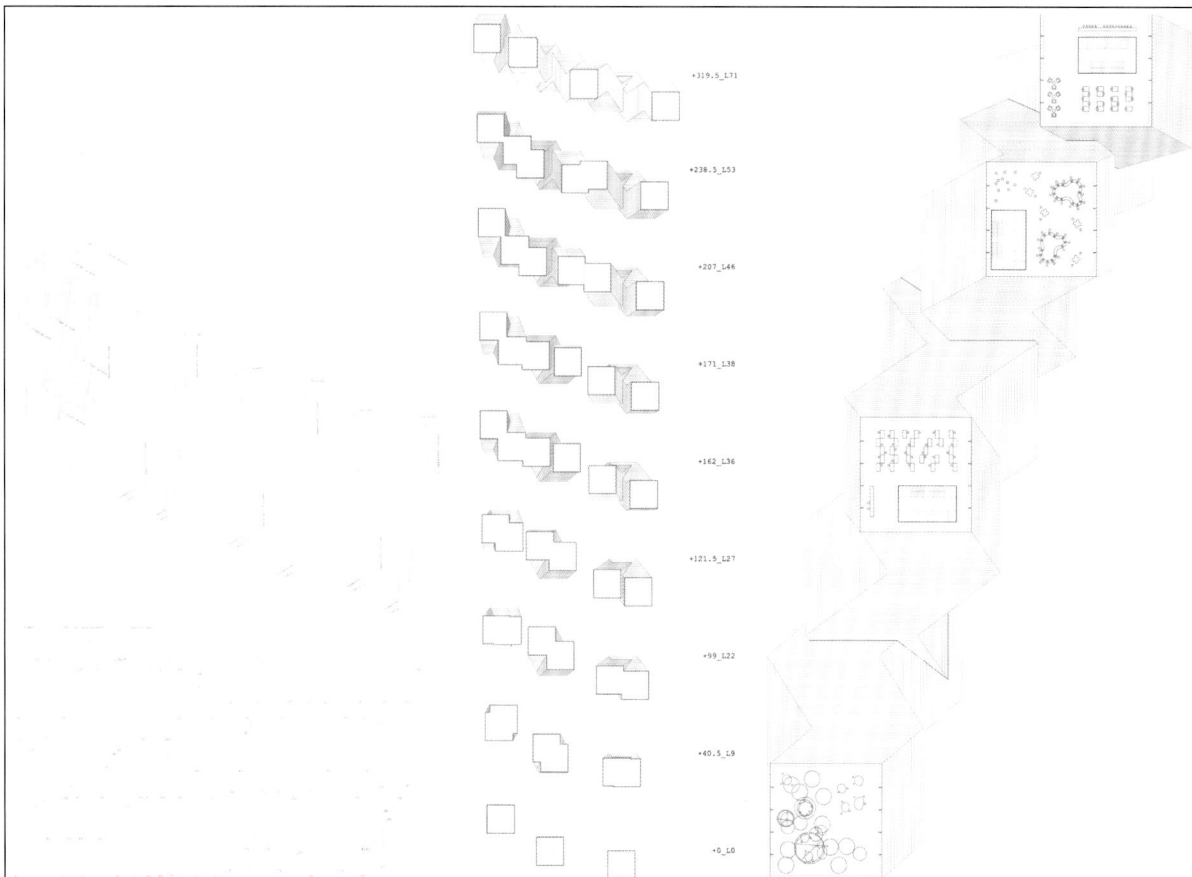

Formally, the Hinging Tower calls for a new 'coarseness' or 'low-resolution curvature'.

Starting with an elemental square plan, a mechanism of repetition driven by the diagram or mathematical function produces a variety of distinctive spaces and great organisational potential.

The displacement of the 'towers' within the tower reveals the coiling effect of the sinusoidal, continuous and periodic functions.

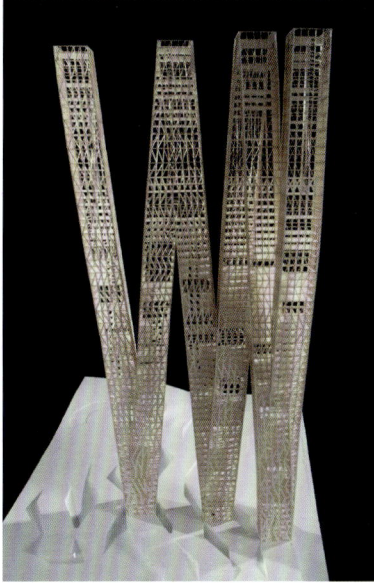

Typical tower configuration is inverted by reducing the footprint and maximizing the area of the upper levels.

The intertwining effect brings a double benefit: structural strength and circulation flexibility.

'low-resolution curvature' to optimise construction. Hence the introduction of fast Fourier transforms (FFTs) allows the possibility of a discontinuous, complex three-dimensional geometry reduced to simple/developable surfaces.

Along the same lines, the goodness of a square plan is acknowledged for its programmatic efficiency and simplicity; in fact, the mathematical notation of the square is equivalent to a 'coarse' circle plotted with only four points. By providing a catalogue of distinctive spaces, qualitatively and quantitatively, through the simple repetition of the square plan, the diagram of the tower aims to generate new organisational potentialities capable of producing difference. The interlocking areas of the 'towers' within the tower form the critical moments of the production of spatial diversity. The morphological configuration of the space determines the programmatic pattern of the tower that begins to take shape: every programme automatically locates itself in the most suitable spot.

The process implies some degree of uncertainty. It is at this juncture that the architect's imagination, understood as the mediation between intuition and understanding, comes into play as a critical tool, operating to identify new potentials. The Hinging Tower exemplifies a speculative architectural practice, conscious of its position within history and aware of its potential as a creative reservoir, probing purposefully the unknown for new models and opportunities. Mathematics here is the way to generate architectural protocols or relational systems that comprehend the whole spectrum of formal variation. ∆

IMPLICIT FIELDS©
MOCAPE SHENZHEN PRC

GEORGE L
LEGENDRE
AND MAX
KAHLEN

During late 2007, guest-editor **George L Legendre** of IJP Corporation and **Max Kahlen** of Dyvik & Kahlen, Architecture, joined forces to develop a competition design for the Museum of Contemporary Art and Planning Exhibition (MOCAPE) in Shenzhen. One of the great challenges of the brief was the subdivision of a great expanse of programmed spaces. In order to tackle this, they created the design concept of 'natural erosion' for which they developed their own parametric surface model, the implicit field©.

George L Legendre and Max Kahlen for IJP, MOCAPE Shenzhen, China, 2007
Perspective rendering and front view towards the People's Palace. In this 'flat-topped' version of the original seed, the distribution of adjacent depressions is statistically controlled by sampling a sinusoidal path cutting across the field.

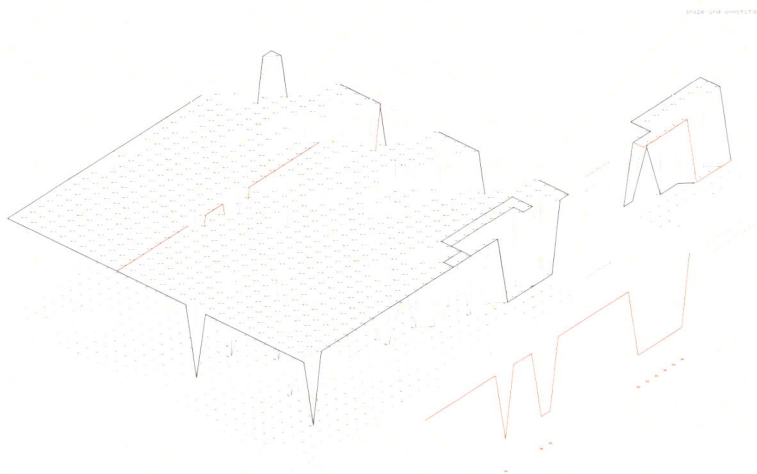

In the summer of 2007, the announcement of an international competition for the Museum of Contemporary Art and Planning Exhibition (MOCAPE) of Shenzhen (People's Republic of China) marked the final major building venture in the newly redeveloped city centre of this fast-growing metropolis. The requirements included an unusual programmatic mixture of art galleries and administrative planning offices splashed over 88,000 square metres (950,000 square feet), challenging competitors to adapt their ultra-specific working methods to the amorphousness and enormity of a contemporary socioeconomic brief.

The joint entry featured here reprised the theme of natural erosion, which offers a practical way of tackling sprawling programmatic masses. Eroding is similar to subdividing larger blocks into smaller units, with the key difference that here subdivision is mathematical, continuous and periodic. Specifically, the concept makes use of the elastic dimensional properties of a parametric surface model known as implicit field©. Based on the aggregation of several periodic functions, the implicit field© is defined by the discontinuities between these functions, which are the salient feature of this surface and form the basis for a building proposal deriving its structure, layout and access to natural light from wherever such discontinuities occur.

The first step was eliminating all curvature from the surface and distributing discontinuities across it by sampling three periodically shaped troughs. Fine-tuning the interval of the sampling revealed more of the sine-, cosine- or tangent-shaped troughs, producing in return an array of punctual, linear or superficial depressions. Early on these depressions were seen as a freely distributed structural arrangement and earmarked as conduits of natural light and bending moments, breaking what might have been, given its 150-metre (500-foot) long side, an implausibly deep building.

The implicit field© occupies almost the entirety of its allotted footprint. The dispersal of depressions erodes its mass from north to south to produce internal and external spaces. The process is orientated: on the south side the extra sampling results in a porous front suitably

Ground Level 1:500
底层平面

Mezzanine Level 1:500
夹层平面

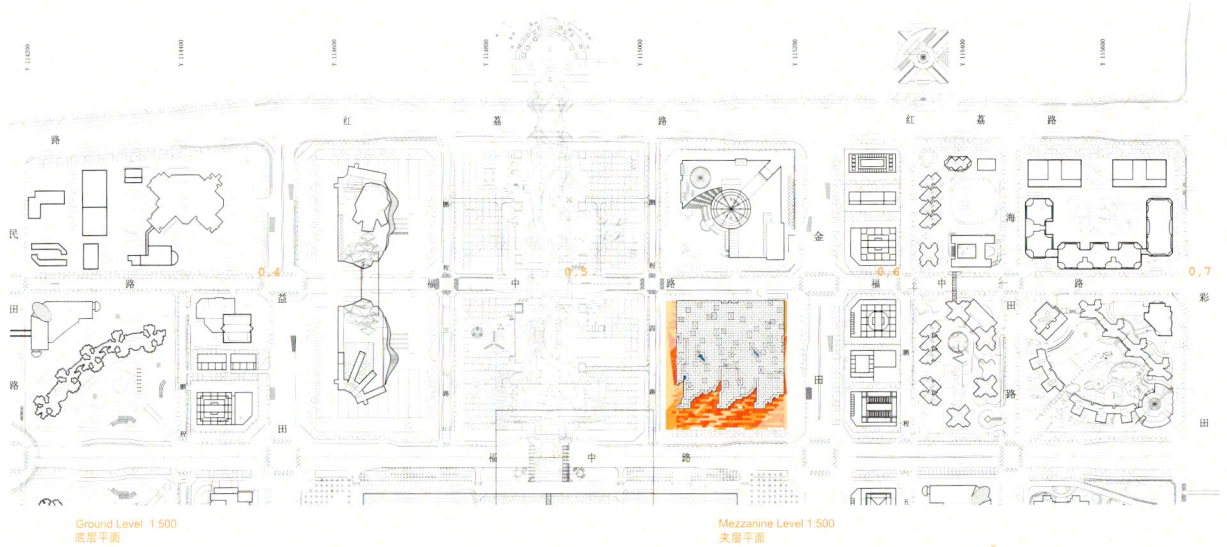

**George L Legendre and Max Kahlen for IJP,
MOCAPE Shenzhen, China, 2007**
Site plan and detailed floor plans. Space flows
freely around cones, whose original position
is statistically calculated to attain sparser
or denser concentrations of matter. Larger
programmatic spaces such as exhibition
galleries fit into the 'empty' areas of the plan.
Smaller offices and workshops colonise the
interstitial spaces in between.

Final model (details).

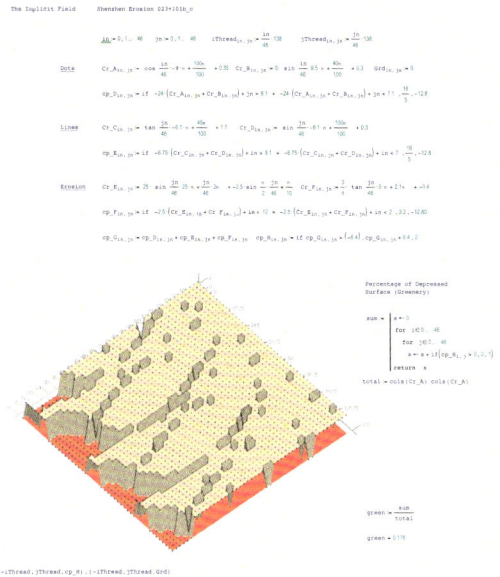

George L Legendre and Max Kahlen, Analytic
Mathematics implicit field©, 2004–7
Worksheet featuring a (simplified) set of
equations for the project.

monumental in use and wide enough to channel the mass movement of visitors.

Based on a single three-dimensional superficial expanse, the 80,000-square-metre (860,000-square-foot) interior can have no extraneous partitions: it is the surface itself that must provide them. This constraint resulted in the integration of the exhibition functions within one open plan, strategically subdivided by the only mode of partition available: a variable density of adjacent discontinuities. On the ground, space wraps freely around closed, semi-open or open depressions creating generally differentiated patterns of access and circulation. The number and final position of the depressions is not predetermined, but is statistically calculated to produce average amounts of aggregation or dispersal. This in turn determines how the space is utilised: rooms requiring clear spans and a generous programmatic footprint, such as exhibition galleries, settle preferably into the 'empty' areas of the plan, whereas small offices, ancillary spaces and production workshops are likely to colonise the compact interstitial spaces nestled between proximate depressions, drawing enclosure, fresh air and natural light as needed.

By size and organisational pattern, like satellite images of the artificial borders of large mid-western US states, the MOCAPE's plans look more like geographic regions than interior layouts, which in the absence of any actual boundary other than the occasional occurrence of depressions is what they actually are.

Paradoxically, the level of control that comes with such a mathematical approach leaves the work vulnerable to the critique that it is deterministic, that is a misperception: beyond the raw statistical aggregations of density versus sparseness, it is not possible to precisely determine anything in this museum. Critically it is an unusually massive building; the variegation of the formula offers an unscripted relief from the artificial problem of composition, as well as from the grim sterilities of repetition. ∆

Text © 2011 John Wiley & Sons Ltd. Images © George L Legendre and Max Kahlen

Philippe Morel

SENSE AND SENSIBILIA

Since the 1960s, innovation has become one of the sole purposes of architecture and membership of the avant-garde an underlying motive force. **Philippe Morel** of EZCT Architecture & Design Research juxtaposes the 'sense and sensibilia' of mathematics, now widely adopted by the 'creative minorities', against the idealism of mid 20th-century modernism.

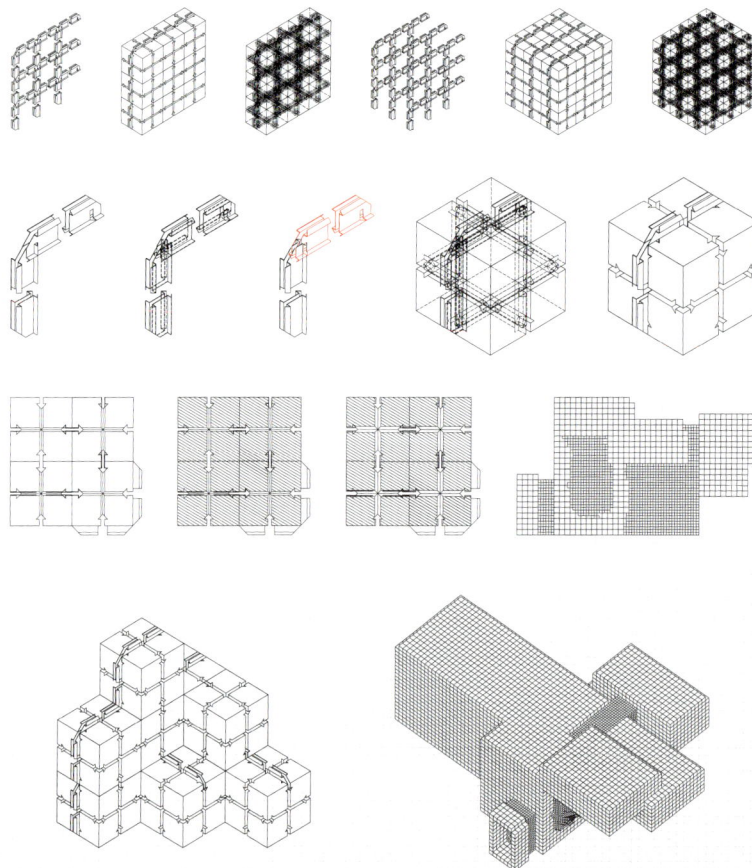

Figure 1. EZCT Architecture & Design Research, Universal House and Assembly Element, 2009–11
The concept of a fully generic and voxel-based architecture (free of topological constraints) comes from EZCT's first investigations, embodied in the Studies on Optimisation: Computational Chair Design using Genetic Algorithm project (2004). The current research, which refers back to that of Nicholas Negroponte and John Frazer, is oriented towards a more precise, articulate and constructive approach.

I can think much better about a formula than about a geometrical object because I never trust that a geometric picture, a drawing, is sufficiently generic.
— Alain Connes in an Interview by Georges Skandalis and Catherine Goldstein, *Newsletter of the European Mathematical Society*, Issue 63, March 2007, pp 27–8[1]

Returning to the Roots of Contemporary Sensibility

A brilliant intuition of the "radical" movement was that normality as a shared value no longer existed, that all society now constituted a set of creating minorities and that the critical and creating methods of the avant-garde had become the only practicable ones. The project therefore changed its status, lost its methodological unity and accepted innovation as the sole purpose of creativity. For these intrinsic reasons, the "radical" movement refused any stylistic unity, any recognisable formal code, to act, on the contrary, as a movement which destroyed within it any trace of the old search for modern certainties. For this reason, it has always been difficult, if not impossible, to file it under a critical category.
— Andrea Branzi, '*Le mouvement radical*', *Architectures expérimentales 1950–2000*[2]

It is with these words that Andrea Branzi commented four decades later on the general philosophy of the Italian movements of the second avant-garde. A philosophy that, in a pop society with omnipresent technology, recognised that the avant-garde had became the new normality. The title of this article, 'Sense and Sensibilia', evokes the significant transformations that were taking place in the early 1960s, and is named after John L Austin's 1962 book of the same title[3] rather than Aristotle's classic philosophical text (*De sensu et sensibilibus*). Austin's work reasserts the pre-eminence of ordinary language placed against a logical background. This language, which moves on the logical ocean that characterises Western civilisation, defines the current relationship between 'sensible things' and mathematics. These things now shared and produced by 'all the creating minorities' are a thousand leagues away from Modernist productions. As for their mathematics, they have evacuated all traces of idealism related to the 'old search for modern certainties'.

It is thus against this context, today and not only in architecture, that we are dealing with mathematics. It is a context inseparable from the social transformations that were established from 1960 onwards – the trigger for which was the hedonistic consumption of goods and services developed during the Second World War – and that defined the theoretical directions taken at this time by architectural research. Beyond their apparent incompatibility, this research forms an extremely coherent set that can be defined as four priority 'topics': 1) the type and role of permanent avant-gardism; 2) mass communication as a source of semiotic pop; 3) the dimensions of the town and its architecture which reach the sizes necessary for their autonomisation; 4) the role of an idealised language of Modern architecture in the face of

Figure 2. Philippe Morel (curator), 'Architecture Beyond Form: The Computational Turn', Exhibition at the Maison de l'Architecture et de la Ville, Marseille, 22 February to 20 April 2007
The exhibition was a reading of the last 45 years of architecture, starting from 1963 and Peter Eisenman's PhD thesis, 'The Formal Basis of Modern Architecture'.

its 'vulgar' versions, and the correspondence between a new codified language of architecture and the general codification that has appeared in linguistics and information sciences.[4]

It is possible to draw up a quick genealogy of these four research directions, which were followed and encountered to varying degrees by the vast majority of architects active in the 1960s. The first was the principal motif of the neo avant-gardes – led by Archizoom and Superstudio – before they turned their attention to the widespread urban condition of global megastructures. The second was in the US, which led the field of mass communications, and was the object of America's pop architecture that was to culminate in the 'Learning from Las Vegas' study by Robert Venturi, Denise Scott-Brown and Steven Izenour, published as a book in 1972.[5] The third was the object of the European functionalism critique from neo-regionalism to Team X and Aldo Rossi's Tendenza.[6] The fourth was that of Peter Eisenman who, in 1963, on finishing his doctorate,[7] broached a 're-examination of the formal'. It was also, a decade later, that of the humanist positivists such as Christopher Alexander.[8]

Of course it goes without saying that this categorisation has in fact never been so clear. Above all, it says nothing about the ideological positions taken by the theoretician architects. Despite this, for an attentive observer, noticing for example that the interest shown by Eisenman in language as such is inseparable from a critique of functionalism, this categorisation clarifies that which has happened since 1960, and principally that which is understood by 'Postmodernism' – a Postmodernism now increasingly appearing as an attempt to create a synthesis of the various issues of the 1960s mentioned above. It is thus through this propensity for summary that it is possible to perceive both the multiple interests in current Japanese architecture (neo-materialism, advanced engineering, information technology and electronics) and the architecture of Coop-Himmelb(l)au or Rem Koolhaas – the most intentionally synthetic of all. It is also thus, although from a different perspective, that we can understand the works of FOA or the intricacy of Greg Lynn,[9] the generic

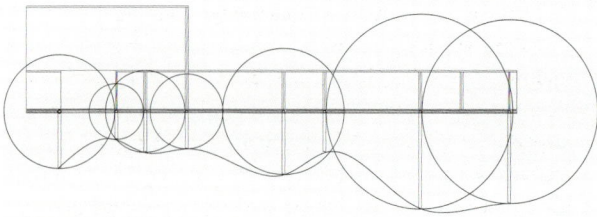

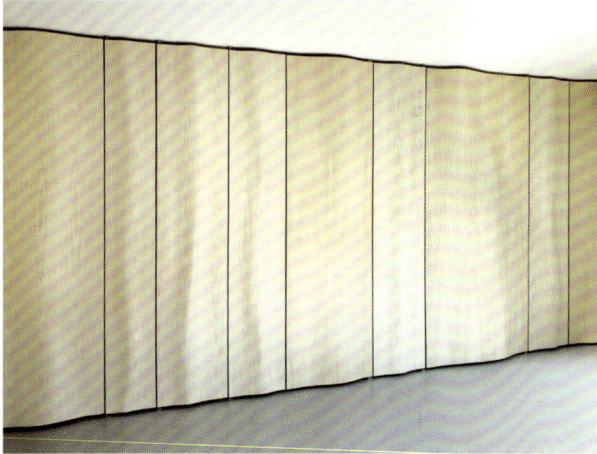

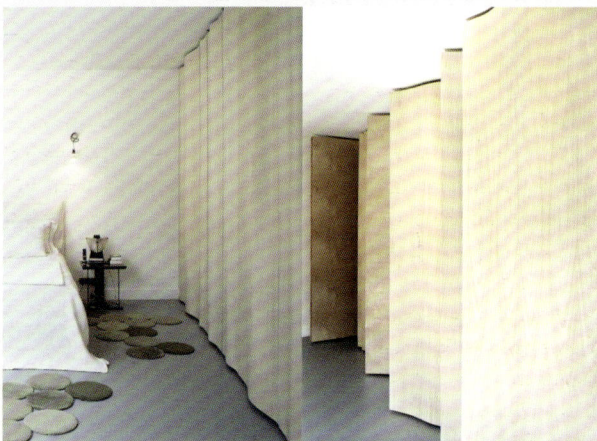

Figure 3. EZCT Architecture & Design Research, Seroussi Cupboard, 2005–8
The fully scripted panel system leads to an entirely automated fabrication process. The double-curvature surfaces of the panels are glued on to a light structure. Everything is built from standard and cheap wood with vertical T-shape steel reinforcements. The algorithms calculate the admissible deformation of the veneer wood (which is supposed to be close to zero) and propose different solutions. Due to very strict constraints, all stainless-steel hinges were conceived by EZCT.

nature of which is derived from a different observation to that of Koolhaas, but indirectly very well summarised by the personal opinion of Anthony Vidler: 'That in which I am involved is another type of identity of the subject, built within self-generated spaces by software which knows nothing of the distinction between animal and human; an identity which, at least for the time being, is more concerned with the morphological and topological transformations of an external skin or a shell, than by the human dimensions of an interior.'[10]

The summary of the major themes of the postwar critical re-readings of Modernism is therefore the major project of Postmodernism. The inherent difficulty in such a project makes it possible to understand both the theoretical inflation which appeared in the 1970s – when architects attempted to link

everything to the quasi-totality of surrounding theories with deliberately funny or sometimes unintentionally grotesque connections – and the relative failure of this summary. Since 1990, the onset of the Internet and information technology has made the use of conceptual and practical tools a dominant focus. Though it has shared with Postmodernism the theorisation of social transformations, apparent in Fredric Jameson's analysis of the Bonaventure Hotel of 1988,[11] it has also introduced a new preoccupation with 'deep structure'. This theorisation was partly carried out by, among others, Lynn and by Alejandro Zaera-Polo, for whom the question of form was in particular the reflection of a reading of the transformations of technological civilisation and not the imprisonment within a new mathematical idealism. Idealism often only offers an anachronistic update of Modernist formal research or a new belief in the participation of architects in the advancement of science. It is by the refusal of this naive belief that Lynn and Zaera-Polo appear as 'experienced intellectuals', the latter being 'those who have understood that they are not at the head of a change but in an experienced rearguard which measures the difference and the progress of technology in relation to the human sphere'.[12]

Conversely, it is due to the half-acceptance translated by the zealous application of science – an application without any scientific foundation or fact – that Alexander may be considered an 'inexperienced intellectual'; intellectual, considering the relationships between the social development and that of the sciences within a historical invariance, deducing from the constant validity of theorems and algorithms the permanence of sensible things. For this belief in the logical continuity which extends from the logico-mathematical laws to the acts had, well before Alexander, been denounced as the pitfall par excellence of moral philosophy, which did not prevent High-Modernism (for example, that of Rudolf Carnap in *The Logical Structure of the World*)[13] from running aground. A pitfall as noted by Nietzsche in the following terms:

> Socrates and Plato, great doubters and admirable innovators were nevertheless incredibly naive in regard to that fatal prejudice, that profound error which maintains that "the right knowledge must necessarily be followed by the right action". … the contrary position is in fact the naked reality which has been demonstrated daily and hourly from time immemorial.[14]

The 'Visible' Is Not 'Sensible'

As such, we cannot be anything other than surprised today to still see in the many works broadly using algorithms and mathematics – and which works can really do without them? – a resurgence of an idealism in the style of Alexander. Just as the latter's relational graphs were influenced at the time by progress in topology and their applications in the form of operational research, the frenzied mathematical idealisms and biomimicry tendencies of today's architecture are nothing less than a new Zeitgeist. As for the less complex approaches, more coolly and visibly logical, although the best remind us by their very radicalism that 'logic is not necessarily as logical as all that', that we 'use it exactly as we wish' and that what is important 'is that things are logical, "in a certain way"',[15] the

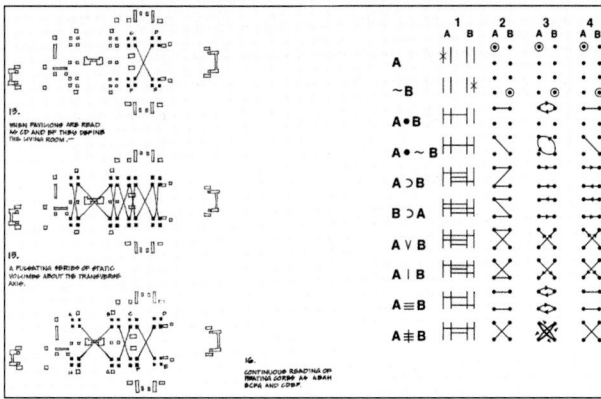

Figure 4. Proposed connection between Peter Eisenman's PhD thesis drawings (1963) and Gerrit Mariè Mes' Logic Diagrams (drawn in the 1960s), illustrating the Zeitgeist of the young Eisenman
Mes, a Dutch-born surgeon based in Krugersdorp, South Africa, developed this variation of logic diagrams of Martin Gardner in the 1960s: directed and undirected lines, and a combination of both (a line without an arrow means that travel may be either way). While being more or less opposed to any kind of Zeitgeist, Peter Eisenman's work is in fact highly related to its surrounding visual and epistemological culture – the sign of a rationalist mind. Original image from Martin Gardner, *Logic Machines and Diagrams*, University of Chicago Press, 1958.

majority of them come down to an opportunistic Postmodern inclusion of an additional variable: a dose of easy spectacular computation and additional effectiveness.

While for Postmodernism there are no longer any aesthetics with an immediate value – 'the ideologem of elegance and chic, of the dear form, is united with its opposite, punk art, trash, the sordid and the wretched'[16] – the mathematics of sensible things becomes foreign to the aim that it is supposed to serve. It is then that the Postmodern paradox appears; at each new attempt to perceptively approach a thing, the result is invariably the distancing from this thing. Such is the Postmodern reality which, on the one hand by the exponential rise in the number of images in circulation and their importance in scientific research submerges us in the field of the apparently sensible, and on the other by the inflation in digital data and the not less exponential growth in algorithmics of IT programming and mathematical methods, freezes all of our immediate perceptions. Although this paradox is not, by essence, Postmodern, it has reached a degree previously unknown thanks to information technology, which has allowed our relationship with the world to enter a new era; and as Marshall McLuhan and Quentin Fiore point out, not without humour: 'Beside it, the wheel is a mere hula hoop, even though the latter should not be entirely neglected.'[17]

The wheel was just a hoop insofar as even in the boldest projections it was still only a representation of the world through the image of a perpetual movement, a representation broadly surpassed today in computer simulations. As observed by the epistemologist Franck Varenne, whose recent works on the integrative and pluri-formalised simulations in botany constitute (using scientific practices) a rigorous critique of any mathematical idealism, science faces two contradictions. The first, a traditional one, is that the researcher 'still believes he is researching the "laws of nature" whilst in practice he is first of all contributing to dispersing this kind of representation';[18] the other, specifically linked to the arrival of information technology and its intrinsic possibilities for repetitions identical to virtual experiences, is that the latter are often preferable to any 'real' experience.

We should point out an amazing opinion among engineers about the use of computer simulation in industry – especially in aeronautics: they are more and more convinced that in many cases, real experiments are superfluous. They think that a good simulation is far better than an experiment on a prototype – apart from the financial considerations. Indeed, when you read Von Neumann, you see that analogue models are inferior to digital models because of the accuracy control limitations in the first ones. Following this argument, if you consider a prototype, or a real experiment in natural sciences, is it anything else than an analogue model of itself? … So the possibilities to make sophisticated and accurate measures on this model – ie to make sophisticated real experiments – rapidly are decreasing, while your knowledge is increasing. These considerations are troublesome because it sounds as if nature was not a good model of itself and had to be replaced and simulated to be properly questioned and tested![19]

This observation of the change in current scientific practices throws precious light on that which is known today as the mathematics of sensible things. Indeed, added to the reductionism which began at the end of the 19th century and ended in the logical positivism and attempts at a complete axiomatisation (which although proved impossible will nevertheless have a holding influence, for example with Bourbakism in France) is a new distancing of the sensible specific to information technology. This distancing is no longer based on the Modernist abstraction as perceived in the universal grids of Piet Mondrian or Mies van der Rohe, but on the contrary on a new 'logical figuration'. Although stylistic Postmodernism had perceived the cultural nature of this figuration, recognising that that which separated it from the void was nothing but its state of 'capitalism transformed into image', it had not really understood the computational logic leading to our logical replication of the world, the latter inheriting as much from Carnap as from the history of scientific notation and symbolism, programming languages or the development of material technologies[20] as from Guy Debord or Jameson. It is in this sense that the synthesis of Postmodern architecture referred to earlier in this article is no

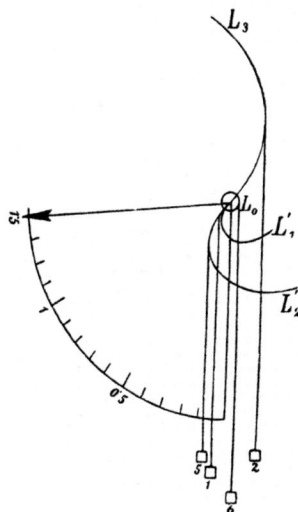

Figure 5. Karl Exner, Balance for Equation, undated
During the 19th century and until the advent of digital computers, scientists searched for mechanical techniques to facilitate complex calculations. From *Uber eine Maschine zur Auflösung höherer Gleichungen* (*About a machine for the resolution of high-order equations*), Vienna, 1881.

52A: General convexity, especially 52A55: Spherical geometr

52B: Polytopes and polyhedr

52B05: Combinatorial properties (number of faces, shortest paths, etc.), See also 05Cxx
52B10: Three-dimensional polytopes
52B11: n-dimensional polytopes
52B12: Special polytopes (linear programming, centrally symmetric, etc)
52B15: Symmetry properties of polytopes
52B20: Lattice polytopes (including relations with commutative algebra and algebraic geometry), See also 06A08, 13F20, 13Hxx
52B22: Shellability [new in 2000]
52B35: Gale and other diagrams

52B40: Matroids (realizations in the context of convex polytopes, convexity in combinatorial structures, etc.), See Also 05B35
52B45: Dissections and valuations (Hilbert's third problem, etc.)
52B55: Computational aspects related to convexity, For computational geometry and algorithms, See 68020, 8025, 68U05; for numerical algorithms, See 65Yxx
52B60: Isoperimetric problems for polytopes
52B70: Polyhedral manifolds
52B99: None of the above but in this section

52C: Discrete geometr

54A: Generalitie
54B: Basic construction
54C: Maps and general types of spaces defined by map
54D: Fairly general propertie

54E: Spaces with richer structures especially metric space

54E35: Metric spaces, metrizability
54E40: Special maps on metric spaces
54E45: Compact (locally compact) metric spaces
54E50: Complete metric spaces
54E52: Baire category, Baire spaces
54E55: Bitopologies
54E70: Probabilistic metric spaces
54E99: None of the above but in this section

54E05: Proximity structures and generalizations
54E15: Uniform structures and generalizations
54E17: Nearness spaces
54E18: p-spaces, M-spaces, sigma-spaces, etc.
54E20: Stratifiable spaces, cosmic spaces, etc.
54E25: Semimetric spaces
54E30: Moore spaces

54F: Special propertie
54G: Peculiar space
54H: Connections with other structures, application
54J05: Nonstandard topology, See also 03H0

57M: Low-dimensional topology, including Knot theor

57M05: Fundamental group, presentations, free differential calculus
57M07: Topological methods in group theory
57M10: Covering spaces
57M12: Special coverings, e.g. branched
57M15: Relations with graph theory, See also 05Cxx
57M20: Two-dimensional complexes
57M25: Knots and links in S^3, For higher dimensions, See 57Q45
57M27: Invariants of knots and 3-manifolds [new in 2000]
57M30: Wild knots and surfaces, etc., wild embeddings
57M35: Dehn's lemma, sphere theorem, loop theorem, asphericity
57M40: Characterizations of E^3 and S^3 (Poincaré conjecture), See also 57N12
57M50: Geometric structures on low-dimensional manifolds
57M60: Group actions in low dimensions
57M99: None of the above but in this section

57N: Topological manifold
57P: Generalized manifolds, see also 18F1
57Q: PL-topology (Triangulation is part of 57R

57R: Differential topology; For foundational questions of differentiable manifolds, see 58AXX; for infinite-dimensional manifolds, See 58BX

57R45: Singularities of differentiable mappings
57R50: Diffeomorphisms
57R52: Isotopy
57R55: Differentiable structures
57R56: Topological quantum field theories [new in 2000]
57R57: Applications of global analysis to structures on manifolds, See also 58-XX
57R58: Floer homology [new in 2000]
57R60: Homotopy spheres, Poincaré conjecture
57R65: Surgery and handlebodies
57R67: Surgery obstructions, Wall groups, See also 19J25
57R70: Critical points and critical submanifolds
57R75: O- and SO-cobordism
57R77: Complex cobordism (U- and SU-cobordism), See also 55N22
57R80: h- and s-cobordism
57R85: Equivariant cobordism
57R90: Other types of cobordism, See 55N22
57R91: Equivariant algebraic topology of manifolds
57R95: Realizing cycles by submanifolds
57R99: None of the above but in this section

57R05: Triangulating
57R10: Smoothing
57R12: Smooth approximations
57R15: Specialized structures on manifolds (spin manifolds, framed manifolds, etc.)
57R17: Symplectic and contact topology [new in 2000]
57R19: Algebraic topology on manifolds
57R20: Characteristic classes and numbers
57R22: Topology of vector bundles and fiber bundles, See Also 55Rxx
57R25: Vector fields, frame fields
57R27: Controllability of vector fields on C^\infty and real-analytic manifolds, See also 490xx, 58F40, 93B05
57R30: Foliations; geometric theory
57R32: Classifying spaces for foliations; Gelfand-Fuks cohomology, See also 58H10
57R35: Differentiable mappings
57R40: Embeddings
57R42: Immersions

57S: Topological transformation groups, See also 20F34, 22-XX, 54H15

58D0

57T: Homology and homotopy of topological groups and related structures

---

Figure 6. Philippe Morel, Visual and Diagrammatic Representation of the Mathematical Subject Classification (MSC) Concerning Geometry, 2005
The diagram was first made to illustrate a lecture entitled 'Some Geometries' at the 'Loopholes Between Theory and Practice' symposium at Harvard Graduate School of Design in April 2005. The idea was to show that geometry is not a classically homogeneous field, but a very complex and intricate landscape.

51: GEOMETRY

VEX AND DISCRETE GEOMETRY

- 51A: Linear incidence geometry
- 51B: Nonlinear incidence geometry
- 51C05: Ring geometry
- 51D: Geometric closure systems
- 51E: Finite geometry and special incidence structures

51F: Metric geometry (distance, lengths and angles; triangulation)

- 51F05: Absolute planes
- 51F10: Absolute spaces
- 51F15: Reflection groups, reflection geometries, *See also 20H10, 20H15; for Coxeter groups, See 20F55*
- 51F20: Congruence and orthogonality, *See also 20H05*
- 51F25: Orthogonal and unitary groups, *See also 20H05*
- 51F99: None of the above but in this section

- 51G05: Ordered geometries (ordered incidence structures, etc.)
- 51H: Topological geometry
- 51J: Incidence groups
- 51K: Distance geometry
- 51L: Geometric order structures, *See also 53C75*

51M: Real and complex geometry

- 51M04: Euclidean problems in Euclidean Geometries
- 51M05: Euclidean geometries (general) and generalizations
- 51M09: Elementary problems in hyperbolic and elliptic geometries
- 51M10: Hyperbolic and elliptic geometries (general) and generalizations
- 51M15: Geometric constructions
- 51M16: Inequalities and extremum problems, For convex problems, *See 52A40*
- 51M20: Polyhedra and polytopes; regular figures, division of spaces, *See also 51F15*
- 51M25: Length, area and volume, *See also 26B15*
- 51M30: Line geometries and their generalizations, *See also 53A25*
- 51M35: Synthetic treatment of fundamental manifolds in projective geometries (Grassmannians, Veronesians and their generalizations), *See also 14M15*
- 51M99: None of the above but in this section

54: GENERAL TOPOLOGY

51N: Analytic and descriptive geometry

- 51N05: Descriptive geometry, *See also 65D17, 68U07*
- 51N10: Affine analytic geometry
- 51N15: Projective analytic geometry
- 51N20: Euclidean analytic geometry
- 51N25: Analytic geometry with other transformation groups
- 51N30: Geometry of classical groups, *See also 20Gxx, 14L35*
- 51N35: Questions of classical algebraic geometry, *See also 14Nxx*
- 51N99: None of the above but in this section

57: MANIFOLDS

- 51P05: Geometry and physics

53: DIFFERENTIAL GEOMETRY

- 53A: Classical differential geometry
- 53B: Local differential geometry
- 53C: Global differential geometry, *See also 51H25, 58-XX; for related bundle theory, See 55RXX, 57RXX*
- 53D: Symplectic geometry, contact geometry *See also 37Jxx, 70Gxx, 70Hxx [new in 2000]*

55: ALGEBRAIC TOPOLOGY

- 55M: Classical topics, For the topology of Euclidean spaces and manifolds, *See 57NXX 57NXX*
- 55N: Homology and cohomology theories, *See also 57TXX*

GEOMETRY MINDMAP

55P: Homotopy theory, For simple homotopy type, *See 57Q10*

- 55P05: Homotopy extension properties, cofibrations
- 55P10: Homotopy equivalences
- 55P15: Classification of homotopy type
- 55P20: Eilenberg-MacLane spaces
- 55P25: Spanier-Whitehead duality
- 55P30: Eckmann-Hilton duality
- 55P35: Loop spaces
- 55P40: Suspensions
- 55P42: Stable homotopy theory, spectra
- 55P43: Spectra with additional structure (E_\infty, A_\infty, ring spectra, etc.) *[new in 2000]*
- 55P45: H-spaces and duals
- 55P47: Infinite loop spaces
- 55P48: Loop space machines, operads, *See also 18D50 [new in 2000]*
- 55P55: Shape theory, *See also 54C56, 55Q07*
- 55P57: Proper homotopy theory *[new in 2000]*
- 55P60: Localization and completion
- 55P62: Rational homotopy theory
- 55P65: Homotopy functors
- 55P91: Equivariant homotopy theory, *See also 19L47*
- 55P92: Relations between equivariant and nonequivariant homotopy theory *[new in 2000]*
- 55P99: None of the above but in this section

55Q: Homotopy groups

- 55Q05: Homotopy groups, general; sets of homotopy classes
- 55Q07: Shape groups
- 55Q10: Stable homotopy groups
- 55Q15: Whitehead products and generalizations
- 55Q20: Homotopy groups of wedges, joins, and simple spaces
- 55Q25: Hopf invariants
- 55Q35: Operations in homotopy groups
- 55Q40: Homotopy groups of spheres
- 55Q45: Stable homotopy of spheres
- 55Q50: J-morphism, *See also 19L20*
- 55Q51: v_n-periodicity *[new in 2000]*
- 55Q52: Homotopy groups of special spaces
- 55Q55: Cohomotopy groups
- 55Q70: Homotopy groups of special types, *See also 55N05, 55N07*
- 55Q91: Equivariant homotopy groups, *See also 19L47*
- 55Q99: None of the above but in this section

- 55R: Fiber spaces and bundles, *See also 18F15, 32LXX, 46M20, 57RXX 57R20, 57R22, 57R25*
- 55S: Operations and obstructions
- 55T: Spectral sequences, *See also 18G40, 55R20*
- 55U: Applied homological algebra and category theory, *See also 18GXX*

Figure 7. Alessandro Mendini, Straw Chair, 1975
A temporary and self-destroying natural chair.

more complete than that of the four fundamental forces in physics, if it can be or if it is desirable. To complete it we should add to Venturi's irony the complete disillusions of Stanley Tigerman,[21] but we most of all should add to the work of the Austrian and Italian radicals, to the deconstructions of the 1980s and to the digital research of the 1990s or the urban and cultural theorisations of Koolhaas, a veritable investigation of the 'computational logic of late capitalism'. Such an investigation would have recourse to algorithms and mathematics beyond an umpteenth passive formalism in order to evaluate them on an entirely new 'critical' base. This goes against the new stylistic unity of algorithmic, parametric or biomimetic architecture, or calls for this unity, the new 'recognisable formal code' which retains the 'trace of the old search for modern certainties'.

De Novo Nature, Life as a 'Good Simulation'

Broaching the mathematics of sensible things is, in reality, the same as dealing with a crucial aspect of a civilisation in which all the artefacts and stimuli are becoming mathematical productions. With Modernist designers who embodied mathematics in physical objects, the problem of the sensible remained 'easy', but we have to admit that it is very different today. Mathematics and logics exist now as a pervasive physical and immaterial environment, as '*a new domestic landscape*', which is perfectly exemplified by the annual production of theorems estimated in 1976 by Stanislaw Ulam as 200,000.[22] Such a landscape, or ecosystem, which is inseparable from information technology is proof of the omnipresence of information technology mentioned above on the subject of a digital nature which itself is a better model than the original. Thanks to this quality, (computer) simulations are not at all a vulgar pretence; this copy which could lead only to the search for the original – a quest that is not just romantic but above all reactionary in its ignorance of the reality of the facts – is a better original.

It is in this recognition of the arrival of digital reality, a major scientific fact, that the entire difference between stylistic and literary Postmodernism and scientific and effective Postmodernism is played out. And this is what Eisenman had summarised perfectly in the title of his essay 'A Matrix in the Jungle' (2003), on this occasion returning to Jameson:

Several years ago, Fredric Jameson said that the computer would be capable of giving us a new nature; not an unnatural nature but a nature derived directly from computerised algorithm and processes. Such a thought means it would no longer be necessary to look at nature with the same eyes through which Le Corbusier observed the natural shapes of D'Arcy Thompson. (It was precisely from the latter's immense body of work that Le Corbusier deduced most of the plastic, spiralled shapes and complex proportional relationships that produced his 'Modulor' system.)[23]

In its relationship to things, and more broadly in its relationship to the environment, current Postmodernism allows little room for hope. Insofar as it is not a language and therefore it 'does not give a representation that can be mobilised by a human spirit (a concept)',[24] computer simulation does not lay itself open for the linguistic research typical of the Postmodernism of the 1980s any more than a 're-examination of the formal' in the manner of the young Eisenman, irrespective of the quality of their transposition into a computational environment. Furthermore, as it is itself experimental proof that nature need not search behind the latest copies, but that it is produced afresh by our computers, Postmodernism appears as a mirror which, to a civilisation whose 'only purpose is to "know"', reflects the image of its own knowledge. From this mirror state comes the fact that each reproach addressed to this civilisation is invariably referred to us as an interrogation of our own choices, at best identical, at worst increased, a sensation felt by everyone when, for example, we wonder how contemporary technology was able to produce such or such a social construction, including architecture.

In this regard we cannot but recall the paradox of the contemporary factory where the staff, workmen or engineers work to increase the performance of the robots that make them obsolete. This paradox was already present in the 19th century in the very term 'manufacture' to design that which is more than mechanical, a paradox that was regularly brought to light by Norbert Wiener[25] and many others without ever finding a satisfactory political response. Furthermore, to say that no response is satisfactory, given the rise in importance of today's global, abstract and computational ambient factory which is the deep cause of the actual crisis, is of course a euphemism.

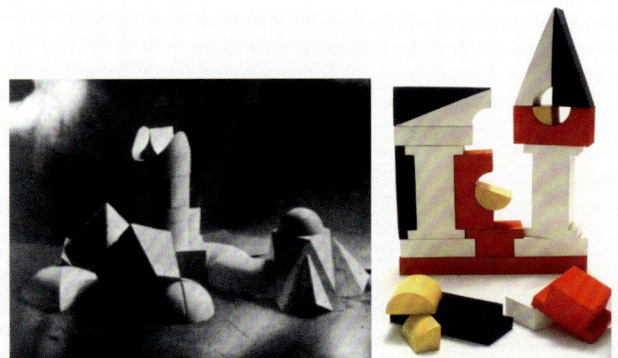

Figure 8. Italian radicals and German expressionists sharing geometry
Hermann Finsterlin, Composition with building blocks, 1916, and
Studio 65, Baby-Ionia, 1973.

In this framework, the mathematics of sensible things, which have neither the elegance of minimal mathematical equations – the Modernist ideal – nor the status of language specific to a pure syntax, become, as stated by Peter Macapia, 'dirty'.[26] They are beta-mathematics, the result of perpetually experimental information technologies.

In fact, the critique of such a 'deviance' of mathematics in architecture devoid of any preferred stylistic expression appears increasingly often in two ways. First, by the expression of an impossibility to finally reach a rationalism which would connect the state of our knowledge and its application in the real, an impossibility translated by a language which appears to be 'inarticulate, arbitrary and non-dialectic'.

This is the language of the most recent Californian architecture which seems to 'produce repetitions not developments' and of which 'consequently the resulting concentric scribble is (specifically through its frustrated ambiguity) the sign of an absolute protest, which "globally" defeats the logic of the real, by refusing to admit the possibility of whatever logic?'[27] Second, by accepting a pop and deeply experimental computationalism in which all historical discourses have been replaced by the gross storage capacities of the now more than one million servers and three million computers of the Google Grid. This grid, by being our Thucydides, embodies the very End of History and henceforth makes the dreams of positivist historiography come true. Everything outside computer memories is not historical facts but literature and dreams. It is thus not a question of rebuilding either history or theories, but of recording or producing a new digital reality by simulation. Here, logical positivism is accepted, as are the resulting technologies that are solving life problems in a way 'theorised' by Andy Warhol:

> The acquisition of my tape recorder really finished whatever emotional life I might have had, but I was glad to see it go. Nothing ever caused me any problems again, because a problem signified a good recording and when a problem turns into a good recording it's no longer a problem.[28]

At this very moment in our computation-based civilisation, the situation is slightly different. On one side life is no more than a good recording, but on the other side it is nothing more than a good computer simulation; a simulation that effectively and physically produces a (synthetic) life.[29] We still have a choice. ∆

Notes

1. Alain Connes in an Interview by Georges Skandalis and Catherine Goldstein, *Newsletter of the European Mathematical Society*, EMS Publishing House (Zurich), Issue 63, March 2007, pp 27–8.
2. Andrea Branzi, *'Le mouvement radical'*, *Architectures expérimentales 1950–2000*, collection from FRAC Centre, Editions HYX, June 2003.
3. John L Austin, *Sense and Sensibilia*, ed GJ Warnock, Oxford University Press (Oxford), 1964.
4. I consider these four theoretical directions as an equivalent to the four known fundamental interactions in physics: electromagnetism, strong interaction, weak interaction and gravitation. As for physics, they ask for a theoretical synthesis in the field of architecture and social sciences. My research agenda is oriented towards such a synthesis.
5. Robert Venturi (with Denise Scott Brown and Steven Izenour), *Learning from Las Vegas*, MIT Press (Cambridge, MA), 1972, revised 1977.
6. Aldo Rossi, *L'architettura della città*, 1966. Translated as *The Architecture of the City*, Oppositions Books and the MIT Press (New York), 1984.
7. Peter Eisenman, *The Formal Basis of Modern Architecture: Dissertation 1963*, Lars Müller Publishers (Baden), 2006.
8. Christopher Alexander (with Sarah Ishikawa and Murray Silverstein), *A Pattern Language: Towns, Buildings, Constructions*, Oxford University Press (Oxford), 1977.
9. The 'Intricacy' exhibition was curated by Greg Lynn at the Institute of Contemporary Art, Philadelphia, and ran from 18 January to 6 April 2003. Catalogue published by ICA, University of Philadelphia.
10. Anthony Vidler, 'From Anything to Biothing', in Cynthia Davidson (ed), *Anything*, MIT Press (Cambridge, MA), 2001.
11. See, for example: Fredric Jameson, *The Prison-House of Language: A Critical Account of Structuralism and Russian Formalism*, Princeton University Press (Princeton, NJ), 1972; *Postmodernism: Or, the Cultural Logic of Late Capitalism*, Duke University Press (Durham, NC), 1991; *The Geopolitical Aesthetic: Cinema and Space in the World System*, Indiana University Press (Bloomington, IN), 1992.
12. Peter Sloterdijk, 'La révolution "pluralisée"', interview with Peter Sloterdijk by Arnaud Spire in *Regards*, No 52, December 1999.
13. Rudolf Carnap, *Der Logische Aufbau der Welt*, 1928. Translated as *The Logical Structure of the World and Pseudoproblems in Philosophy*, trans RA George, University of California Press (Berkeley, CA), 1967.
14. From F Nietzsche, *Aurore*, Second book, trans Julien Hervier, Gallimard (Paris), 1970 (original: *Morgenröte – Gedanken über die moralischen Vorurteile*, 1881).
15. Donald Judd in 'La petite logique de Donald Judd' (trans Pascale Haas), interview with Catherine Millet in *Artpress* 119, November 1987.
16. Frederic Jameson, *Signatures of the Visible*, Routledge (London), 1992.
17. Marshall McLuhan and Quentin Fiore, *War and Peace in the Global Village*, Bantam (New York), 1968, p 34.
18. Franck Varenne, 'Le destin des formalismes: à propos de la forme des plantes – Pratiques et épistémologies des modèles face à l'ordinateur', PhD thesis, Université Lumière – Lyon II, 29 November 2004, p 10. Partial content of the thesis is included in Franck Varenne, *Du modèle à la simulation informatique*, Vrin (Paris), 2007.
19. Franck Varenne, 'What does a Computer Simulation Prove? The Case of Plant Modeling at CIRAD', in N Giambiasi and C Frydman (eds), *Proceedings of the 13th European Simulation Symposium*, Marseille, France, 18–20 October 2001, SCS Europe Bvba (Ghent), 2001, pp 549–54.
20. Ray Kurzweil is one of the few with a general and historical overview of the problem, as had Marshall McLuhan, Guy Debord and Andrea Branzi in different ways from the 1960s.
21. It seems to me that Tigerman's irony is the sign of a complete disillusion, not only towards any kind of political action but also towards the cynical and opportunistic positions of most architects.
22. Stanislaw M Ulam, *Adventures of a Mathematician*, Scribner's (New York), 1976, p 288.
23. Peter Eisenman, 'A Matrix in the Jungle', in *Written into the Void: Selected Writings 1990–2004*, Yale University Press (New Haven, CT), 2007, p 121.
24. Franck Varenne, 'La simulation conçue comme expérience concrète', in *Le statut épistémologique de la simulation, actes des 10èmes journées de Rochebrune: rencontres interdisciplinaires sur les systèmes complexes naturels et artificiels*, Editions de l'Ecole Nationale Supérieure des Télécommunications (Paris), 2003, pp 299–313.
25. See the talks that mathematician and scientist Norbert Wiener, inventor of cybernetics, gave to the unions in the US about the evolution of production towards automatic factories.
26. See 'Turbulent Grid', *arch'it*, February 2007, and 'Dirty Geometry', *Log*, Issue 10, Summer/Fall 2007.
27. The metaphysical and metaphorical principle of Ferreri 'is inarticulate, arbitrary and non-dialectic, to the point that it produces repetitions, not developments and that, consequently the resulting concentric scribble is (specifically through its frustrated ambiguity) the sign of an absolute protest, which "globally" defeats the logic of the real, by refusing to admit the possibility of whatever logic?' Pier Paolo Pasolini, *Ecrits sur le cinéma*, Editions des Cahiers du Cinéma (Paris), 2000, p 199.
28. From Andy Warhol, *The Philosophy of Andy Warhol (From A to B & Back Again)*, Harcourt Brace Jovanovich (New York), 1977, pp 26–7.
29. See the work by Craig Venter on synthetic DNA in, among other numerous articles, Victoria Gill, '"Artificial Life" Breakthrough Announced by Scientists', BBC News Science & Environment, 20 May 2010 (www.bbc.co.uk/news/10132762).

COUNTERPOINT

Will McLean

LESS ANSWERS MORE QUESTIONS

Is architecture heading for a 'procedural mathematic cul-de-sac'? Are architects just too ready to settle for the 'well-defined certainty of parametricism', having got stuck on a mathematics of pattern? **Will McLean**, Senior Lecturer at the University of Westminster, urges designers to open themselves up to the wider delights of mathematics and the full range of possibilities that the discipline has to offer.

A mathematical proof, the argument goes, should not just answer a question, it should also provide some insight.
— Simon Singh, 'Packing Them In', *New Scientist*, 28 June 1997, pp 20–1[1]

The realisation that the pre-'scientific calculator' logarithmic table books that I used at school were in any way related to specific curves was a kind of minor revelation. That the 19th-century mechanical calculators of computer pioneer (and scourge of street performers) Charles Babbage[2] were developed to compute and print these tables was yet another. Mathematics to the non-mathematician but interested observer is a world of infinite possibilities, which are elegantly posed in a mathematical problem discussed by Ian Stewart.[3] In a column for *Scientific American* magazine, Stewart tries to solve a problem first posed by Victor Klee in 1969, which is, if you lit a match

somewhere in a totally reflective room, no matter what shape the room was, would you see the light from the match anywhere in that room? The answer is perhaps more complex than one might imagine and it is indeed possible to create darkness (or not to fully extend illumination) through a specific geometric disposition.

Such paradoxes are mathematical fertile ground and present a more aberrant and less algorithmic precision than the well-defined certainty of parametricism; this year's answer to everything.

It seems unfortunate that architects are generally so easily satiated with such deterministic procedural numericism that would not seem to enjoy the full potential of mathematical exploration. *Mathematics*, David Bergamini's excellent popular science survey of the subject from the late 1960s,[4] reads like a manual of proto-architectural projects, which includes the topological problem of the seven bridges of Königsberg (neatly solved by Leonhard Euler), conic sections, statistical chicanery, Boolean logic and any amount of relations between number and human endeavour. Another remarkable book of mathematics, art and life is *Connections* by self-confessed Design Scientist Jay Kappraff,[5] which while extending detailed mathematical concepts, genuinely attempts to connect the essence of mathematics to proportion, sculpture, music and architecture. Architects seem to get unnecessarily stuck on a superficial mathematics of pattern, which is the kind of maths which can be printed, etched or cast into some willing substrate or crudely abstracted into some planned urban metropolis, its edges denoted variously in a keenly deployed chamfered-edge building, the hard landscaping of angular anti-skate bench/bollard ensembles and the interminable layouts of the non-deciduous anti-personnel shrub.

The useful generalism and eclecticism of the architect should employ the full range of mathematical possibilities and engage in a more thorough exploration of the world of mathematical models. We might ask:

Bruce McLean, Will McLean and Mel Gooding, The Pythagorean School, 2000
left: A mathematically imperfect model for a school. The drawing was etched onto bronze plate and exhibited as a part of the exhibition 'Bruce McLean, Works 1969–1999' at the Talbot Rice Gallery, Edinburgh, in January 2000.

Test assembly of the Pythagorean School, in South Acton, in 1999.
right: The photo features Swiss steel fabricator Simon Veglio, artist Bruce McLean and designer Mark Boyce.

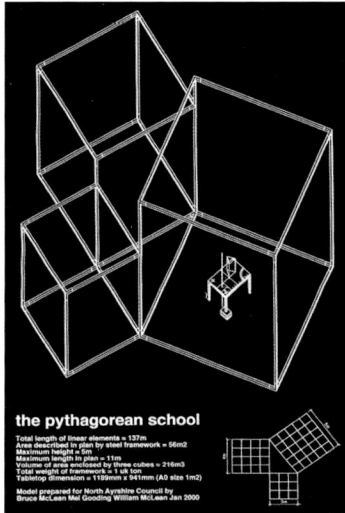

How would we inhabit the single-surface Klein bottle building and where would the environmental envelope begin or end, and what about the perceptual problematic of the skewed perpectival conundrum of the Ames room or Ian Stewart's paradoxical mirrored world? Edwin Abbott's elegant paean to dimensionality, *Flatland: A Romance of Many Dimensions*,[6] takes us cumulatively through the non-dimensional pointland, lineland, flatland and three-dimensional spaceland, and Thomas F Banchoff takes us *Beyond The Third Dimension*[7] into a world of four, five or six mathematical dimensions.

Autodidact geometer Buckminster Fuller explored the platonic solids and specifically the icosahedron in his quest for doing 'the most with the least' in the enclosures business, and was spurred on by his dissatisfaction with the structurally unstable but ubiquitous archetype of the cube. Architects and designers should learn to enjoy more mathematical delights, which might suggest organisational nomenclature as well as the visual treat. How about the self-similarity of Benoît Mandelbrot's fractal world, so neatly captured in Koch's snowflake and the non-integer growth exponents of the Sierpinski gasket.

Alternatively, why not engage in a thought experiment and thoroughly immerse ourselves in the elegant complexity of the Navier–Stokes equations where the mathematics of flows will not discriminate between air, water, blood or smoke. The mathematics of computational fluid dynamics (CFD) is not only scaleable and non-discriminatory in its viscous medium; it also produces a wonderfully interactive graphic interface making visible the not always visible eddies and turbulence of fluid dynamics. Similarly, the algebraic complexity of finite element analysis (FEA) has got a whole lot more interesting since it became a visual medium with a high-speed turnaround structural-optimisation rendered immediately in colour-coded stress.

And while we go about digitising the physical world and its behaviour, we should also revisit Craig Reynolds's work on simulating human and animal behaviour, notably his 'Boids' project from 1986,[8] which neatly modelled the group flocking and schooling behaviour of birds and fish. Or what about Karl Sims's Virtual Creatures,[9] where he developed virtual creatures from simple digitally modelled blocks and then articulated and animated these forms through virtual muscles. These models were then placed in virtual analytical environments such as a CFD program and given a goal, such as swimming or moving towards a light source.

These genetic algorithmic (GA) based developmental models, gifted with simple sensing abilities, evolved behaviours, some of which were recognisably zoomorphic (animal-type motions) while interestingly others were not.

And how about cybernetician Gordon Pask's Random Number Machine built for the office of Cedric Price during the development of the Fun Palace project in the early 1960s. Cedric Price observed: 'It is surprisingly difficult to randomise with one's own brain – try and think of 45 random numbers … randomly.'[10] As interesting (in architectural history terms) as the hyperbolic paraboloid frozen music of the Philips Pavilion (Brussels, 1958) might be, it is surely the subsequent stochastic and granular synthesis compositional experiments of Iannis Xenakis that are of greater 'mathematic' interest.[11] A composer of international renown is surely how Xenakis is remembered and not as the truculent job architect for a trade-sponsored Expo goody by Le Corbusier.

Architects might spend less time parametrically polishing the proverbial and usefully employing the rubric of mathematics for the positive production of new alternatives, employing simple rule-based techniques such as John Horton Conway's cellular automata or the predictive statistical

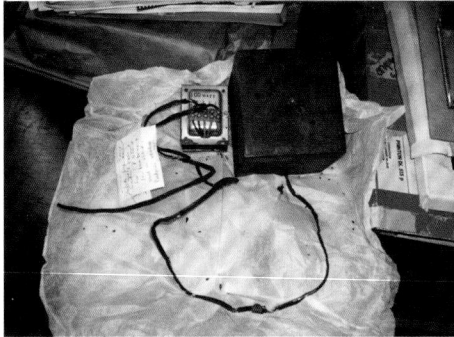

Gordon Pask, Random Number Machine, c 1963
The Random Number Machine, designed by Gordon
Pask for the office of Cedric Price, and now housed in the
Cedric Price Archive, Canadian Centre for Architecture
(CCA), Montreal.

**Bruce McLean and Will McLean, Abacus, Dalry
Primary School, North Ayrshire, 2007**
One of the artworks that were specially designed for each
classroom space of Dalry Primary School, fabricated by
Simon Veglio.

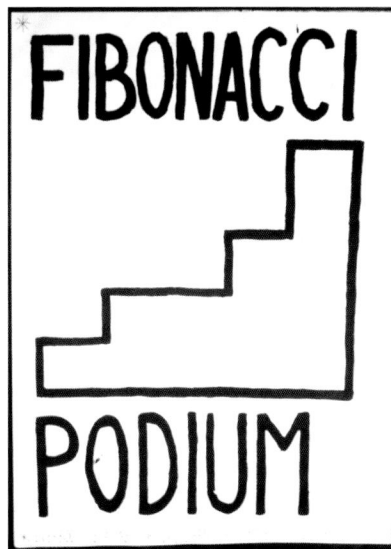

**Will McLean/PAL (Performing Arts Labs), Fibonacci
Podium, 2008**
The Fibonacci Podium, where whoever wins, everyone is
part of an elegant arithmetic progression.

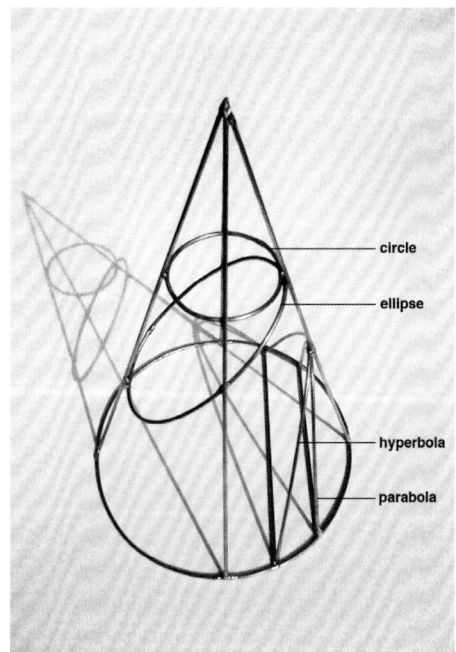

Will McLean, Conic Section Model, 2010
Conic section model showing four different curve types
from the dissection of a single solid.

BUILDING AS AN INSTRUMENT OF
MEASUREMENT / 7 ZONES

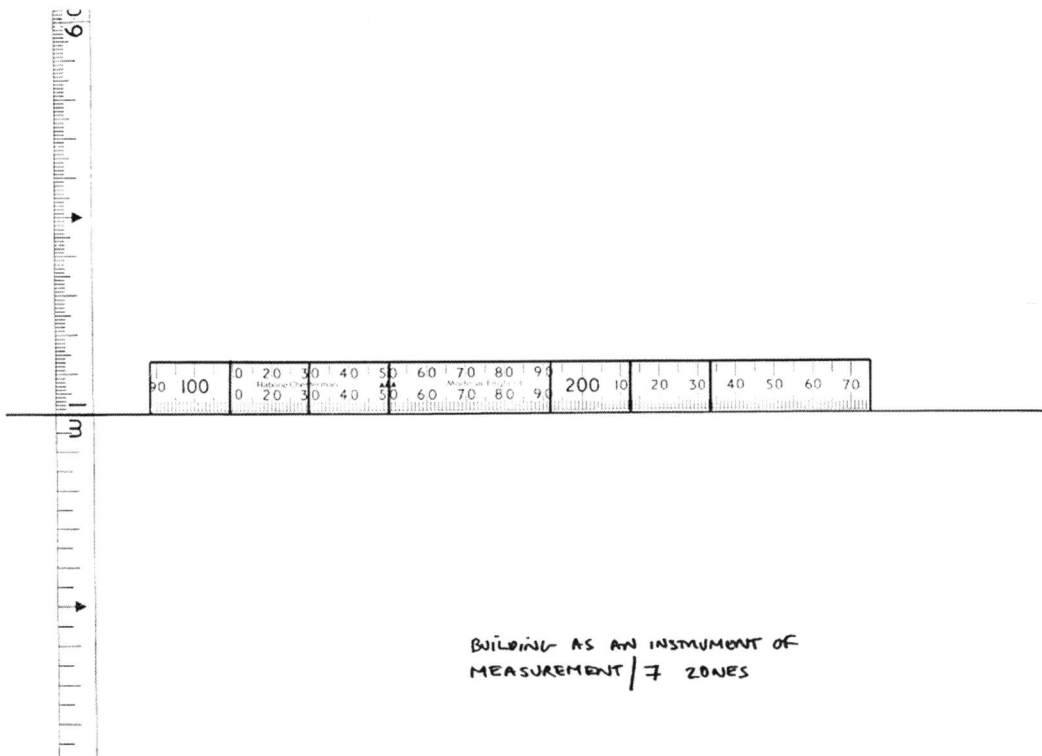

Will McLean and Bruce McLean, School as a Rule, 1998
Proposal for a self-measuring linear sculpture at
Lawthorn Primary School in North Ayrshire.

analysis and algorithmic compilation used to predict which queue we choose to join, what music we buy and the general evolution of our purchasing habits. There is a model from the 1970s in London's Science Museum of the UK's economy rendered in plastic tubes, and using water and controllable valves for computation and statistical analysis of such data as our gross domestic product (GDP). With increasingly serious computational processing power available to anyone with a computer, we might begin to ask more pertinent questions as to the nature of what the designer does and could do, and spend our processing power on causation (new possibilities) and not on images of saleable iterations and no ideas at all.

Why, as designers, is our interest in mathematics strictly limited to its artefacts and not its use as a genuinely generative tool? I am not specifically talking of GA shape optimisation, which in application to turbine blade design seems useful, but its application to the crudely conceived programmatic congruence of a building might be less relevant. If in prefabricated architecture it is possible, as John Frazer suggested, that we

have too often prefabricated the wrong bit, then with mathematics it is possible that we continue to under-utilise its potential as a developmental tool and continue to employ the mathematic product as a mere appliqué or numerical coordination system. We can all enjoy the sequential niceties of the Fibonacci sequence without mindlessly rendering it in double-curved steel sections and top-of-the-line curtain walling.

In November 1979 artists Bruce McLean and Paul Richards staged and performed *The Masterwork*,[12] a kind of multi-headed performance artwork at Riverside Studios in London. *The Masterwork* (programmed as the 'definitive work in mediocrity') was subtitled *An Award Winning Fishknife* and was a highly choreographed scabrous tale about an architect whose major *coup de grâce* was the development of some stonkingly good tableware. Over 30 years later, could we retitle a contemporary performance of this piece as the award-winning 'parametrically designed' fishknife? Architects, generally gifted with little humour or self-doubt, are only too willing to redesign dead ends for any number of despicable clients and are

currently indulging in a kind of procedural mathematical cul-de-sac while presumably the world awaits another masterwork. ⌂

Notes
1. Simon Singh, 'Packing Them In', *New Scientist*, 28 June 1997, pp 20–1.
2. Charles Babbage, *Passages from the Life of a Philosopher*, William Pickering (London), 1994, pp 30–50.
3. Ian Stewart, 'Mathematical Recreations: Shedding a Little Darkness', *Scientific American*, August 1996, pp 81–3.
4. David Bergamini, *Mathematics*, Time-Life Books (New York), 1969, pp 159–64.
5. J Kappraff, *Connections*, McGraw-Hill (New York), 1991, pp 1–34.
6. Edwin Abbott, *The Annotated Flatland: A Romance of Many Dimensions*, The Perseus Press (Oxford), 2002, pp 33–7.
7. Thomas F Banchoff, *Beyond the Third Dimension*, Scientific American Library (New York), 1996, pp 1–11.
8. See www.red3d.com/cwr/boids/.
9. Thomas S Ray, 'Evolution as Artist, Morphology/ Neobiology', *Form + Zweck* 17, 2000, pp 14–21.
10. Samantha Hardingham (ed), *Experiments in Architecture*, August 2005, pp 44–6.
11. Iannis Xenakis, *Formalized Music: Thought and Mathematics in Composition*, Indiana University Press (Bloomington, IN), 1971, pp 50–1.
12. Bruce McLean, *Process, Progress*, Projects Archive, Chelsea Space (London), 2006, pp 50–9.

Francis Aish is a Partner in Foster + Partners' Specialist Modelling Group, where his role is the research and development of systems to model and solve complex, multi-disciplinary design problems. This role takes two forms. Firstly, he conducts project-driven R&D, for which he has worked on over 100 projects and competitions, including the SwissRe HQ in London and the new Airport for the Beijing Olympics. Secondly he conducts collaborative research with leading universities and companies. Prior to joining Foster + Partners, he spent two years in the Advanced Technology division of Nortel Networks. Francis received his undergraduate degree in Aerospace Systems Engineering from the University of Southampton in 1996, and is currently undertaking an Engineering Doctorate at University College London. He has published a number of papers on design and simulation systems, and lectured on the same subject in Europe and North America.

Daniel Bosia, an experienced structural designer with a masters in architecture and engineering, is an expert in complex geometries and computation. He is a lecturer in architecture and engineering schools, and now an associate director at Expedition Engineering after leading the Advanced Geometry Unit (AGU) at Arup for many years, with realised projects including the Pedro and Inês Bridge and the Weave Bridge. In the last 15 years in practice, he has worked in a series of high-profile collaborations with architects such as Daniel Libeskind, Toyo Ito, Enric Miralles and Nicholas Grimshaw. More recently he has supported emerging practices such as BIG and LAVA, and collaborated with artists including Anish Kapoor and Matthew Ritchie.

Mark Burry is Professor of Innovation (Spatial Information Architecture) and director of the Spatial Information Architecture Laboratory (SIAL) at RMIT University. He is also founding director of RMIT's Design Research Institute which brings together investigators from a range of design disciplines and harnesses their collective expertise to address major social and environmental dilemmas. He is Executive Architect and Researcher to the Temple Sagrada Família in Barcelona and was awarded the title Il.lustrísim Senyor by the Reial Acadèmia Catalana de Belles Arts de Sant Jordi in recognition of his contribution. He holds various senior positions at academic institutions in Australia, New Zealand and Europe, including Velux Visiting Professor at CITA, Royal Academy of Fine Arts in Copenhagen, Denmark. He is a member of the Advisory Board of Gehry Technologies in Los Angeles

and was a member of the Australian Research Council College of Experts from 2003 to 2007. In 2006 he was awarded the Australian Research Council's most prestigious funding award, a Federation Fellowship, for five years.

Bernard Cache holds professional degrees in architecture and business management, as well as a PhD in architectural history. In 1995 he introduced the concept of non-standard architecture in his MIT Press book Earth Moves, a concept given the name 'Objectile' by Gilles Deleuze in his own book *The Fold: Leibniz and the Baroque* in 1992. A year later, together with his partner Patrick Beaucé, he founded the company Objectile, in order to conceive and manufacture non-standard architecture components. He is currently dedicated to fundamental research both on antiquity and new CAD/CAM software in collaboration with Missler Software Corporation, where he teaches teams of software developers to read century-old treatises of geometry. He has taught widely in Europe and America, most recently holding a visiting chair at the Politecnico di Torino. In the spring of 2010 he gave the keynote address of the conference 'The Mathematics of Sensible Things' on the subject of Vitruvius's *De Architectura*.

Amy Dahan-Dalmedico is a professor at the Paris-based Institute École des Hautes Études en Sciences Sociales where she directs a masters degree in the history of science, technology and society. Her history of science PhD thesis charted the configuration of French mathematics at the beginning of the 19th century. From 2000 she turned her attention to the modelling of complex systems, and has since directed numerous doctoral theses on issues of climate change considered in scientific, societal and political terms. She taught mathematics at university level until 1983 and has held prestigious appointments in the history of science at the Paris-based École Polytechnique, the École des Hautes Études, the Free University of Brussels and France's Centre national de la recherche scientifique (CNRS). She is the author of four books and numerous papers. Her first book (with Jeanne Peiffer), *History of Mathematics: Highways and Byways* was translated into English and published in 2010 by the Washington-based Mathematical Association of America.

Adam Davis is an associate in Foster + Partners' Specialist Modelling Group where he has worked since 2006. He is currently researching machine perception as part of the Virtual Environments, Imaging and Visualisation

programme at University College London. He worked as a web technologist for Internet and open-source software companies before attending the University of Pennsylvania School of Design, where he received Master of Architecture and Master of Landscape Architecture degrees. He has taught parametric and computational design at the University of Pennsylvania and the Architectural Association (AA) in London, and has been a tutor and organiser for SmartGeometry workshops and symposia in Delft and Barcelona.

Ana María Flor Ortiz is a young Spanish architect and currently works at the Chicago-based firm Studio Gang Architects. She graduated from the Escuela Técnica Superior de Arquitectura de Madrid (ETSAM) and completed an exchange programme at the École Polytechnique Fédérale de Lausanne (EPFL) in Switzerland in 2003. Upon being awarded a fellowship from the Real Colegio Complutense and the Caja de Burgos, she moved to Boston to earn a masters of architecture with distinction from Harvard GSD.

Max Kahlen works as an architect in London and Germany. He is founding director of Dyvik & Kahlen, Architecture based in London. After graduating from the Architectural Association (AA) with honours in 2008, he worked as an associate at IJP Corporation. He previously taught as a diploma-unit tutor (2008–10) at the AA and is currently running a media studies course.

Will McLean is the joint coordinator of technical studies teaching in the Department of Architecture at the University of Westminster. He has co-authored two books with Pete Silver and is currently working on a third with both Pete Silver and Peter Evans, entitled *Structures in Action: Structural Engineering for Architects*, to be published by Laurence King in 2012. In 2008 he established Bibliotheque McLean, an independent publisher of art and architecture books. The first publication was *Quik Build: Adam Kalkin's ABC of Container Architecture* (2008), and forthcoming publications include *Sabbioneta: Cryptic City* by James Madge (2011) and *Accelerating Architecture* by Professor John Frazer (2011).

Panagiotis Michalatos and Sawako Kaijima have been involved in the design development of a vast range of architectural projects undertaken in collaboration with widely acclaimed architectural practices including Zaha Hadid Architects, Foster + Partners, BIG architects and Heatherwick Studio. Their consultancy work and applied research is focused on complex form and its structural implications. Their research has been extensively published in international conferences on architectural and engineering computing such as eCAADe, ACADIA and the IASS. Michalatos received a masters of science from the art and technology programme jointly organised by Chalmers and IT-Universitet in Gothenburg, Sweden. He also studied architecture and engineering at the NTUA in Athens. He is currently working as a lecturer at Harvard University Graduate School of Design. Kaijima studied at MIT where she received her masters of architecture. She holds a BA in environmental information, majoring in media design from Keio University, Japan. She is currently working as a research scientist at the Singapore University of Technology and Massachusetts Institute of Technology (MIT).

Philippe Morel is a cofounder of EZCT Architecture & Design Research and an associate professor at the École Nationale Supérieure d'Architecture Paris-Malaquais where he founded and leads the Digital Knowledge educational programme. He has written extensively about the consequences of technological phenomena on global disurbanism as well as on our most recent technological and economical shifts. He has also lectured and/or exhibited at 'Loopholes within Discourse and Practice' (Harvard GSD, 2005), 'Script' (Firenze, 2005), 'The Architecture of Possibility' (Mori Art Museum, Tokyo, 2005) and 'GameSetMatchII' (TU Delft, 2006), at Columbia GSAPP and the MIT Department of Architecture and, recently, at the Berlage Institute and the IaaC, and in Toronto. He has taught at the Architectural Association (AA) and was the organiser and curator of the exhibition 'Architecture Beyond Forms: The Computational Turn' at the Maison de l'Architecture et de la Ville PACA in Marseille (spring 2007). He is also a PhD candidate at the Archives Henri Poincaré, Department of Philosophy and History of Science.

Antoine Picon is the G Ware Travelstead Professor of the History of Architecture and Technology at Harvard GSD where he also co-chairs the doctoral programmes. In addition he holds a research position at the École Nationale des Ponts et Chaussées. He has published numerous books and articles mostly dealing with the complementary histories of architecture and technology. His most recent book, *Digital Culture in Architecture* (Birkhäuser, 2010), proposes a comprehensive interpretation of the changes brought by the computer to the design professions.

Fabian Scheurer is a founding partner of designtoproduction and leads the company's office in Zurich. After graduating from the Technical University of Munich with a degree in computer science and architecture, he worked as assistant for the university's CAAD group, as software developer for CAD provider Nemetschek, and as new media consultant for Eclat AG in Zurich. From 2002 until 2006 he studied the use of artificial-life methods in architectural construction as a member of Ludger Hovestadt's CAAD group at the ETH Zurich and managed to transfer the results to a number of collaborative projects between architects, engineers and fabrication experts. In 2005 he co-founded designtoproduction as a research group to explore the connections between digital design and fabrication. At the end of 2006 designtoproduction teamed up with architect Arnold Walz and became a commercial consulting practice, since then having implemented digital production chains for projects including the Hungerburg-Funicular in Innsbruck (Zaha Hadid Architects), the EPFL Rolex Learning Center in Lausanne (SANAA) and the Centre Pompidou in Metz (Shigeru Ban). Since 2009 he has been a visiting professor at the Architectural Association's EmTech programme in London.

Dennis R Shelden is an associate professor of Practice in Design Computation at MIT and a founder and the chief technology officer of Gehry Technologies. He lectures and conducts research in building industry process advancement and in design computation and cognition. He holds a Bachelor of Science in architectural design, a Master of Science in civil and environmental engineering, and a PhD in computation and architectural design from MIT, and is a licensed architect in the state of California.

Hanno Stehling graduated with a diploma in architecture from the University of Kassel, Germany, where he studied under Professor Manfred Grohmann (Bollinger + Grohmann) and Professor Frank Stepper (Coop Himmelb(l)au). He has a strong background in computer programming and worked as a freelance programmer and web developer as well as computational designer for renowned architects like Bernhard Franken before he joined designtoproduction in 2009. He is a co-founder of the online platform RhinoScript.org and has given RhinoScript classes.

Martha Tsigkari is an associate in Foster + Partners' Specialist Modelling Group where she has created and developed numerous generative design systems within the context of

geometrically and programmatically challenging projects around the world. She is also a tutor at the Bartlett, teaching programming to graduate students. A member of the SmartGeometry group and co-organiser of its Open Platform workshop, she has taught and presented in conferences and workshops internationally. She holds an Architect-Engineer's degree from the Aristotle University in Macedonia, Greece, and an MSc in adaptive architecture and computation from University College London, graduating in both with distinction. A registered architect in Greece and the UK, she has worked for various architectural and engineering firms.

Rodia Valladares Sánchez is a Spanish architect based in Chicago and currently works for Studio Gang Architects. He studied at the Escuela Técnica Superior de Arquitectura de Madrid (ETSAM), where he was a Marcelino Botín Fellow. In 2003 he completed an exchange programme at the Illinois Institute of Technology in Chicago, during which he worked with Studio Gang Architects, for the first time. As a recipient of a La Caixa Fellowship, he earned his masters of architecture with distinction from Harvard GSD.

Michael Weinstock is an architect, and currently Director of Research and Development and Director of the Emergent Technologies and Design programme at the Architectural Association (AA) in London. He studied architecture at the AA from 1982 to 1988 and has taught at the AA School of Architecture since 1989 in a range of positions from workshop tutor, intermediate and then diploma unit master, master of technical studies through to academic head. Over the last decade his published work has arisen from research into the dynamics, forms and energy transactions of natural systems, and the application of the mathematics and processes of emergence to cities, to groups of buildings within cities and to individual buildings. He has published and lectured widely, and taught seminar courses, studios and workshops on these topics at many other schools of architecture in Europe, including Brighton, Delft, Rome, Barcelona, Vienna and in Stuttgart; and in the US at Yale and Rice.

Andrew J Witt is Director of Research at Gehry Technologies. Trained as both an architect and mathematician, he was previously a director at the practice's Paris office where he consulted on parametric design, geometric approaches and new technologies for clients including Gehry Partners, Ateliers Jean Nouvel, UNStudio and Coop Himmelb(l)au. He received an MArch and an MDes from Harvard GSD.

What is Architectural Design?

Founded in 1930, *Architectural Design* (Δ) is an influential and prestigious publication. It combines the currency and topicality of a newsstand journal with the rigour and production qualities of a book. With an almost unrivalled reputation worldwide, it is consistently at the forefront of cultural thought and design.

Each title of Δ is edited by an invited guest-editor, who is an international expert in the field. Renowned for being at the leading edge of design and new technologies, Δ also covers themes as diverse as: architectural history, the environment, interior design, landscape architecture and urban design.

Provocative and inspirational, Δ inspires theoretical, creative and technological advances. It questions the outcome of technical innovations as well as the far-reaching social, cultural and environmental challenges that present themselves today.

For further information on Δ, subscriptions and purchasing single issues see: www.architectural-design-magazine.com

How to Subscribe

With 6 issues a year, you can subscribe to Δ (either print or online), or buy titles individually.

Subscribe today to receive 6 issues delivered direct to your door!

INSTITUTIONAL SUBSCRIPTION
£230 / US$431 combined
print & online

INSTITUTIONAL SUBSCRIPTION
£200 / US$375 print or online

INDIVIDUAL RATE SUBSCRIPTION
£120 / US$189 print only

STUDENT RATE SUBSCRIPTION
£75 / US$117 print only

To subscribe:
Tel: +44 (0) 1243 843272
Email: cs-journals@wiley.com

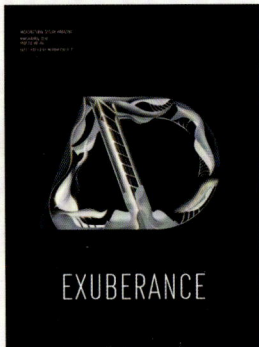

Volume 80 No 2
ISBN 978 0470 717141

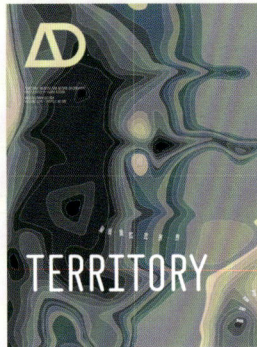

Volume 80 No 3
ISBN 978 0470 721650

Volume 80 No 4
ISBN 978 0470 742273

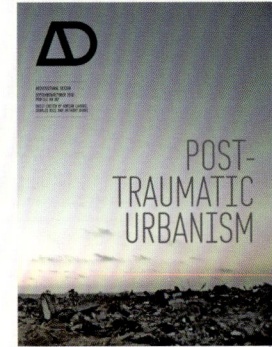

Volume 80 No 5
ISBN 978 0470 744987

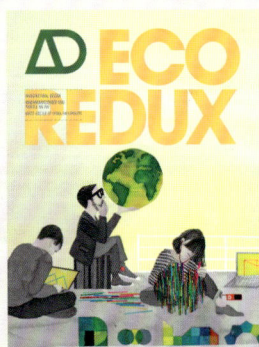

Volume 80 No 6
ISBN 978 0470 746622

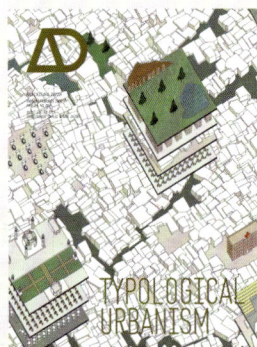

Volume 81 No 1
ISBN 978 0470 747209

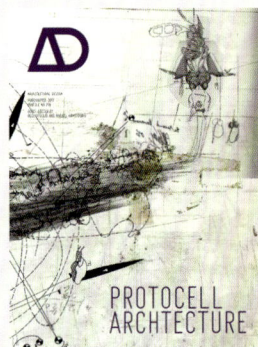

Volume 81 No 2
ISBN 978 0470 748282

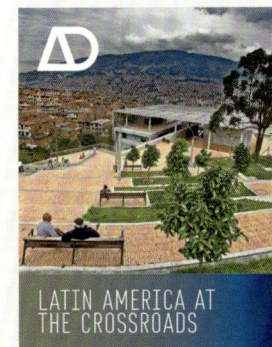

Volume 81 No 3
ISBN 978 0470 664926